The Fashion Business

The Fashion Business

Theory, Practice, Image

Edited by

Nicola White and Ian Griffiths

Oxford • New York

First published in 2000 by
Berg
Editorial offices:
1st Floor, Angel Court, 81 St Clements Street, Oxford OX4 1AW, UK
175 Fifth Avenue, New York, NY 10010, USA

Paperback edition reprinted in 2004

Berg is an imprint of Oxford International Publishers Ltd.

Library of Congress Cataloging-in-Publication Data
A catalogue record for this book is available from the Library of Congress.

British Library Cataloguing-in-Publication Data
A catalogue record for this book is available from the British Library.

ISBN   1 85973 354 9 (Cloth)
         1 85973 359 X (Paper)

Typeset by JS Typesetting, Wellingborough, Northants.
Printed in the United Kingdom by Biddles Ltd, King's Lynn.

Contents

Contents

Part 4 Image and Marketing

Notes on Contributors

Valerie Steele is Chief Curator of the Museum at the Fashion Institute of Technology in New York, and Editor of the quarterly journal *Fashion Theory: The Journal of Dress, Body and Culture*. Her numerous published works include *Handbags: A Lexicon of Style* (with Laird Borrelli) (Rizzoli); *Shoes: A Lexicon of Style* (Rizzoli); *China Chic, East Meets West* (with John S. Major) (Yale University Press); *Fifty Years of Fashion: New Look to Now* (Yale University Press, Adam Biro); *Fetish: Fashion, Sex and Power* (Oxford University Press); *Women of Fashion: 20th Century Designers* (Rizzoli); *Men and Women: Dressing the Part* (with Claudia Kidwell) (Smithsonian Institution Press); *Paris Fashion: a Cultural History* (Oxford University: revised edition Berg); and *Fashion and Eroticism* (Oxford University Press).

Her books have been reviewed in dozens of periodicals and newspapers as diverse as the Italian fashion magazine *Donna* and *The Los Angeles Times Book Review*, and she is a regular contributor of essays to many publications, including *Isabel and Ruben Tolelo: A Marriage of Art & Fashion* (Korinsha), *Claire McCordell: Redefining Modernism* (Abrams) and *The Style Engine* (Monacelli). Dr Steele has organized several major exhibitions at the Fashion Institution of Technology, often centred on the themes explored in her books. Dr Steele lectures frequently and her articles have been published in periodicals ranging from *Aperture* and *Artforum* to *Visionnaire*, *Vogue* and of course, *Fashion Theory*.

Caroline Evans is a Senior Lecturer in the Cultural Studies department at Central Saint Martins College of Art and Design, London, where she is currently also Senior Research Fellow in Fashion. Additionally she is a visiting Tutor at Goldsmiths College, London, and is on the editorial board of *Fashion Theory: the Journal of Dress, Body and Culture*. She has taught and written widely on the history and theory of fashion, ranging from exhibition catalogues to academic articles. With Minna Thornton, she is co-author of *Women and Fashion: a New Look*. She is currently working on a book on contemporary fashion and its historical origins in modernity to be published by Yale University Press.

Christopher Breward is Reader in Historical and Cultural Studies at the London College of Fashion, the London Institute. He is the author of *The Culture of Fashion* and *The Hidden Consumer* (both Manchester University Press) and joint editor of *Material Memories* (Berg). He sits on the editorial board of the journal *Fashion Theory* and has published several articles and chapters on nineteenth- and twentieth-century fashion in its cultural context. His current research focuses on the role played by fashionable clothing in the history and culture of London.

Stephen Gundle is Senior Lecturer and Head of the Department of Italian at Royal Holloway, University of London. He is the author of *Between Hollywood and Moscow: The Italian Communists and the Challenge of Mass Culture, 1943–91* (Duke University Press, 2000) and of many articles on Italian history, politics and popular culture. He is currently completing studies of glamour and of feminine beauty and national identity in Italy.

Réika C.V. Buckley is completing a PhD at Royal Holloway, University of London on female film stars and popular culture in post-war Italy.

Amy de la Haye is a Senior Research Fellow at the London College of Fashion, Creative Consultant to Shirin Guild and Consultant for the forthcoming 'Fashion and Style' gallery at Brighton Museum & Art Gallery. From 1991 to 1998 she was Curator of Twentieth Century Dress at the Victoria & Albert Museum. Published works includes *Fashion Source Book* (MacDonald 1989); *Chanel: the couturier at work* (1994); *Surfers, Soulies, Skinheads and Skaters* (1996); *The Cutting Edge: 50 Years of British Fashion* V&A Publications (1997). Recently published titles include (with Valerie Mendes) *Concise History of Twentieth Century Fashion* (Thames & Hudson, World of Art series, 1999); (with Elizabeth Wilson) *Defining Dress: Dress as Object, Meaning and Identity* (Manchester University Press, 1999).

Luigi Maramotti is Vice-Chairman and CEO of MaxMara Fashion Group. With an annual turnover in excess of £600m and over 1,000 stores worldwide, MaxMara is one of the best known and successful names in fashion. Luigi Maramotti has a specialist interest in the promotion of fashion as an academic subject, has provided funding for the enhancement of the contextual studies element of the fashion course at Kingston University, has initiated the sponsorship of research degrees including Nicola White's, the MaxMara lecture series, and an annual award of outstanding third-year dissertations. Luigi Maramotti, who holds a degree in Business Administration from the

University of Parma, was awarded an honorary Degree of Doctor of Design by Kingston University in 1997.

Professor Ian Griffiths was Head of the well-known School of Fashion at Kingston University for eight years from 1992, and simultaneously a Design Consultant to the MaxMara Group. He was responsible for Kingston University's *Perspectives In Fashion* lecture series, which ran for five years, and was the starting point for this book. He relinquished his headship of the School of Fashion in June 2000 to focus on his creative role at MaxMara, but continues to teach on an occasional basis and is currently researching a book dealing with the history and theory of fashion from a practitioner's perspective.

Brian Godbold's career, culminating in his appointment as Design Director at Marks & Spencer, is documented in detail in the chapter which he has written for this book. His championship of design within the fashion industry has resulted in his appointment as Deputy Chairman of the British Fashion Council, and as a Council Member of the Royal College of Art. In addition to honorary doctorates from the Universities of Southampton and Westminster, he is an Honorary Fellow of the Shenkar College in Israel, a Fellow of the Royal Society of Arts and the Chartered Society of Designers and President of the Royal College of Art Society.

Lou Taylor is Professor of Dress & Textile History at the University of Brighton, author of *Mourning Dress, a Costume and Social History* (Allen & Unwin), the Study of Dress History (Manchester University Press), and co-author (with Elizabeth Wilson) of *Through the Looking Glass: History of Dress from 1860 to the Present Day* (BBC Book). She is a member of the Editorial Board of *Fashion Theory*.

Rebecca Arnold is a Lecturer in the Cultural Studies department at Central Saint Martin's College of Art & Design, London. She has written widely on twentieth-century fashion and her first book, *Fashion, Desire & Anxiety, Image and Morality in the 20th Century* is published by I. B. Tauris in January 2001.

Nicola White is a lecturer in History of Art and Design, specializing in Fashion at Kingston University, where she is also a Research Post Graduate. She has also lectures at Central St Martin's College of Art and Design. Her MPhil thesis, sponsored by the MaxMara group was published under the title *Reconstructing Italian Fashion* (Berg) and she has also published works on *Versace* and *Armani* (Carlton Books).

List of Figures

Introduction
The Fashion Business:
Theory, Practice, Image

Nicola White and Ian Griffiths

This book derives from a series of lectures organised by Kingston University in collaboration with the Italian manufacturer retailer MaxMara. The lectures, entitled 'Perspectives in Fashion', were launched in 1994 to explore emerging themes in the history and theory of fashion, with the objective of considering them in the context of contemporary industrial practice. Both Kingston and MaxMara shared the view that this would primarily benefit students of fashion design, opening their eyes to the intellectual significance of their chosen field, and would consequently be of service to the industry itself.

The lecture series represented an opportunity to consolidate the diverse lines of approach that were being pursued in the name of fashion, often in isolation. Since its inception, around five lectures have been presented each year by a broad spectrum of speakers: historians, academics and curators, designers, industrialists, magazine editors, journalists and public relations consultants. It was envisaged that this would constitute a multi-disciplinary arena which would enable the progressive formulation of a more useful, holistic view of this complex subject than single prescriptive approaches could allow. It was hoped that understanding of contributory disciplines would be enriched by the dynamic established between them.

Although the historical ambivalence towards fashion in academic circles is widely acknowledged, the lecture series was established at a time when this situation seemed to be changing.

The history and theory of fashion has, over the past decade, become a field of unprecedented academic interest, some interdisciplinary tensions and lively methodological disputes, which the lecture series has naturally reflected.

During the same decade, the media profile of the fashion business has been raised to heady levels.

ID Magazine reported in 1999 that 'the 90's have been a decade of heightened celebrity and fashion designers some of its brightest stars. The grand narratives of fashion fame are as fascinating as any pop or celluloid',[1] whilst the sociologist and anthropologist, Joanne Finkelstein notes that fashion 'now functions as a form of global entertainment reported in the nightly television news broadcast . . . the romances, wild escapades and indiscretions of the fashion industry's supermodels and the occasional political insensitivities of its flamboyant designers all fuel the gossipy tabloids, and sometimes ignite the mad indignation of the international press'.[2] The contemporary appetite for fashion is insatiable, and yet it seems that the practical realities of the fashion business are little known to very few other than those who work within it, including it appears to the many authors of academic discourses on the subject. It must also be noted that very few of those who practice within the fashion industry are even dimly aware of the body of academic research which has grown up around its theory and history. That a subject's theory should be thus divorced from its practice is unusual; the MaxMara lectures aim to address this divide, for the benefit of practitioners and academics alike and, with this book, we hope to bring it to the attention of a wider audience. This, we believe, is the first sustained attempt at a conciliation of such diverse views.

With the analysis of the fashion arena in the post-war period as its central theme, the book is divided into three principal sections which have emerged from the lectures as the sites of important debates: the theory and culture of fashion, design and industry, image and marketing. The text begins with Valerie Steele's contextual overview of the history of fashion in the second half of the twentieth century.

The first section which addresses theory and culture of fashion begins with Christopher Breward's analysis of recent methodological debates, now at least partly resolved, that have engendered a multidisciplinary approach which promises to be highly effective for unravelling complex contemporary issues. Evidence of this can be found, for example, in Amy de la Haye's study which demonstrates the recent return of interest in the relationship between fashion and craft. Through observation of contemporary practice and artefacts considered in the light of design historical and ethnographical studies, de la

1. Cole, B., 'Receive the Look. Replicate the Look. . .' *I.D. Magazine*, October 1999, p. 159.
2. Finkelstein, J., 'Chic – A Look that's Hard to See', *Fashion Theory*, vol 3, issue 3, Oxford: Berg, 1999, pp. 363.

Haye provides us with an analysis of the phenomenon which is as useful and meaningful to the practitioner as it is to academics from any of the fields which have informed it. Réka C.V. Buckley and Stephen Gundle's chapter illustrates the potential for apparently obliquely related academic disciplines to throw light on issues which lie at the very heart of fashion. In this case, cultural history helps to develop our ideas about glamour. Importantly, this chapter does not simply use fashion as a specimen on which the authors' theories about their discipline can be tested. Rather, the aim is to use the author's perspective as a key to unlock the issue.

The second section encompassing design and industry introduces the practitioner's perspective, which has been largely ignored in the academic development of the field of fashion. Redress of this imbalance can do much to locate fashion practice at the centre of its own academic study, rather than as a subject incidental to others. We have nevertheless to note the general reluctance of practitioners to involve themselves in academic work. Ian Griffiths' chapter draws on his simultaneous experiences as an academic lecturer and designer to give a practitioner's view of the body of discourses which is generally understood to constitute the academy of fashion. He argues that a body of work informed more directly by the agencies and activities which generate fashion would lead to a more complete understanding of the subject. The contributions of both Luigi Maramotti and Brian Godbold illustrate how an academic understanding of the theoretical aspects of fashion may be enhanced by inside information. Luigi Maramotti's chapter gives an incisive view of creativity within the industry, a topic about which there is a good deal of miscomprehension, whilst Brian Godbold offers a wealth of anecdotal evidence on which to test our theories about fashion, demonstrating the kind of empirical evidence which will be critical to the development of an academic study capable of tackling the complexity of contemporary fashion. Godbold's testimony might prompt a reappraisal of some of the perceived tenets of fashion theory, such as the way in which design functions in relation to the mass market.

The third section, which tackles image and marketing, gives an academic insight into the means, mechanisms and devices which the fashion industry uses to present and promote itself. Lou Taylor effectively illustrates how contemporary fashion uses images to ascribe value to products which goes beyond their material worth. Caroline Evans examines modernity and spectacle through contrasting analysis of the later nineteenth-century department store and world fair, with the 1990s fashion shows of John Galliano. Rebecca Arnold, in her study of 1990s minimalism, shows how fashion's endlessly redefined constructs perpetuate our interest. Nicola White's chapter, which investigates the significance of style and national identity in

Italian fashion, demonstrates how understanding of industry and practice are central to issues of identity in dress and shows that the 'look' of Italian clothes cannot be separated from Italy's industrial capabilities.

We hope that the reader will appreciate how key issues in fashion are highlighted from different angles. For example, Luigi Maramotti's thoughts about the creation or intuition of desire dovetail with Rebecca Arnold's study of changing meanings in luxury. Whilst we believe this book to the first of its type, we also hope that it will be the first of many. A cumulative body of multi-disciplinary work, with inside information will unlock many more riddles than this book can hope to do and in that case we look forward to its being joined and surpassed by others.

Part 1

Context

1

Fashion: Yesterday, Today & Tomorrow

Valerie Steele

As we enter a new millennium, fashion journalist Teri Agins proclaims *The End of Fashion*. Of course, fashion has not ceased to exist. We are not all identically dressed in a unisex uniform of tee-shirts and chinos. Nor are we likely to be. Many people still care passionately about the way they look. Yet fashion, as we have known it, is definitely disappearing. Certainly, over the past fifty years, fashion has been completely transformed.

The empire of fashion has fragmented into hundreds of competing looks – what Ted Polhemus calls "style tribes". Polhemus has spent years studying the effect of youth culture on street styles, and he uses the term "style tribes" to describe the looks associated with groups such as goths, punks, and rappers. I would argue, though, that adults also fall into different style tribes, epitomized by different fashion labels. The Modernists, for example, (represented by, say, Jil Sander) are an entirely different breed than the Sex Machines (Tom Ford for Gucci). The Rebels (Alexander McQueen) can easily be distinguished from the Romantics (John Galliano). This is not a question of socio-economic status or age. Members of the Status Symbol tribe (Marc Jacobs for Louis Vuitton) have neither more nor less money than members of the Artistic Avant-Garde (Rei Kawakubo for Commes des Garçons), but they do have very different values and lifestyles.

As a result of this stylistic proliferation, we can safely predict that there will be no New Look next year, at least not in the sense that Christian Dior launched his "New Look" in 1947. At that time it was still possible for a fashion designer radically to transform the way women dressed. Dior's first couture collection featured dresses with small shoulders, a voluptuously curved torso with a nipped-in waist and padded bust and hips, and long, full skirts. It was a dramatic change from the broad shoulders, boxy torsos, and short skirts of the war years. Some women tried to salvage their old clothes by lowering hemlines and removing shoulder pads; others focused on acquiring an entirely new wardrobe. There were protests in Great Britain from Labour Party politicians and some members of the public, who argued that the New Look was profligate and retrograde.

But the style was wildly popular with many women, who felt starved for glamour and femininity after the war years. "We are saved," wrote Susan Mary Alsop, "becoming clothes are back, gone the stern padded shoulders, in are soft rounded shoulders without padding, nipped-in waists, wide, wide skirts about four inches below the knee. And such well-made armor inside the dress that one doesn't need underclothes; a tight bodice keeps bust and waist small as small, then a crinoline-like underskirt of tulle, stiffened, keeps the skirt to the ballet skirt tutu effect that Mr. Dior wants to set off the tiny waist."

The cost of a couture dress was "very high", she admitted. However, the New Look was soon "knocked off" at all price points. Already the structure of the fashion system was changing, as the haute couture was transformed from a system based on the atelier to one dominated by the global corporate conglomerate. Paris was the capital of fashion, but its mode of influence owed much to American-style licensing and mass-manufacturing. To a far greater extent than hitherto, this was a mass society when "fashion for all" became a reality. This trend has only accelerated in subsequent decades.

The profile of fashion designers was already very different in the 1950s than it had been in the 1920s. "Women are bad fashion designers. The only role a woman should have in fashion is wearing clothes," declared Jacques Fath in 1954. Behind Fath's provocative rhetoric lurked an undeniable fact. In the 1920s and 1930s, women had dominated the French couture. After the war, however, the new stars of the couture were men like Christian Dior, Christobal Balenciaga, and Jacques Fath. As fashion was reconceived as big business and high art, rather than a small-scale luxury craft that required a minimal investment, women designers lost ground. At the turn of the century Jeanne Lanvin had opened her own business with a loan of 300 francs. Marcel Boussac invested $500,000 in establishing the House of Dior.

Only a few women were able to marshal this type of financial backing, notably Coco Chanel whose perfume business was lucrative. Chanel herself was not above exploiting the prejudices of her day. Fath claimed that "Fashion is an Art and men are the Artists." But Chanel insisted that "Men were not meant to design for women." The sight of women in Dior's New Look fashions acted on her as "a red flag to a bull", recalled Franco Zeffirelli. In his autobiography he described how Chanel voiced ugly homophobic sentiments: "Look at them. Fools, dressed by queens living out their fantasies. They dream of being women, so they make real women look like transvestites."

It took a very long time before women designers began to approach gender equality, and when they did it was the result both of social changes (such as women's liberation) and further structural changes in the fashion industry (especially the growth of ready to wear). Although there are many gay fashion designers, homosexuals continue to face widespread social prejudice, which has been exacerbated in the age of AIDS.

If we look back at the post-war period, it is clear that, almost immediately after World War II ended, the Cold War began, ushering in an atmosphere of conformity and paranoia. As one American advertisement for men's clothing put it: "You're being watched! Dress right – you can't afford not to!" If men were pushed towards stereotyped masculinity and sartorial uniformity, women were pressured into the world of the Feminine Mystique.

Fashion writer Eve Merriam noted how the women's fashion press emphasized conformity: "The language is hortatory, a summons. . . You have been Called. Would you keep the Lord waiting?. . . Therefore accept the dicta from on high and do not question. Today, thick textures, nubby, palpable. Tomorrow, diaphanous draperies, fluid, evanescent.... Mauve Is. Don it, or go back to supermarket suburbia where perhaps you really belong."

"Think pink!" ordered the fashion editor in the 1950s movie *Funny Face*, and immediately women obeyed. (Only the fashion editor herself remained above the diktat.) Today, of course, this type of direct order is no longer seen in fashion magazines, because it would arouse anger and ridicule, rather than obedience. To understand why this shift occurred, it is necessary to examine the course of fashion in the 1960s and 1970s, in particular the rise of Youthquake fashions and the spread of anti-fashion sentiment.

Self-trained British designer Mary Quant reacted against the conformity of mainstream women's fashions. As early as 1955, she opened her first boutique on the King's Road, a fashion promenade for London's Mods and Rockers, youth groups obsessed with music and style. In her autobiography, she wrote: "I had always wanted young people to have a fashion of their own. To me adult appearance was very unattractive, alarming and terrifying, stilted, confined, and ugly. It was something I knew I didn't want to grow into." The clothes she made were simple and inexpensive variations on the Chelsea Girl or Art Student look, unmistakably young in feeling, and with rising hemlines.

"People were very shocked by the clothes, which seem so demure and simple now," Quant's husband and partner, Alexander Plunket Greene, told *Rolling Stone* in 1987. "At the time they seemed outrageous. I think there was a slightly sort of paedophile thing about it, wasn't there?" The fashionable woman of the Fifties, "all high heels and rock-hard tits", was replaced in London by a girl with a "childish. . . shape" and "a great deal of long leg".

In 1961, the year the Beatles were discovered, Quant began to mass-produce miniskirts. It was several years before the hemlines of adult women started to rise above the knee, but the styles of "Swinging London" gradually made an impact around the world, even in Paris. In 1961 French designer André Courrèges showed his first miniskirts. Courrèges later claimed, "I was the man who invented the mini. Mary Quant only commercialized the idea." But Quant dismissed his claim: "It wasn't me or Courrèges who invented the miniskirt anyway – it was the girls in the street who did it." Although Quant's success did not herald the rise of a new generation of women designers, it did mark the official beginning of a revolution in fashion based on youth.

Styles began on the street, among a core group of working-class youths who were obsessively concerned with issues of personal style. They were known as "mods" – an abbreviation of "modern". In the 1950s, menswear tended to be staid and sober. But as England's youth culture blossomed, clothing for young men became increasingly colourful, modish, and body conscious, advertising the wearer's sex appeal. This transformation was called the "Peacock Revolution".

Youth culture was based on music and fashion, sex and drugs. According to boutique owner John Stephen, when the Beatles and the Rolling Stones adopted a style, "fans noticed what they wore and wanted to buy the same clothes." Just as the miniskirt was probably indirectly influenced by the greater availability of contraception, especially the birth-control pill, so also did changing sexual attitudes influence men's fashions. Sir Mark Palmer recalled that "There was a time when men wouldn't wear coloured clothes for fear of being thought queer." However, after homosexuality was decriminalized in Britain in 1967, gay men felt less need to disguise their sexual orientation to avoid persecution.

"Sexual intercourse began in 1963," declared the poet Philip Larkin with pardonable exaggeration. Certainly, the sexual revolution influenced the course of fashion history. As we move into the twenty-first century and fashion becomes ever more erotic and taboo-breaking, it is clear that the youthquake of the 1960s played a pivotal role in the development in modern fashion.

Soon the "mod" style became an international phenomenon. "Even the peers are going "mod"" declared *Life International* in a piece on the "Spread of the Swinging Revolution", published in July 1966.

It all began with the teenage 'mods' who spent most of their pocket money on flamboyant clothes. Now the frills and flowers are being adopted in other strata of Britain's society, and the male-fashions born in London have joined the theatre among the British exports that aren't lagging. The way-out styles already have appeared in such disparate metropolises as Paris and Chicago and may eventually change the whole *raison d'etre* of male dress.

Meanwhile, some designers in Paris also began to explore new directions in fashion. Yves Saint Laurent designed his controversial "Beat Look" for the House of Dior in 1960. Inspired by the beatniks, Saint Laurent drew on other rebellious youth styles, such as the biker's black leather jacket. A few years later, Saint Laurent also developed a ready-to-wear line, Rive Gauche. "Ready to wear, for me, is not a last resource, a sub-couture; it is the future," said Saint Laurent. "One dresses women who are younger, more receptive. With them, one can finally be more audacious."

Fashion futurism also served as a metaphor for youth. This was especially important in France, which had no real youth culture or music scene comparable to that in Britain or America. André Courrèges designed his "Space Age" or "Moon Girl" collection in 1964, which included white pantsuits and minidresses worn with vinyl go-go boots and other space-age accessories. "The Courrèges message is loud and clear: bold stark simple clothes, exquisitely balanced with scientific precision to achieve a dazzling new mathematical beauty," declared a British magazine. "It's a look that couldn't have been dreamed of in pre-Sputnik days." High tech – from plastic and stretch fabric to industrial zippers – was associated with progress and a happy future. "Zip up, pop on and just go – zing!" advised American *Vogue* in 1965. "No hooks, no ties . . . everything clings, swings, ready to orbit."

The rise of the hippies, first in America and then around the world, heralded a new shift in youth culture. Fashion historian Bruno de Roselle has analysed the significance of "anti-fashion sentiment" among young people associated with the hippy culture. Fashion, the hippies believed, was a "system that Society imposes on all of us, restricting our freedom". Fashion change turns us into "consumers" who have to buy new clothes "even if the old ones are not worn out". In part an economic criticism of capitalism, the hippies' argument also implied, philosophically, that "fashion is a perpetual lie".

Fashion is damaging, because "this uniformity and this change keep us from being ourselves. Clothing is a means of communication about the self, but we are not allowed to be honest and individual." The solution to this dilemma, according to the hippies, was "to abandon received fashion, in order to invent our own personal fashions". Theoretically, each individual would create his own unique style. He would "express himself" and "do his own thing" – as the clichés of the time put it. In this way, the individual would defeat "the System", whether this was conceived of as the fashion system, advanced global capitalism, or society in general.

Rejecting contemporary fashion, the hippies looked for inspiration in the clothing of long ago and far away. The ethnic look and the romantic-pastoral look were especially significant. Hippy women gravitated toward long skirts, while men adopted evocative garments such as fringed suede shirts, like those worn by native Americans. Initially handmade or scavenged from thrift shops, these clothes were soon produced by savvy entrepreneurs.

Hippy styles rapidly entered the fashion mainstream. In 1967, American *Vogue* solemnly announced that "Timothy Leary's paradigm "Turn on, tune in, drop out" remains the classic statement of the hippy weltanschauung." Rock critic Richard Goldstein wrote: "Now beauty is free. Liberated from hang-ups over form and function, unencumbered by tradition or design. A freaky goddess surveying her. . . realm. Kite-high, moon-pure. Groovy, powerful and weird! . . . The style of the 60s is creative anarchy."

People are mistaken in thinking of the 1970s as a period of calm after the "uproar" of the 1960s. Although political radicalism faded after the end of the Vietnam War, both the drug culture and the sexual revolution became mass phenomena. From about 1970 through 1974, fashion was characterized by a continuation of many late 1960s themes, such as conspicuous outrageousness (epitomized by platform shoes and hot pants), retro fantasies, and ethnic influences. In its orientation toward youth, freedom, and other counterculture virtues like equality and anti-capitalism, the first phase of 1970s style might be described as late hippie diffusion.

From 1975 through 1979, however, fashion became simultaneously harsher and more conservative. On the level of street fashion, the peace and love ethos of the hippies was followed by the sex and violence of the punks and the macho style of gay "clones". In the world of high fashion, a deliberately decadent style of "Terrorist Chic" dominated. Yet at the same time, middle-class people increasingly gravitated toward sportswear separates and Dress-for-Success uniformity.

When the 1970s began, however, the most striking development was the sound of hemlines falling. In January 1970, the Paris collections emphasized long skirts. After almost a decade of rapidly rising hemlines, the new, longer length made news around the world. *Life* published a cover article on "The Great Hemline Hassle", bemoaning the demise of the mini-skirt, symbol of youth and sexual allure. Many women reacted against the new fashion of midi skirts, because they were tired of fashion's excesses – and sympathetic to the hippies' creed of dressing to suit oneself. (The hippies themselves, of course, had already adopted long skirts, and within a few years hemlines would, in fact, fall.) Yet the resistance to the midi was historically significant. Never again would the majority of women change their hemlines just to be in fashion.

Increasingly, women chose to wear trousers, the traditional symbol of masculine power. They even began wearing trouser suits to work, another important turning point in twentieth-century fashion. Meanwhile, for casual occasions, both men and women favoured denim jeans. Although blue jeans

are popularly associated with the 1960s, in fact they became more
in the 1970s than ever before. Even as jeans became "co-opted" by tl
system (with the appearance of various fashion jeans), their signifyi
grew more powerful, as they symbolized youth, freedom, and sex ap   .

"Let us grant to the seventies its claim to antifashion, for the freedom to
wear what you want, where and when you want, is finally here," declared
journalist Clara Pierre in her 1976 book, *Looking Good: The Liberation of
Fashion*. The hippies had destroyed every rule, except the injunction to please
oneself. Now the arbiters of fashion, editors and designers alike, risked being
dismissed as "fashion fascists" if they dared tell women what was "in" or
"out". As a result, fashion journalists quickly adopted a new language of
"freedom" and "choice". They constantly reassured readers that "fashion
now is the expression of women who are free, happy, and doing what they
want to be doing". As British *Vogue* put it: "The real star of the fashion
picture is the wearer . . . you."

Certain designers understood the mood of the time. Yves Saint Laurent is
"today's Chanel", declared *Women's Wear Daily* in 1972. Like Chanel, he
pioneered the masculine look in women's fashion, but he did not neglect
erotic allure. According to actress Catherine Deneuve: "Saint Laurent designs
for women with double lives. His day clothes help a woman confront the
world of strangers. They permit her to go everywhere without drawing
unwelcome attention and, with their somewhat masculine quality, they give
her a certain force, prepare her for encounters that may become a conflict of
wills. In the evening when a woman chooses to be with those she is fond of,
he makes her seductive."

Seduction took many forms in the 1970s, however. Many young people
adopted "wild styles", such as hot pants and platform shoes. Traditional
rules of taste and propriety were deliberately violated. "Trashy" styles
proliferated, including see-through blouses, crushed vinyl burgundy maxi-
coats, electric blue lycra "second-skin" bodystockings, and silver lurex halter
tops. Polyester shirts were open to the waist, and dresses were slit up to the
crotch. "Is bad taste a bad thing?" demanded British *Vogue* in 1971, with
the clear implication that the freedom to violate social conventions was
liberating. No wonder the 1970s have been called "The Decade that Taste
Forgot".

At the same time, however, fashion designers such as Halston and Calvin
Klein spear-headed a new kind of minimalist modernism. Simple cashmere
or Ultrasuede dresses gave women a sensuous but grown-up appearance. In
the evening, sex came out of the closet and music continued to be a major
influence on fashion. Disco was originally a gay phenomenon, but soon it
had spread to the wider society. Disco dressing emphasized materials that

picked up the light, and clothes that showed off the body. Indeed, disco helped introduce underwear as outerwear. Especially popular were silken slip dresses with spaghetti straps.

By contrast, punk rock spawned a deliberately "revolting style". The punks are most notorious for their ripped tee-shirts, Doc Marten boots, and "tribal" hairstyles. As Dick Hebdige writes in *Subculture: The Meaning of Style*:

> Safety pins were . . . worn as gruesome ornaments through the cheek, ear or lip. 'Cheap' trashy fabrics (plastic, lurex, etc.) in vulgar designs (e.g. mock leopard skin) and 'nasty' colors, long discarded by the quality end of the fashion industry as obsolete kitsch, were salvaged by the punks and turned into garments . . . which offered self-conscious commentaries on the notions of modernity and taste . . . In particular, the illicit iconography of sexual fetishism was . . . exhumed from the boudoir, closet and the pornographic film and placed on the street.

More important than safety-pins and mohawks was the way the punks used the visual strategy of *bricolage*, throwing together wildly unrelated elements, like army surplus and fetish underwear. The punk style was initially greeted with horror. Yet within a very short time, it was a major influence on international fashion. Vivienne Westwood was a pivotal figure in the transmission of punk style, with her notorious pornographic tee-shirts and bondage trousers. Soon Jean Paul Gaultier was producing underwear-as-outerwear, and black leather became mainstream.

Fashion photographers like Guy Bourdin and Helmut Newton also drew on violent and pornographic iconography. Newton often depicted women fighting, in positions of dominance, or posed as sex workers. He was hired as a consultant for the horror film *The Eyes of Laura Mars*, which depicted Faye Dunaway as a fashion photographer whose work mixed sex and violence. In one scene, two models wearing nothing but underwear, high heels and fur coats engage in a violent hair-pulling catfight in front of a burning car. Guy Bourdin focused explicitly on the connections between sex and death. His shoe advertisements for Charles Jourdain were especially notorious: In one advertisement he depicted what appeared to be the aftermath of a fatal car crash; one of the victim's shoes lay at the side of the road. Fashion advertising of the 1990s continued this trend, especially with the vogue for "heroin chic". Aspects of aggression proved erotically alluring to many people.

Saint Laurent exploited the eroticism of sexual ambiguity, most famously in his female version of the tuxedo suit, *le smoking*, which Helmut Newton photographed for French *Vogue*. Saint Laurent's evening clothes, on the other hand, revelled in the "retro" and "ethnic" influences so beloved of the hippies. With his Russian – or Ballets Russes – collection of 1976–7 Saint Laurent launched a phantasmagoria of Oriental influences, creating spectacularly luxurious costumes, such as sable-trimmed gold brocade Cossack coats and long gypsy skirts in iridescent silks. "A revolution . . . that will change the course of fashion around the world," proclaimed the *New York Times* in a front-page article. "The most dramatic and expensive show ever seen in Paris," declared the *International Herald Tribune*.

Some observers complained that the collection was "nostalgic" and too close to "costume" to be really wearable, but American *Vogue* defiantly insisted that "What Yves Saint Laurent has done . . . is to remind us that fashion, in its radical form of haute couture, *is* costume . . . It strikingly illustrates the degree of sophistication attained by fashion's analysis of history." This issue continues to recur in fashion today, as designers like John Galliano pillage the past to create romantic fantasy fashions.

Paris remained the capital of fantasy fashion, but in the late 1970s, the rise of ready to wear in Milan began to threaten French fashion hegemony. Whereas the Roman couture was essentially an imitation of Paris, Milan offered a genuine alternative to Paris. "Weary of French fantasy clothes and rude treatment on Parisian showroom floors, buyers were happy to take their order books next store," announced *Newsweek* in 1978. The clothes coming out of Milan were, admittedly, not couture, but they were extremely stylish. "They were classically cut but not stodgy, innovative but never theatrical. They were for real people – albeit rich people – to wear to real places."

Backed by the Italian textile producers, designers in Milan produced high-quality ready-to-wear – clothes that combined the casual qualities of American sportswear with European luxury and status. "The Italians were the first to make refined sportswear," recalled John Fairchild of *Women's Wear Daily*. Significantly, the international clientele for Italian style included both men and women. Moreover, they increasingly wore clothing that was not only "made in Italy", but that also expressed some version of "the Italian Look".

In 1982, when Giorgio Armani was featured on the cover of *Time Magazine*, the lead article began with a quote from Pierre Bergé, the business partner of Yves Saint Laurent. Asked about Italian fashion, Bergé insisted that except for "pasta and opera, the Italians can't be credited with anything!" Bergé demanded, "Give me one piece of clothing, one fashion statement that Armani has made that truly influenced the world." It was a rash challenge to make to an American journalist, and Jay Cocks impudently replied, "Alors, Pierre. The unstructured jacket. An easeful elegance . . . Tailoring of a kind thought possible only when done by hand . . . A new sort of freedom in clothes."

Already in the mid-1970s, Armani had begun to soften men's clothes. He rejected the stiffly tailored business suits that traditionally symbolized masculine rectitude, introducing instead "deconstructed" jackets, without padding and stiff interlinings. The shoulders dropped and broadened, the lapels and buttons crept downward. Armani used softer, more easily draped "luxury" fabrics (such as cashmere and silk-and-wool blends), which have a greater tactile appeal than the tightly woven wools more typical of men's suits. He also expanded the repertoire of colours available to men; in addition to traditionally masculine colours like navy blue and steel grey, he added softer warmer shades, like camel. Then Armani turned around and interpreted his menswear look for the female.

Much of Armani's popularity – and the appeal of the Italian look in general – derived from the way it "came to bridge the gap between the anti-Establishment 60's and the money-gathering 80's" (as fashion journalist Woody Hochswender astutely noted). If the tailored suit had long signified business-like respectability, now it also projected an image combining sensuality and physical power – for men and women alike. An Armani suit symbolized easy self-assurance and understated elegance. As gender stereotypes became less rigid, women appreciated the powerful image created by an Italian suit, while men were increasingly willing to present themselves as sex objects.

Gianni Versace was the other pivotal figure in the emergence of Italian fashion. The favourite designer of extroverted musicians and actors, he brought colour and Baroque vitality to rock 'n roll fashion. Not since Pucci's psychedelic prints had fashion seen such a riot of colour and design. His use of leather was also brilliant, especially in his so-called S&M collection of 1991, which introduced hundreds of socialites to a style derived from the gay leatherman look. Perhaps his most famous single dress, however, was the neo-punk safety-pin dress worn by Elizabeth Hurley. The murder of Gianni Versace brought an untimely end to a larger-than-life talent, but his sister Donatella continued to design for the company.

New talents have continued to flourish in Italy. Miuccia Prada, for example, is the designer of choice for many chic fashion editors. The heir to a leather goods company, she first received international attention in the mid-1980s with her black nylon backpack, which brilliantly undermined contemporary status symbols, like the "gilt 'n quilt" Chanel purse. Prada soon became known for her fashion-forward styles, which unerringly combined classicism and audacity. For younger and/or more playful women, she launched her secondary line Miu Miu.

Meanwhile, over the course of the 1990s, Tom Ford, the American designer at Gucci, transformed that near-moribund company into one of the world's hottest fashion labels, known for ultra-sexy clothes and must-have accessories. Yet, as Ford demonstrates, fashion today is no longer rigidly segmented by country.

An American designer can work for an Italian company, an Englishman can design for a French couture house, and an Austrian can set up shop in New York. The German Jil Sander and the Belgian Anne Demeulemeester are major international talents. Of course, there is evidence of cross-culturalism in the past as well: neither Schiaparelli nor Balenciaga were French, although both flourished in Paris. Yet the internalization of fashion has become especially noticeable ever since the Japanese invasion of the 1980s, which also marked a new phase in avant-garde fashion.

Suzy Menkes has described the sensational effect of Kawakubo's Spring/Summer 1983 collection for Commes des Garcons: "Down the catwalk, marching to a rhythmic beat like a race of warrior women, came models wearing ink-black coat dresses, cut big, square, away from the body with no line, form, or recognizable silhouette." Menkes recognized that Kawakubo was "search[ing] for clothing that owes nothing to outworn concepts of femininity". Most journalists were just shocked, and they used the language of mourning, poverty, and atomic warfare, arguing that the clothes made women look like "nuclear bag ladies".

When American *Vogue* featured Kawakubo's clothes in 1983, an outraged reader demanded to know why anyone would want to pay $230 for "a torn . . . shroud". Joan Kaner, then vice-president and fashion director at Bergdorf Goodman said that "Rei's clothes are interesting to look at, difficult to wear. How much do people want to look tattered?" The new Japanese clothes also tended to be oversized and loose; to a hostile viewer, big and bulky. "They do nothing for the figure," complained Kaner, "and for all the money going into health and fitness, why look like a shopping bag lady?"

As time went on, however, avant-garde fashion began to be accepted, at least among certain artistic style tribes. The cognoscenti recognized that Kawakubo's infamous "ripped" sweater, for example, was not ripped at all. The seemingly random pattern of holes was the result of careful thought and technology. According to Kawakubo: "The machines that make fabric are more and more making uniform, flawless textures. I like it when something is *off*, not perfect. Handweaving is the best way to achieve this. Since this isn't always possible, we loosen a screw of the machines here and there so they can't do exactly what they're supposed to do." Her sweater is today in the fashion collection of the Victoria and Albert Museum, where it is recognized as an important development in late twentieth-century design.

In addition to Rei Kawakubo, the most influential Japanese designers were Yohji Yamamoto and Issey Miyake. Both are the kind of designer that other designers admire. Miyake was recognized early as a true artist of fashion, whose explorations into textile technology have revolutionized fashion.

Yamamoto has become ever more influential, as he combines the aspirations of the haute couture with the daring of the iconoclast.

By the 1990s, the Japanese avant-garde had given birth to a European avant-garde, spearheaded by Martin Margiela, who, like Kawakubo, espoused an aesthetic of deconstruction and radical experimentation. Margiela's use of recycled clothing was especially influential. He unravelled French Army socks and knitted them into sweaters, and cut up old leather coats to make into evening dresses. The young Belgian designer Anne Demeulemeester revels in the inky black that Kawakubo herself has now renounced in favour of newly transgressive colors – like pink.

Sex and gender continue to be central issues in the cultural construction of contemporary fashion. But whereas Yves Saint Laurent politely combined seduction and subversion, designers like Jean-Paul Gaultier have upped the ante. "A woman, like a man, can be feminine," insisted Gaultier, whose work travesties traditional gender expectations. His collection 'And God Created Man' featured the skirt for men, while 'Wardrobe for Two' focused on androgyny. As Gaultier said in 1984: "Gender-bending, huh! It's a game. Young people understand that to dress like a tart doesn't reflect one's moral stance – perhaps those *jolies madames* in their little Chanel suits are the real tarts? I'm offering equality of sex appeal."

Gaultier was also notorious as the apostle of bad taste. "Me, I like everything," he said. "Everything can be beautiful or ugly . . . I like different kinds of beauty." He showed his strange clothes on unconventional models – fat women, old people, heavily tattooed and pierced people. When French *Vogue* went to Brooklyn to photograph Jean-Paul Gaultier's collection of Hasidic fashions, many Jews complained. His use of fetishism has been especially influential, epitomized in his corsets created for Madonna. Less obvious are the ways in which he has subverted traditional ideas of class distinction.

Social class is no longer clearly defined in terms of fashion, in part because of the excess associated with the nouveaux-riches styles of the 1980s. The 1980s have been stereotyped as a "decade of greed" and "excess". Journalists have focused on themes such as the money culture, junk bonds, and status symbols. As it happened, the stock market crash of 1987 coincided with Christian Lacroix's New York opening, and there were those who drew a connection between the two events. In her essay, "Dancing on the Lip of the Volcano: Christian Lacroix's Crash Chic", society journalist Julie Baumgold argued that "Lacroix makes clothes of such extravagant, gorgeous excess as to divide the classes once and for all."

The frivolous and theatrical look of Lacroix's dresses – extended over hoops or bustles, and adorned with garlands, fringe and ribbons, in a riot of red, pink and gold, stripes, polka dots and roses, and costing some $15,000 to

$30,000 per dress – seemed to signify a decadent society wholly abandoned to the cult of conspicuous consumption. The reality, however, was much more complex. Class distinctions were important in the 1980s, as they are today, but now the desire for status increasingly coexists with the desire to look young and "cool", however this is defined by one's style tribe.

Even venerable couture houses have required injections of youthful style. Thus, in 1982 Karl Lagerfeld was invited to design for Chanel. Journalist Javier Arroyello credits Lagerfeld with being:

> the man who broke the spell of the Chanel mummy. He likes to picture himself as an emergency doctor who . . . rejuvenated the famous Chanel suit, the exhausted uniform of the *grandes bourgeoises*, through repeated shock treatments (he brought leather and even denim to the kingdom of gold-trimmed tweed) and intensive corrective surgery (wider shoulders, roomier jackets, a sharper silhouette that included even pants).

There were occasional complaints that Lagerfeld had "vulgarized" the Chanel look. But sales increased dramatically, and the average age of the Chanel customer dropped from the mid-fifties to the late thirties. "All the stuff before pre-Karl was so-o-o square," said Caroline Kellett, a young English fashion editor. Innovative and iconoclastic, Lagerfeld wore the Chanel mantle lightly. He admitted that "Chanel has to stay Chanel in a way," but he also stressed that there was room to expand beyond "those knit suits".

Drawing on influences from the street, Lagerfeld put his Chanel models in rappers' chunky gold chains, big gold earrings, and the kind of skin-tight shorts worn by New York City bicycle messengers. The influence moved both ways, however. Some rappers have mixed baggy shorts and baseball caps by Home Boyz with combat boots by Chanel. "We have the Chanel combat boots now, which are more upscale," explained one performer. "They're also really easy to dance in."

Together with popular music, sports are one of the most important influences on contemporary fashion. This trend has long been evident throughout society, and can even be observed in, for example, the Mattel toy catalogue in 1984, the year when "Great Shape Barbie" was launched. As the advertising copy put it: "Hot new trend in fashion – aerobics," adding that the Barbie doll looked "trim 'n terrific" in her "trendy looking" athletic clothes. The 1980s were indeed characterized by a pronounced emphasis on physical fitness – especially aerobics, jogging, and body-building – which had a significant impact on the culture of fashion.

The trend towards more body-conscious clothing was as radical a development as the rise of the miniskirt in the 1960s. Whereas Dior's New Look squeezed and padded women into an approximation of the ideal shape (and men were covered with boxy grey flannel suits), by the end of the twentieth century women could simply pull on a leotard and leggings. Meanwhile, young men cruised through the urban landscape wearing lycra bicycle shorts and sleeveless undershirts. New fabric technologies provide impetus for fashion-forward styles. Along with various stretch fabrics, there are an increasing variety of "smart" materials that can do useful things, such as providing warmth with minimal bulk and weight. Today many designers in both Europe and America cater to the sculpted bodies of fashion trendsetters. It is, however, incumbent upon men and women alike to *internalize* the corrective aspects of fashion, and to mould their bodies into a fashionably muscular shape.

As the culture of fashion has changed, so also has the fashion industry and the image of fashion. But fashion itself remains alive and well, always new, always changing.

Part 2

Theory and Culture

2

Cultures, Identities, Histories: Fashioning a Cultural Approach to Dress

Christopher Breward

The first serious use to which research in historical dress was applied in British academia during the post-war period lay in the area of art historical studies. The careful dating of surviving clothing and its representation in paintings was seen as a useful tool in processes of authentication and general connoisseurship. The emphasis on the creation of linear chronologies and stylistic progressions that art historical directions dictated at the time has to some extent influenced the nature of much fashion history writing since. Various approaches have subsequently been adopted following the self-conscious establishment of a school of new art historical thinking in the late 1970s, in which social and political contexts were prioritized over older concerns of authorship and appreciation or connoisseurial value. The arising debates undoubtedly challenged those assumptions that had underpinned the serious study of fashion in the first place. Indeed many of the defining aspects of new art historical approaches, which drew on ideas from Marxism, feminism, psychoanalysis and structuralism or semiotics, encouraged a fresh prominence for debates incorporating problems of social identity, the body, gender and appearance or representation. These are issues that lie at the centre of any definition of fashion itself, though it might be argued that their effect has been to nudge concentration away from the artefact towards an emphasis on social meaning.[1] Rees and Borzello (1986), in their introductory text on the new art history, use instructive examples of the resulting paradigm shift which had broad implications for the study of fashion history. In their

---

1. Palmer, Alexandra, "New Directions: Fashion History Studies and Research", *Fashion Theory*, Vol. 1.3, 1997.

definition of the more cultural scope of new art historical approaches, they state that "when an article analyzes the images of women in paintings rather than the qualities of the brushwork, or when a gallery lecturer ignores the sheen of the Virgin Mary's robe for the Church's use of religious art in the counter-reformation, the new art history is casting its shadow".[2]

However close it came to interrogating the cultural meanings of objects depicted in paintings and other forms of cultural production, the new art history remained largely concerned with issues of representation, the relationship between culture and image. Design history, a relatively young discipline compared to the history of art, has perhaps been able to take on board the complexities of social considerations, economic implications and cultural problems that inform and are informed by objects in a less fixed and self-conscious manner. The relationship between production, consumption and the designed artefact, which has always been central to any definition of the discipline, demands an investigation of cultural context, and is well-suited to the study of historical and contemporary clothing. As design historian Josephine Miller has stated:

> This is a multi-faceted subject and in some ways can be seen to relate to almost every area of design and many aspects of the fine arts. It needs to be placed firmly within a cultural context, against a background of technological and industrial change, literary and aesthetic ideas. In the post-industrial period, the marketing and retail outlets, together with developments in advertising and publishing techniques, have brought a new set of considerations with them. Moreover, the study of dress and its production cannot be separated from women's history.[3]

Ten years on, the expansion of post-colonial studies and the examination of masculinity and sexuality might broaden her list, but it stands as an indication of the potential held in clothing for a design historical and broadly cultural approach. It is surprising then, that despite its fitness for the field, the study of dress and fashion still remains marginal to wider design historical concerns. This perhaps reflects the discipline's roots in industrial and architectural design practice, with their modernist sympathies. A theoretical and inspirational aid to students of industrial and graphic design, design history as originally taught in art and design colleges tended to prioritize production in the professional "masculine" sphere, re-enforcing notions of a subordinate "feminine" area of interest, into which fashion has generally been relegated. The relatively late establishment of fashion-design courses in

2. Rees, A. and F. Borzello, *The New Art History*, London: Camden Press 1986.
3. Conway, Hazel, *Design History. A Student's Handbook*, London: Allen & Unwin 1987.

British art colleges and polytechnics during the 1960s further encouraged a separate provision for contextual and historical studies in clothing and textiles that has probably influenced the semi-detached nature of fashion in the design historical canon ever since.

Related disciplines, including cultural studies and media studies, have arguably taken the politics of identity and appearance – "fashion" – closer to their core, but tend to concentrate on contemporary issues and confine themselves, in tandem with art history, mainly to the study of representation and promotion, using social anthropology and semiotics as tools to define meaning. Significantly, cultural studies finds its history in a literary rather than a visual tradition, and objects of study reflect those roots, existing as texts to be decoded in the present, rather than reflections or remains to be recovered from the past. Whilst much of this work has found its way through to the teaching of fashion students with their more pressing contemporary interests, broader historical issues have remained largely beyond their concern. This brings me to my own limited intervention in the field, a textbook designed to present fashion history in the context of contemporary historio-graphical debate.[4] In the face of a potentially confusing and contradictory conflict of interests, I aimed to incorporate elements of art historical, design historical and cultural studies approaches in an attempt to offer a coherent introduction to the history and interpretation of fashionable dress. Used together carefully, these methods promised to provide a fluid framework for the study of fashion in its own right. They could also be set within a wider argument concerning the nature of cultural history generally, which has fostered concepts of diversity rather than prescriptive or narrowly defined readings of historical phenomena. Roger Chartier in his essay that appeared in Lynn Hunt's anthology of new historicist writings outlines the problems in his discussion of the concepts of "popular" and "high" culture, an area especially pertinent to the history of fashionable clothing and the dynamics of cultural studies:

> First and foremost, it no longer seems tenable to try and establish strict correspond-ences between cultural cleavages and social hierarchies, creating simplistic relationships between particular cultural objects or forms and specific social groups. On the contrary, it is necessary to recognize the fluid circulation and shared practices that cross social boundaries. Second, it does not seem possible to identify the absolute difference and the radical specificity of popular culture on the basis of its own texts, beliefs or codes. The materials that convey the practices and thoughts

4. Breward, Christopher, *The Culture of Fashion*, Manchester: Manchester University Press 1995.

of ordinary people are always mixed, blending forms and themes, invention and tradition, literate culture and folklore. Finally the macroscopic opposition between "popular" and "high" culture has lost its pertinence. An inventory of the multiple divisions that fragment the social body is preferable to this massive partition.[5]

It is the central contention of much recent work which places clothing in the cultural sphere that clothing has played a defining, but largely uncredited role in the formulation of such differences, microscopic, highly subjective, and deeply personal though their manifestation in dress may be. Fashion therefore requires a method of analysis that takes account of multiple meanings and interpretations. Reductive connections between social influences and fashionable appearance have dogged much fashion history, unaware as it has sometimes seemed to be of the difficulties and complexity of agency. It is here that the new cultural history, in tandem with more recent work in cultural studies, is of use, presenting a more questioning framework which allows for explanations that are multi-layered and open ended. The historians Melling and Barry have presented a model that acknowledges difference and tensions between new cultural approaches, suggesting a more positive use for the harnessing of divergent directions:

> It would be misleading to present all these changes as moving in harmony and in a single intellectual direction. For example, there is a clear tension between the emphasis laid by some, notably literary critics, on the autonomous power of the text and language, compared to the interest of others in recovering the intentions of historical actors. Put crudely, the former are seeking to deconstruct the identity and rationality of historical actors, while the latter strive to reconstruct them. To some extent we are seeing, within the concept of "culture" as a basis of historical explanation, a revival of the standard sociological debate between "structure" and "action". Should culture be considered as a given system or structure within which past actors are predestined to operate? Or does the emphasis on culture place higher priority on human creativity, on self conscious action by the individual or society to change their condition. It would be ironic should this false dichotomy become too well entrenched, since the notion of culture has in many ways been invoked precisely to avoid the need to choose between structure and action, but the danger remains, if concealed by the inherent ambiguity of "culture" as an explanation.[6]

These are useful suggestions for considering the relationship between fashion and culture, though the passage also introduces the deeper problem of pinning

5. Hunt, Lynn (ed.), *The New Cultural History*, Los Angeles: University of California Press, 1989.

6. Melling, J. and J. Barry, *Culture in History*, Exeter: Exeter University Press, 1992.

down the notion of culture as a neutral descriptive category in the first place. T.S. Eliot in a famous passage from his *Notes towards the Definition of Culture* could state categorically that "culture . . . includes all the characteristic activities and interests of a people: Derby day, Henley Regatta, Cowes, the Twelfth of August, a cup final, the pin table, the dart board, Wensleydale cheese, boiled cabbage cut into sections, beetroot in vinegar, nineteenth century gothic churches, and the music of Elgar."[7] Ten years later at the birth of cultural studies in Britain as a specific discipline, Raymond Williams rejected this largely pastoral, romantic and commodified vision to present what he saw as a more inclusive, realist definition of culture that encompassed "steel making, touring in motor cars, mixed farming, the Stock exchange, coal mining and London transport".[8] Forty or fifty years on, both readings of English culture are marked by the effects of nostalgia and the subjective positions of their narrators, but Williams, together with Richard Hoggart,[9] incorporated the idea that culture is a contested and social field in which production and consumption find no easy union and the activities, customs and philosophies of the working class conflict with, or differ from, those of the gentry. Their work established that culture is political as well as aesthetic in its forms and effects.

Between the two positions evolved the formation of a modern school of British cultural studies which aimed to examine precisely the circulation of such constructions and their social power. A purer history of the discipline would trace its roots back to the Frankfurt School and the Institute for Social Research established in Germany in 1923, before moving to the United States, with its largely pessimistic and critical take on the effects of mass culture. There isn't the space here to outline the continuing development of cultural studies as a discrete discipline, and I'm not sure that I could do it the justice it deserves anyway. Graeme Turner's recent *British Cultural Studies: An Introduction* provides a more than adequate overview of the historiography and its emergent methods.[10] What I do propose to offer instead is a broad discussion of the key areas in which cultural considerations have made a direct impact on the writing of fashion history over the past decades. These fall largely under the categories of textual analysis (semiotics, film and magazines), the consideration of audience and consumption (ethnography, history and sociology), the role of ideology (hegemony, subcultures and pleasure) and the political question of identities (race, gender, sexuality). These

7. Eliot, Thomas Stearns, *Notes towards a Definition of Culture*, London: Faber, 1948.
8. Williams, Raymond, *Culture and Society 1780–1950*, London: Penguin, 1958.
9. Hoggart, Richard, *The Uses of Literacy*, London: Penguin, 1958.
10. Turner, Graeme, *British Cultural Studies*, See above, London: Routledge, 1996.

are obviously neither comprehensive nor mutually exclusive divisions, but they do indicate the key ways in which clothing and fashion have finally become a vehicle for debates that now lie at the heart of visual and material culture studies.

Fashion and Signification

The deconstruction of image or product as text lies at the heart of any totalizing definition of a cultural studies methodology. In direct opposition to traditional art and design history and literary criticism methods, cultural studies offers a way of studying objects as systems rather than as the simple product of authorship. Borrowed from European structuralism, most specifically the work of linguist Ferdinand de Saussure,[11] the theory of language "looms as the most essential of cultural studies concepts, either in its own right, or through being appropriated as a model for understanding other cultural systems" (Turner 1996). The structures of language, deployed through speech or text, have been shown to reveal those mechanisms through which individuals make sense of the world: "Culture, as the site where that sense or meaning is generated and experienced, becomes a determining, productive field through which social realities are constructed, experienced and interpreted" (Turner 1996). In the most basic of terms, the science of semiology pioneered by Saussure and later Roland Barthes[12] offered a more refined mechanism for applying the structural model of language across the wider range of cultural signifying systems, allowing the scholar to examine the social specificity of representations and their meaning across different cultural practices: gesture, literature, drama, conversation, photography, film, television and, of course, dress. Central to this method is the idea of the sign, an anchoring unit of communication within a language system, which might be a word, an image, a sound, an item of clothing, that placed in juxtaposition with other items produces a particular meaning. That meaning is further communicated by the process of signification, the division of the sign into its constituent parts: the signifier (its physical form) and what is signified (the mental concept or associations that arise). Any meaning generated by the sign emerges from the subconscious or automatic relationship of these parts, which is usually arbitrary and culturally relative rather than fixed. It is a meaning that shifts through time and context, so that the ways in which such a shift or relationship might occur are of central importance

11. Saussure, Ferdinand de, *A Course in General Linguistics*, London: Peter Owen, 1960.
12. Barthes, Roland, *Mythologies*, London: Paladin, 1973.

to cultural studies, because, as Turner (1996) notes "it is through such phenomena that it becomes possible to track cultural change", and also cultural value and cultural associations. Barthes famously attributed the term "myth making" to this production of social knowledge and meaning through the manipulation of the sign, and its cultural and political power is difficult to over estimate.

Fashion historians have of course been utilizing this power for a long time. Every time the clothing in a portrait is "read" (for its literary associations, the symbolic power of its various textiles and elements of decoration, the value entailed in its material and production that might together offer evidence of status, nationality, age, sexuality or date) representation is being decoded as text, associative meanings combed out and cultural systems established. But the process has rarely been perceived in a self-reflective or critical light. Culture is often taken as an historical given rather than a constructed system in which the portrait or the dress plays its constitutive part. Elizabeth Wilson must take the credit in her highly influential work on the cultural meaning and history of fashion for questioning and opening up the field.[13] In her aim to ally fashionable dressing with other popular or mass leisure pursuits she has taken the graphic and literary reproduction of dress into a system of mass communication and consumption, hinting at the possibility that more traditional dress history has been toiling unnecessarily in its efforts to use fashion journalism, historical advertising and other popular documentary forms as evidence for actual fashion change or cultural conditions. In her account of the role of clothing in the formation of normative understandings of status and gender, and its capabilities in terms of dissent and deviance from those roles, Wilson has liberated the fashion plate and magazine column from the narrower, linear readings of established dress history:

> Since the late nineteenth century, word and image have increasingly propagated style. Images of desire are constantly in circulation; increasingly it has been the image as well as the artefact that the individual has purchased. Fashion is a magical system, and what we see as we leaf through glossy magazines is "the look". Like advertising, women's magazines have moved from the didactic to the hallucinatory. Originally their purpose was informational, but what we see today in both popular journalism and advertising is the mirage of a way of being, and what we engage in is no longer only the relatively simple process of direct imitation, but the less conscious one of identification.

The conception of fashion as a magical system, which might benefit from textual or linguistic scrutiny, is an area also well tested in the field of film

13. Wilson, Elizabeth, *Adorned in Dreams*, London: Virago, 1987.

theory and history. The dress historian can draw useful methodological parallels from the way in which authors such as Jane Gaines,[14] Pam Cook[15] and Christine Gledhill[16] take examples of cinema and describe the manner in which filmic images interact with women's perceptions of themselves in terms of fashion, sexuality, maternal and marital duty and work. Gaines makes the connections with cultural studies' linguistic and political concerns explicit:

> There is a significant link between the notion of woman displayed by her dress and woman displayed by other representational systems. In addition, one might say that contemporary feminists have understood woman's inscription in the codes of contemporary representation because they themselves know too well what it is to be fitted up for representation. We are trained into clothes, and early become practised in presentational postures, learning, in the age of mechanical reproduction, to carry the mirror's eye within the mind, as though one might at any moment be photographed. And this is a sense a woman in western culture has learned, not only from feeling the constant surveillance of her public self, but also from studying the publicity images of other women, on screen, certainly, but also in the pages of fashion magazines.

Recent dress history, predicated on a cultural studies understanding of the power of the sign, together with film theory, revels in the ambiguity of fashion and its shifting signifiers, which moves the discipline away from earlier reductive or moralistic approaches. From Thorstein Veblen[17] through Quentin Bell[18] to James Laver,[19] historians and commentators from all political persuasions had perhaps taken too many liberties over their ownership of a received understanding of female psychology and supposed predisposition towards luxury, whilst second-wave feminism simply equated fashion with patriarchal oppression. A similarly puritanical strain in early cultural studies echoed a mistrust of fashionable or popular consumption. Such a condemnation of fashion and fashion history implied a dismissal of the women and men who enjoyed its possibilities, and ignored what Gaines has termed "the strength of the allure, the richness of the fantasy, and the quality of the compensation", which their consumption of image and object allowed.

14. Gaines, Jane and Charlotte Herzog (eds.), *Fabrications: Costume and the Female Body*, London: Routledge, 1990.

15. Cook, Pam, *Fashioning the Nation*, London: BFI, 1996.

16. Gledhill, Christine, *Home Is Where the Heart Is*, London: BFI, 1987.

17. Veblen, Thorstein, *The Theory of the Leisure Class: An Economic Study in the Evolution of Institutions*, New York: Macmillan, 1899.

18. Bell, Quentin, *On Human Finery*, London: Hogarth, 1947.

19. Laver, James, *A Concise History of Costume*, London: Thames and Hudson, 1969.

Though to follow recent cultural theory on the instability of the sign to its illogical limits presents a particular set of problems that both cultural studies and fashion history have had to address. As Gaines states: "the more extreme contention of post modernist theory – the idea that the image has swallowed reality whole – obliterates the problems endemic to comparisons between images and society. If the image now precedes the real, engulfs it and renders it obsolete as a point of comparison, do we any more need to show how representation is ideological?" (Gaines 1990).

The artificiality of fashion texts and representations would certainly seem open to similar interpretation, so how can they in this sense be tied in to any discussion of inequality, power and manipulation, or the simple actions of consumers themselves? Here the poststructuralist approach of Gaines and others and the broader concerns of cultural studies, with the argument that the image of fashion and femininity is a construction, a textual product of its society, relying only on the reality of the moment, allows for a clearing up of any confusion. The constructed image can be held up for further scrutiny, the construction made clear and the seventeenth-century broadside, the nineteenth-century fashion journal or the twentieth-century film revealed as representational systems. In this way fashion and its associated publicity can be shown to rely on current ideologies, and the "obliterated" problems of image and society reinstated for discussion. The arising affinity between fashion and textual analysis has probably constituted cultural studies' major contribution to the discipline of dress history or, more precisely, dress studies.[20]

I choose the term "dress studies" over "history" because that contribution has remained largely within the field of twentieth-century and contemporary concerns. The incursion of cultural studies methods into historical discussions of dress has remained more circumspect, and where examples of a convergence between dress, history and the focus of cultural studies on theory and discourse exist, the texts lie on interdisciplinary boundaries, largely on the peripheries of social, literary and art history, and are by authors who often find it necessary to stress their distance both from traditional forms of their own disciplines and from dress historians themselves. The relationship between cultural studies and history has never been a straightforward or easy one, but some of the crossovers have produced interesting studies of historical clothing practices. The source of the disparity between historical and cultural approaches lies in the necessity of the latter to frame itself within a broad theoretical structure. The problem of conceptualizing the social relationships that make up popular cultures is that it defeats contained

20. Craik, Jennifer, *The Face of Fashion*, London: Routledge, 1994.

empirical analyses and therefore led to a split in terms of methodology and theory between structuralists and culturalists at the moment when cultural studies was gaining ground in Britain during the 1960s.

Structuralists viewed culture as their primary object of study, with the forms and structures that produced meaning drawing their attention at the expense of cultural specifics, empirical quantitative evidence and the process of historical change. Culturalists, amongst whom most British social historians of the left placed themselves, resisted this trend as overly deterministic and comprehensive – in a word "ahistorical". For E.P. Thompson in particular, human agency retained a stronger hold than abstract ideology and the work of British culturalists tended to look inwards to English historical experience rather than outwards to European theory.[21] The two positions rather falsely represent polar opposites for the sake of illustration and more recent work predicated on a broad cultural studies perspective productively knits ideology and experience together through the notion of "discourse". This is a term, owing much to the work of French theorist Michel Foucault,[22] that "refers to socially produced groups of ideas or ways of thinking that can be tracked in individual texts or groups of texts, but that also demand to be located within wider historical and social structures or relations" (Turner 1996). Here the scope for dress history has been wide, as it has for art history and literary criticism, and in my view some of the most exciting examples for a cultural dress history have resulted from this vein. I would offer the work on shopping, department stores and the negotiation of class and gender in the nineteenth century as one manifestation of the approach, incorporating as it does authors as varied as Rosalind Williams,[23] Rachel Bowlby,[24] Valerie Steele,[25] Philippe Perrot,[26] Mica Nava[27] and Elaine Abelson.[28] It is perhaps significant that only two of these would associate themselves with the discipline of dress history, though all have something to contribute to the development of the discipline.

21. Thompson, E.P., *The Making of the English Working Class*, London: Penguin, 1963.

22. Foucault, Michel, *Discipline and Punish: The Birth of the Prison*, Harmondsworth: Peregrine, 1979.

23. Williams, Rosalind, *Dream Worlds: Mass Consumption in Late Nineteenth Century France*, Berkeley: University of California Press, 1982.

24. Bowlby, Rachel, *Just Looking*, London: Methuen, 1985.

25. Steele, Valerie, *Fashion and Eroticism*, Oxford: Oxford University Press, 1985.

26. Perrot, Philippe, *Fashioning the Bourgeoisie*, New York: Princeton University Press, 1994.

27. Nava, Mica and Alan O'Shea (eds.), *Modern Times: Reflections on a Century of English Modernity*, London: Routledge, 1996.

28. Abelson, Elaine, *When Ladies Go A Thieving*, Oxford: Oxford University Press, 1989.

Pleasure and Politics

Another outcome of the argument between structuralists and culturali
a repositioning of focus in cultural studies and history that has had f̨
ramifications for the study of fashion. Abstract debates about theory
methodology were superseded in the late 1970s by the opening up of n
previously hidden areas of study and fresh perspectives on old politi̧
problems. In social history, those receptive to cultural studies concerṇ
oriented around the formation of the *History Workshop Journal*, which aimec̨
to move discussion away from the academy and into the realm of working
people's lives, stressing the importance of feminist and other hidden voices,
utilizing the power of oral and non-traditional historical sources that lay
outside of the "official record", and claiming that theory might provide
answers to social and political problems learnt from the past. In cultural
studies, associates of the Birmingham Centre for Contemporary Cultural
Studies, founded by Richard Hoggart in 1964, and later directed by Stuart
Hall, drew in methods from sociology and anthropology and saw a similar
shift in emphasis. Histories of everyday life focused especially on subcultures,
examining their construction, their relation to dominant hegemony, and their
histories of resistance and incorporation. Much of this work examined the
rituals and practices that generated meaning and pleasure within, precisely,
that fragment of the cultural field which earlier pioneers from Frankfurt
through to Hoggart had dismissed: urban youth subcultures. Dick Hebdige's
work on this phenomenon[29] arguably laid the foundation for several studies
of fashion and the young which have fed back in to the dress history
mainstream,[30] culminating in both the Streetstyle Exhibition[31] at the V&A
and the earlier collected essays published under the title *Chic Thrills*.[32]

The whole notion of a "pleasurable" consumption of clothing, which
subcultural studies partly raised, is an idea that has now become familiar in
fashion histories spanning a broad chronology. But its substance formed the
basis of the last political crisis to rock the cultural studies field. The rise of
postmodernism, with its questioning of value and authenticity together with
the economic effects of Thatcherism and the Lawson boom in the mid-1980s,
placed the issue of pleasure and consumption at the centre of the cultural

29. Hebdige, Dick, *Subculture: The Meaning of Style*, London: Methuen, 1979.
30. Polhemus, Ted, *Streetstyle. From Sidewalk to Catwalk*, London: Thames and Hudson, 1994.
31. de la Haye, Amy and Cathie Dingwall, *Surfers, Soulies, Skinheads and Skaters*, London: Victoria & Albert Museum, 1996.
32. Ash, Juliet and Elizabeth Wilson, *Chic Thrills*, London: Pandora, 1992.

lies debate. Summarized by the term "New Times", the discussion was
.en up by *Marxism Today* and signalled, according to Angela McRobbie,
ne diversity of social and political upheavals in Britain . . . including the
iccess of Thatcherism, the decline of a traditional working class politics,
he emergence of a politics of identity and consumption, and most importantly
the challenge these represent to the left".[33] It cannot be easily claimed that
fashion history has arisen out of a political consensus in the way that cultural
studies obviously has, but nevertheless the implications of the New Times
debate have important repercussions for the study of objects which cannot
be divorced from questions of status, gender, sexuality and national identity.
Though the terms of New Times were complex and inward-looking, the
emergence of a new politics of identity and consumption offered genuine
opportunities for novel approaches and arguments, represented particularly
in works on clothing, fashion, shopping and gender. Recent publications,
from Caroline Evans' and Minna Thornton's overview of fashion and
femininity in the twentieth century,[34] through to Frank Mort's study of
Burton's in the 1950s[35] or Sean Nixon's examination of menswear and men's
magazines in the 1980s,[36] show some residue of the arguments. Any
discussion of consumption and its (dis)contents requires precisely the kind
of close political analysis that cultural studies methods can provide, and used
in conjunction with other, more empirical methodologies its application can
often lead to the most provocative and exciting insights.

It is a shame then that the cultural studies slant often seems to raise
aggressive or defensive shackles amongst dress historians, as it does amongst
historians generally. It is undoubtedly a field riven with disagreements, and
coming to a consensus on what the study of culture actually entails is a
minefield. In this sense it would be a mistake to isolate cultural studies at all
as a desired or necessarily coherent position, more valid than any other. It is
an interdisciplinary field where certain concerns and methods have converged.
The usefulness of this convergence is that it can enable us to understand
cultural phenomena and social relationships that were not accessible through
other disciplines, thus enriching our knowledge of an object category (fashion)
that has clearly always played a central role in cultural/social processes. It is
not a unified field, but one of argument and division as well as convergence,
and therein lies its strength and promise. The dress historian Lou Taylor's

33. McRobbie, Angela, *Postmodernism and Popular Culture*, London: Routledge, 1994.

34. Evans, Caroline and Minna Thornton, *Women and Fashion. A New Look*, London: Quartet, 1989.

35. Mort, Frank, *Cultures of Consumption: Masculinities and Social Space*, London: Routledge, 1996.

36. Nixon, Sean, *Hard Looks*, London: UCL Press, 1997.

recent review (1996) of John Harvey's book *Men in Black* (itself a model of interdisciplinary endeavour)[37] offers encouraging signs for the future:

> In Harvey's book we see a very effective shattering of the protective barriers we have erected between academic disciplines. Of course no one person can be "expert" on everything but an open ... mind ... set on reading the inner meanings of externals, has demonstrated ... the great advantages of knocking away the walls of academic protectionism. What is this book? Dress History? Literary Criticism? Cultural History? Gender Study? Visual Culture? Who cares? Read it.[38]

Note

The author is grateful to the editors of this collection for allowing the re-publication of this chapter. It originally appeared in Fashion Theory Volume 2 Issue 4 (1998). The response of students and staff from Kingston University to its arguments made an important contribution to its final form.

37. Harvey, John, *Men in Black*, London: Reaktion, 1995.
38. Taylor, Lou, "Men in Black", *Journal of Design History*, Vol. 9.4, 1996.

3

Fashion and Glamour

Réka C.V. Buckley and Stephen Gundle

Few words are as ubiquitous in the contemporary mass media as glamour. 'The new glamour burns bright' headlined *Interview* in March 1997, while *Elle* of December 1996 tempted readers with the following cover title: 'Glamour! The people who live it – the clothes that scream it – the make-up that makes it'. Yet quite what glamour is frequently remains unclear. When fashion and women's magazines from time to time conduct enquiries into the meaning of glamour, they invariably seek opinions from a range of experts and celebrities, whose views are strikingly contradictory. Confusion arises over the gender connotations of glamour, whether it is an intrinsic (charismatic) phenomenon or a manufactured one, and whether it is permanent or temporary. In addition there is disagreement over its application to age ranges, places and situations. Such is the lack of common ground that it is tempting to agree with lexicographer Eric Partridge who, as long ago as 1947, included glamour in his list of 'vogue words' which had gained a momentum of their own whatever the original impulse had been.[1] For Partridge, glamour was a word without meaning that had been invested with high status and picturesque connotations by authors and journalists.

One enduring feature of glamour is its identification with fashion. In a recent analysis of fashion photography, Clive Scott contrasted 'glamour' with 'sophistication'. He found that in the fashion press glamour was: youthful, dynamic, pleasure-seeking, extrovert, voluble, short-term, gregarious, uncultured, volatile, public (and thus downmarket). On the other hand sophistication was seen as: mature, poised, restrained, introvert, taciturn, long-term, solitary, cultured, controlled/severe (and thus upmarket).[2] In other

---

1. Partridge, Eric, *Usage and Abusage: A Guide to Good English*, London: Hamish Hamilton, 1947, p. 361.
2. Scott, Clive, *The Spoken Image: Photography and Language*, London: Reaktion, 1999, p. 156.

accounts fashion and glamour are taken to be synonymous. Jeanine Basinger takes this view in her analysis of classical Hollywood cinema and its female audiences. However, she also states that 'Glamour goes beyond mere fashion. Although the concept of glamour includes fashion, it ultimately involves more than what a woman puts on her body. It deals with the lady herself.'[3] The movie stars she refers to usually occupied a median position between the two poles identified by Scott, thus rendering his differentiation meaningless.

In the context of such confusion, an attempt to identify what glamour is, where it comes from and how it works is surely timely. In this chapter three moments of glamour will be explored. In keeping with glamour's associations with the immediate and the commercial, the first of these will be the present. Older meanings will be considered in relation to contemporary uses in the press and advertising. Second, the root of many of the gestures and stereotypes of modern glamour – Hollywood cinema of the middle decades of the twentieth century – will be examined. In the final section, consideration will be given to the transformation of the nineteenth-century city which, it will be argued, was the original site of glamour as it is used and understood today.

Contemporary Glamour

The term glamour is employed continuously in connection with fashion, showbusiness and entertainment, beauty and beauty marketing and the social worlds that are determined by, or associated with, these industries. It is scarcely possible to open a copy of *Marie Claire*, *Vogue* or *Hello!* without finding the word used to underline the allure of an occasion, a dwelling, a product or a person. Even the broadsheets make use of the word's evocative power in presenting leisure, fashion and entertainment features. In all these publications, glamour is used primarily, although by no means exclusively, in association with the public presentation of fashion. The 'fashion weeks' of London, Paris, Milan and New York give rise to ample coverage of runway shows by leading designers which are conceived precisely to capture press and media attention. The concentration of designer brands, fabulous frocks, name models and celebrity guests, all under the glare of publicity and fêted with lavish hospitality, amounts to an irresistible cocktail of all that is desirable in contemporary commercial culture. The pre-eminence often given

3. Basinger, Jeanine, *A Woman's View: How Hollywood Spoke to Women 1930-1960*, London: Chatto and Windus, 1994, p. 137.

to the presentation of the new Versace collection on such occasions is testimony to that design company's mastery of the language of allure.[4]

Glamour's appeal is by no means limited to top-of-the-range publications. It is equally used by teenage magazines like *17* and *19* and by the in-house magazines of stores like Debenhams and Fenwicks. In these sorts of publications, it is rare to see top fashion models and designer garments. Rather the emphasis is on explaining to ordinary people on average incomes, and teenage girls of limited means, how they can acquire a touch of glamour for a special occasion or a night out. For example, the Winter 1997 issue of the Debenhams magazine featured on the cover the model Caprice. Inside, she modelled three versions of a 'dressed-up' look, each featuring clothes available in the store. Caprice's function in this context is clear. She is neither an aloof catwalk model nor a homely Page Three Girl, but the sort of woman whose polished California-style beauty functions as a vehicle of general aspiration.[5] Although young and apparently flawless, she has enough personality and sophistication (she first came to public attention in Britain as a friend of socialite Tara Palmer-Tomkinson in the 1996 ITV documentary 'Filthy Rich: The It Girls') to be able credibly to impart fashion and beauty advice in her own right. Her image is that of the high-maintenance, groomed woman whose immaculate look is achieved by judicious choice of clothes, cosmetics and beauty treatment.[6]

As an American, Caprice stands outside the British class system. Her Californian origins give her what Jason Cowley describes as 'a certain exotic appeal, a glamorous *difference*'.[7] But her glamour also derives, in addition to her beauty, from the flash-bulb narrative of her life. Thanks to the able management of public relations expert Ghislain Pascal, Caprice was constantly in the public eye following her launch in the 1996 documentary. She featured on the front pages when she appeared at the 1997 National Television Awards wearing a transparent black lace Versace gown. Her calendar enjoyed enormous sales. She advertised pizzas, California prunes, Wonderbra, hair products and even the cricket world cup. She presented her own travel show and posed for men's magazines *GQ* and *Playboy*. In addition,

---

4. See Réka C.V. Buckley and Stephen Gundle, 'Flash Trash: Gianni Versace and the Theory and Practice of Glamour' in Stella Bruzzi and Pamela Church Gibson (eds), *Fashion Culture* London: Routledge, 2000.

5. For a selection of men's views of Caprice, see 'Nice One?', *Front*, April 2000, pp. 44–53.

6. Not by chance perhaps, Caprice resembles nothing so much as an Escada advertisement come to life. These advertisements, in *Vogue* and elsewhere, set the contemporary benchmark for highly polished sophistication.

7. Jason Cowley, 'Caprice', *New Statesman*, 6 March 2000, p. 18.

her relationships, including in 2000 the hint of a liaison with Prince Andrew, have been carefully staged and widely reported.[8]

Caprice appeals because she is an invented personality. In reality she is not a socialite, but a brightly-packaged vehicle for individual dreams and aspirations. As a product she can exist only in the world of the media, where the values she embodies are highly regarded and well-rewarded. Her surface image and shallowness ensure that she conserves certain general qualities that allow people to identify with her. She offers herself as a perfected version of the ordinary woman, while at the same time, through advertising and advice columns, promising to assist women to improve themselves.

Even brief consideration of an example such as Caprice enables us to identify the elements which go to make up what everyone would recognize today as glamour: fashionably attractive, a polished, slightly unreal appearance, physically and sexually appealing, mysterious origins, a touch of the exotic, highly visible. Glamour, in short, seems to be a quality which is rooted to some extent in the real but which is largely manufactured and which exists in the realm of that second-order reality that is sustained by and in the mass media. As a quality that is intended to fascinate a mass audience, it is not very subtle and, indeed, might be said to verge on bad taste. An example of this may be seen in the magazine *Take a Break*. In a story published in June 1995, two women who had paid for a photograph of themselves after a 'Hollywood makeover' lamented the fact that, far from achieving the sophistication they had dreamed of, they seemed like 'a couple of tarts'.[9] Ignoring the sexual and showy elements that are always present in glamour, they had aspired to the polished, confident look so frequently found in upmarket women's magazines.

In order to render these notions more precise, let us examine dictionary definitions of the term. Despite the vagueness of its usage, the etymology of glamour is reasonably clear. According to *The New Fowler's Modern English Usage* (1996) the word was originally Scottish. It was an alteration of the word grammar that retained the sense of the old word gramarye ('occult learning, magic, necromancy'). The *Oxford English Dictionary* (1989) also highlights its Scottish origins and derivation from grammar, although this is indicated to mean magic, enchantment and spells rather than necromancy and the occult. According to Fowler's, glamour passed into standard English usage around the 1830s with the meaning of 'a delusive or alluring charm'.

8. See Alison Boshoff, 'The Prince and the Show-Off Girl', *Daily Mail*, 24 February 2000, pp. 24–5.
9. Joanne Richardson, 'We Look Like a Couple of Tarts', *Take a Break*, 22 June 1995, p. 43.

For *Websters Third New International Dictionary* (1961), glamour is 'an elusive, mysteriously exciting and often illusory attractiveness that stirs the imagination and appeals to a taste for the unconventional, the unexpected, the colourful, or the exotic'. In its secondary meanings glamour is said to be 'a strangely alluring atmosphere of romantic enchantment; bewitching, intangible, irresistibly magnetic charm; [. . .] personal charm and poise combined with unusual physical and sexual attractiveness'.

Today, this world of illusion, mystery, seduction and enchantment is to be found almost exclusively in media representations but, as the magazines referred to above show, this world is connected to everyday reality in many ways. Through consumer products women are promised instant transformation and entry to a realm of desire.[10] In December in particular, women's magazines suggest ideas to assist their readers in preparing for the Christmas party season by presenting photographic spreads of red gowns, black evening dresses and sultry cosmetic treatments. On occasion, the message can be remarkably simple. In *19* of September 1994, for example, the 'glamour look' is reduced to bright red lipstick, a party frock and high heels.

Where did these ideas come from? When and how did glamour become a general phenomenon, indeed even a routine feature of contemporary culture? Why is it associated almost exclusively with the feminine? Quentin Bell and Daniel Roche both suggest that glamour's origins are to be found in the *ancien régime*.[11] Sumptuary laws reserved the use of certain colours and precious fabrics for the aristocracy and the court in feudal Europe. In consequence, elegance, luxury and seductive appearances were confined to the top of the social system. Other authors, including John Harvey, have shown that the bourgeois revolution witnessed the renunciation of colour and flamboyance by men of all classes.[12] In the nineteenth century, black became the habitual masculine colour, while decorativeness, luxury and seduction became a feminine prerogative. According to another interpretation, glamour as it is understood today, as a structure of enchantment deployed by cultural industries, was first developed by Hollywood. In the 1930s, the major studios, having consolidated their domination of the industry, developed a star system

---

10. It might be argued that by the 1980s men were also being offered such promises. However, consumption and shopping were connoted as feminine when they first emerged in the nineteenth century and have retained some of these associations. See Rappaport, Erika, *Shopping for Pleasure: Women and the Making of London's West End*, Princeton: Princeton University Press, 2000.

11. Bell, Quentin, *On Human Finery*, London: The Hogarth Press, 1976; Roche, Daniel, *The Culture of Clothing: Dress and Fashion in the 'ancien régime'*, Cambridge: Cambridge University Press, 1994.

12. Harvey, John, *Men in Black* London: Reaktion, 1995.

in which dozens of young men and women were groomed and moulded into glittering ideal-types whose fortune, beauty, spending power and exciting lives dazzled the film-going public. Writing in 1939 about American film stars, Margaret Thorp defined glamour as 'sex appeal plus luxury plus elegance plus romance'. 'The place to study glamour today is the fan magazines,' she noted. 'Fan magazines are distilled as stimulants of the most exhilarating kind. Everything is superlative, surprising, exciting . . . Nothing ever stands still, nothing ever rests, least of all the sentences . . . Clothes of course are endlessly pictured and described usually with marble fountains, private swimming pools or limousines in the background . . . Every aspect of life, trivial and important, should be bathed in the purple glow of publicity.'[13]

Neither of these seems to us to be persuasive as a starting point for the analysis of glamour, although both, with their common emphasis on image and spectacle, are important components of any examination of the phenomenon. Hollywood, in particular, as the most systematic producer of glamorous images in the twentieth century, requires analysis if the functioning of glamour in contemporary commercial culture is to be understood. Before embarking on this, however, let us set out our own definition of the phenomenon. Glamour, it may be argued, is an enticing image, a staged and constructed image of reality that invites consumption. That is to say, it is primarily visual, it consists of a retouched or perfected version of a real person or situation and it is predicated upon the gaze of a desiring audience. The subjects of glamour, which may be things or people (usually reified through a process of manufacture), seduce by association with one or more of the following qualities (the more the better): beauty, sexuality, theatricality, wealth, dynamism, notoriety, leisure. To this list might be added the feminine, because display and consumption have been heavily connoted as feminine since at least the nineteenth century. Femininity moreover is often considered to be a masquerade, the construction of an image that matches cultural expectations. As Basinger observes, 'a woman *is* her fashion and glamour, rather than her work'.[14]

13. Farrand Thorp, Margaret, *America at the Movies*, New Haven, Conn., 1939. Quoted in Richards, Jeffrey, *The Age of the Dream Palace: Cinema and Society in Britain 1930–1939*, London: Routledge, 1984, pp. 157–8.

14. Basinger, Jeanine, *A Woman's View: How Hollywood Spoke to Women 1930–1960*, London: Chatto and Windus, 1994, p. 129.

The Golden Age of Hollywood

By the last two decades of the twentieth century, Hollywood had shed many of the trappings of glamour that had characterized it in the 1930s and 1940s. Only on select occasions, such as Oscar Night, does the modern-day movie industry seek to dazzle its public with a glittering gathering of stars dressed to the height of elegance. If Sharon Stone is sometimes referred to as the only current star of the old type, it is largely because she made it her business from the 1990s always to present herself as elegantly groomed, perfectly coiffed and sexually alluring. Yet the image of the stars of the past and their lifestyles is still strongly evident in contemporary commercial culture. Perhaps more than anything else, the Hollywood golden age constitutes the benchmark for what today is understood as alluring and glamorous. On numerous occasions fashion magazines feature models made up and photographed in black and white as Lauren Bacall, Marlene Dietrich or Ava Gardner. Moreover, in recent times, Pretty Polly tights has deployed in advertisements images of Rita Hayworth, while Mercedes and World of Leather have used Marilyn Monroe, Elena Mirò Ava Gardner, Luciano Soprani fragrances Hedy Lamarr and Gap Steve McQueen. All these images refer back to the period between the 1930s and the 1950s, when Hollywood cinema conquered the world and shaped the collective imagination with its stories, style and stars.

The 'glamour of Hollywood' was precisely an image that was constructed through a variety of media: the films themselves, still photographs and portraits, publicity material and press and radio coverage of the lives and loves of the stars. In reflecting on this image, two elements deserve particular attention. Sex appeal on the one hand and luxury on the other constituted the cornerstone of Hollywood's strategy to capture and hold mass interest.

On screen, all direct references to sexual intimacy inside and outside of marriage were strictly taboo following the adoption of the Hays Code in 1932. By introducing this element of self-regulation, the American movie industry hoped to pacify respectable opinion and win recognition as a mainstream component of American society. Yet sex appeal was always important in Hollywood movies. In 1950, anthropologist Hortense Powdermaker observed in her study of America's 'dream factory' that the physical presence of actors was vital to the films' appeal.[15] Heroes were always virile he-men, she noted, while heroines exuded an obvious sex appeal. The immediate and unambiguous attraction between the two protagonists (even if at first disguised by a comedy of hatred) was part of the theme of most

15. Powdermaker, Hortense, *Hollywood: The Dream Factory*, Boston: Little, Brown, 1950, p. 207.

movies. Hollywood, she argued, stressed the 'look at me', 'look at my body' type. Close-ups emphasized the intimate details of the physical being of actors. They were also known by parts of their bodies, that which was deemed most worthy of attention. Thus a husky voice, beautiful breasts, or a dimple in the chin came to sum up the entire persona of a star. The reduction to parts affected women more than men, although Powdermaker did reveal that one (unnamed) male star was known as 'the penis'. Newcomers to Hollywood were obliged to perform a long apprenticeship, part of which involved them in revealing as much flesh as possible for 'cheesecake' and 'beefcake' shots. As Edgar Morin remarked, 'stars reveal their spirits, starlets exhibit their bodies'.[16]

Prior to the Hays Code, many films featured a more obvious sexuality and laid considerable stress on experience. In the 1920s and early 1930s, stars like Greta Garbo and Marlene Dietrich played world-weary women who had seen everything and were shocked by nothing. Frequently, as in Garbo's *Susan Lennox* and Dietrich's *Shanghai Express*, they played women who had been abandoned by lovers and had turned to prostitution. As Lea Jacobs has shown, 'fallen women' movies exercised a great appeal during the Depression years because they legitimated the use of sexuality as a means by which women could escape poverty and hardship.[17] These images also drew on the theatrical tradition of the femme fatale that had been established in the nineteenth century by writers like Théophile Gautier and actresses such as Sarah Bernhardt. Garbo and Dietrich were both enigmatic, even exotic, European women whose allure was enhanced by costumiers like Adrian at MGM and Travis Banton at Paramount, as well as the art of the best cinematographers in Hollywood.

The movie capital sometimes liked to give the impression that the seductiveness and beauty of its stars was a natural phenomenon. All the industry had to do was discover the star quality and present it unalloyed to the public. One example of this can be seen in *The Barefoot Contessa*. In an evening scene, Humphrey Bogart tells Ava Gardner (playing a simple Spanish singer, Maria Vargas) that the moon illuminates her face just like a key light, revealing her potential for movie stardom. Of course, Gardner was already a star and the 'moon' was in fact a key light. The fiction of naturalness served to disguise the fact that the beauty and photogenic qualities of the stars were in reality highly constructed. To turn Margherita Cansino, a simple girl of Spanish-Mexican origin, into the all-American glamour girl Rita

---

16. Morin, Edgar, *Les Stars*, Paris: Seuil, 1972, p. 53.

17. Jacobs, Lea, *The Wages of Sin: Censorship and the Fallen Woman Film 1928–1942*, Madison: University of Wisconsin Press, 1991.

Hayworth required considerable art and expertise, and the same talents moulded Norma Jean Baker into Marilyn Monroe. Even Garbo and Dietrich were very ordinary, rather gauche women before being thoroughly reshaped by the studios. The sex appeal of the stars was not an intrinsic feature, although 'personality' was a quality the industry regarded as vital to star creation; on the contrary it was a manufactured, artificial phenomenon that the studios conferred on their protegés.

The inventor of sex appeal in American cinema was the English novelist Elinor Glyn, who arrived in Hollywood at the invitation of Jesse Lansky in 1920 and subsequently worked for MGM. Glyn, author of the scandalous novel *Three Weeks* and the short story *It*, believed that sex should be disguised as romance. She also believed in the creation of an aura of mystery to arouse public interest.[18] Working with Gloria Swanson and Rudolph Valentino, she taught them poise, elegance and seductive techniques (such as Valentino kissing the palm rather than the back of a woman's hand) which fuelled the atmosphere of sensuality. In the course of the 1920s and 1930s, Hollywood set design and costume applied the lesson of deflected or displaced sexuality by incorporating the exotic or the sensual (shimmering fabrics, shiny surfaces) into the structure of film-making. Actors were also moulded through cosmetic surgery, cosmetics and flattering lighting.

Perhaps the most extraordinary and enduring examples of Hollywood glamour are provided by the stills of great studio photographers like George Hurrell and Clarence Sinclair Bull. These portraits, for which the stars often posed reluctantly at the end of a day on the set, are today gathered in numerous volumes. Moreover, when an occasion presents itself, contemporary actors are more than willing to allow themselves to be photographed in the studio manner of the 1940s because they know that the allure of those images is unrivalled.[19] In the sultry black and white photographs of the past, actors were turned into icons. They appeared almost as gods and certainly as archetypes, their individuality giving way to a generalized image of seduction. The perfection of the images did not derive from the beauty of the subject but rather from the invention of the photographer.

Speaking in the 1980s, Hurrell said that he regarded glamour as a synonym for 'giving a sexier attitude' or creating a 'bedroom look'. 'You know, glamour to me was nothing more than just an excuse for saying sexy pictures. In

18. See Rosen, Marjorie, *Popcorn Venus: Women, Movies and the American Dream*, London: Peter Owen, 1973, pp. 117–20 and Glyn, Anthony, *Elinor Glyn*, London: Hutchinson, 1955, chapter six.

19. See, for example, the 'old Hollywood' portraits of present-day actors in Prince, Len, *About Glamour*, New York: Simon and Schuster, 1998.

other words my interpretation was entirely one of saying "Come on, we're going to take some sexy pictures".'[20] To achieve this effect, he employed light, floating materials, posed his subjects lying on their backs or wet, or bathed them in light and shade. Each of the images was heavily worked over and blemishes were eliminated through retouching. Although the typical shots involved women, men were given the same treatment. Lead was put on the negative, sometimes on both sides, or images were improved through dyes and brush work. Hurrell claimed that his job was easier if the actor already had a sensual quality or attitude, but where this was absent sex appeal could be conferred as a total invention.

As far as luxury was concerned, this became a hallmark of Hollywood with Cecil B. De Mille, who believed that opulent scenes and fabulous costumes would make people stop and gasp. Several of the moguls had begun their working lives in the garment industry and were alert to the importance of fine clothing in weaving an image that audiences would find seductive. With the aid of Glyn and a few other style advisors, Hollywood conferred on itself an upper-class image of wealth and elegance. The widespread use of eye-catching wardrobes including furs, feathers and jewellery roused some contemporary critics to anger. It was felt that, by covering 'fallen women' with the trappings of luxury in tales of irregular social mobility, a direct exchange between sex and money was being suggested. The accusation that Hollywood was condoning prostitution and offending moral standards was a key factor in the adoption of the Hays Code. However, the emphasis on luxury in the films of larger studios like MGM and Paramount did not diminish. Even by today's standards, the opulence of the upper-class settings of many movies of that era is breathtaking.

What was the reason for this emphasis? First, it should be remembered that Hollywood before the Second World War was not respectable. The moguls who had founded and run the studios were typically Jewish immigrants who were social outsiders. For all his power, Louis B. Mayer of MGM could not join the Los Angeles Country Club because Jews were not allowed. Given this situation, it is not surprising that Hollywood shared the emphasis on exterior appearance that marked immigrant behaviour in early twentieth-century America. Stuart and Elizabeth Ewen have spoken of an impulse to finery in immigrant communities, in which marginalized individuals struggled to fit in by emulating their 'betters'.[21] Even among the poor, self-hood could

20. Kobal, John (ed.), *George Hurrell: Hollywood Glamour Portraits*, London: Schirmer Art Books, 1993, p. 11.
21. Ewen, Stuart and Ewen, Elizabeth, *Channels of Desire: Mass Images and the Shaping of American Consciousness*, Minneapolis: University of Minnesota Press, 1992, pp. 154–8.

be achieved through the construction of an appearance that contained no outsider traits. Given the American ethic of success and social mobility, the upper-class look of those whom Veblen described as the 'leisure class' stood as the maximum aspiration.[22]

A second, connected, reason for the sumptuousness of Hollywood films concerns the rapid development of consumerism in America in the 1920s. In this decade, the Ewens argue, consumption became central to Americanism.[23] The message was communicated particularly strongly to immigrants that by purchasing goods they could transform themselves and become fully-fledged citizens. As Hollywood was developing and becoming a national and international industry at precisely this time, it naturally evolved in tandem with the consumer society. Indeed, even more than advertisements, the movies offered a compelling, enticing image of capitalism. Hollywood's linkages to consumerism were numerous but perhaps the most striking involved the stars. Because the stars were conceived as marketing devices for films, they could also be used to market a range of other products, and these secondary advertisements or endorsements could drum up further business for given films. In an important essay, Charles Eckert examined how tie-ins became a key part of the way stars were presented to the public.[24] Industry found that sex appeal generated excitement which could assist in the sale even of the most demure products.

Stars were the perfect consumers. They were new men and women who were upwardly mobile and rich. They, more than anyone else, were obliged to consume and to display their wealth in order to prove their status; their lifestyles acted as a focus for the aspirations of the masses. However, their explicit association with the material culture of consumerism was not felt by all to be positive. Producer David O. Selznick, for example, thought that tie-ins undermined the mystique that the studios had built up. He also disapproved the free endorsements that actresses gave to Max Factor and Lux soap. Morin, by contrast, sees no contradiction between the star as goddess (*star-déese*) and the star as product (*star-merchandise*). It may be suggested that the growing links between the film industry and consumerism did in fact herald a change in the nature of stars. As Morin himself notes, stars of the sound era were less exotic and exceptional and more projections of the typical. In this context they became themselves industrial products,

22. Veblen, Thorstein, *Theory of the Leisure Class*, New York: A.M. Kelley, 1899.

23. Ewen, Stuart and Ewen, Elizabeth, *Channels of Desire: Mass Images and the Shaping of American Consciousness*, Minneapolis: University of Minnesota Press, 1992, chapter three.

24. Eckert, Charles, 'The Carol Lombard in Macy's Window' in Christine Gledhill (ed.), *Stardom: Industry of Desire*, London: Routledge, 1991.

manufactured in series like Ford cars. Sometimes, the objectification of the star, especially where the personality was weak and the elements of 'type' strong, resulted in a sense that the objects had taken over. For example, there are some photographs of Lana Turner taken in the 1940s which depict her coiffed, made up and adorned in every conceivable fashion accessory: hat, gloves, fur stole, brooch, earrings.[25] The human element appears to have disappeared almost completely.

There is something standardized about all the icons of glamour produced during the Hollywood golden age. Like shop mannequins and the fashion models of more recent times, their blankness and apparent hollowness leaves a space which enables people to 'buy into' them and project themselves and their aspirations on to them. While upper-class and established middle-class people regarded Hollywood as vulgar, brash and impossibly *nouveau*, lower-class people viewed it as the epitome of refinement. Certainly, it was a great educator, with its stories of physical and social mobility, its encouragements to self-transformation and its mail order catalogue aesthetics. Yet, Elizabeth Wilson has pointed out that star images are frequently characterized by an air of the haunting and the unnatural.[26] So still and lifeless are the composed images that their subjects appear almost embalmed and laid to rest.

The capacity of capitalism for reification, for turning everything, even people, into things was first noted by Gyorgy Lukacs in 1923.[27] It can be argued that the de-humanized, dead look that marks glamour proves its intrinsic link to urban, industrial society. Divorced from nature, this society poses the transcendence of nature as an objective. For the first time, abundance was configured as a real possibility by industry. 'Consumerism posed nature as an inhospitable force, a hopeless anachronism,' write the Ewens. 'Industrial production and enterprising imaginations claimed for themselves the rights and powers of creation.'[28] Because these forces were developed most fully in the United States, so too is glamour a phenomenon that in its purest form can be analysed through the prism of Americanism. The level of abstraction required could be developed most easily in the context of a country that was itself invented and unburdened by the weight of the past. Within the context of America, Hollywood was the maximum expression of the artificial, a community created in the middle of nowhere and dedicated to fiction. The lives of the stars, no less than the backlot, was a staged reality,

25. See Fahey, David, and Rich, Linda (eds), *Masters of Starlight: Photographers in Hollywood*, New York: Ballantine, 1987, p. 159.

26. Wilson, Elizabeth, *Adorned in Dreams: Fashion and Modernity*, London: Virago, 1985.

27. Lukacs, Gyorgy, *History and Class Consciousness*, London: Merlin, 1977.

28. Ewen, Stuart and Ewen, Elizabeth, *Channels of Desire: Mass Images and the Shaping of American Consciousness*, Minneapolis: University of Minnesota Press, 1992, p. 47.

a theatrical construct designed to entice an audience. Consequently, it offered the most powerful and seductive form of glamour and the Hollywood film star became the most glamorous figure to have existed.

The Nineteenth-Century City

At the root of glamour, however, is a set of social and cultural changes that took place in the late nineteenth century, in particular in the great modern cities. Broadly speaking, this period may be said to have seen the decline of rigid social hierarchies and the eclipse of aristocratic control of culture, politics and society. Instead, a civilization based on money took shape, in which luxury, visibility and elegance were not reserved for a closed elite, but were open to whoever could pay or be paid for. Increasingly, a cosmopolitan category of *nouveaux riches* bought into the old high society or, where access was obstructed, emulated its forms and rituals. As part of this process, monetary values of ostentation and display enjoyed prominence as industrialists and financiers struggled to establish their status through conspicuous consumption. At the same time, a range of secondary changes served to render more open and visible the public dimension of the life of the elite, which took on the characteristics of a tableau or narrative for lower social classes. For example, the theatre and high society enjoyed closer relations, and both for the first time in the modern period established links with the street, which was redefined as a place of shopping and display. In Paris, Benjamin's 'capital of the nineteenth century', the boulevards,[29] the arcades and the theatres of Montmartre became centres of frivolity and luxury that were not hidden behind the closed doors of the palaces of the aristocracy.

In such a context, dazzling facades produced by families and individuals seeking to win recognition mingled and mixed with commercial displays, the bustle of the boulevards and the gaiety of the world of entertainment. Enticing images became part and parcel of the modern city. What were the sources of this new visual language of display? In part they were conventional ones. Royal courts, like that of the French Second Empire prior to its downfall, or the events of the London Season, provided a focus of attention. But as an established elite lost its monopoly of splendour, the sources were widened to include the *demi-monde* or what eventually was termed 'café society'. Among the low cultural forms that provided inputs into the dynamic image of the city were popular theatre, the *cafés chantants*, the display windows of the

29. Benjamin, Walter, *The Arcades Project*, Cambridge, Mass.: Harvard University Press, 1999.

arcades and the department stores, and the world of commercial sex. The seductive imagery that defines glamour, it may be argued, was forged through the mixing of these low and high sources. From the latter came the exotic, bright colours (notably red), and a sleazy, vulgar element, while the former supplied an injection of luxury balanced by good taste and refinement.[30] Sex and the theatrical mixed openly in the vibrant red-dominated posters of Toulouse Lautrec.

The figure who symbolized the new language was the courtesan. Like the film star of later years, the courtesan was an emblematic figure who was recounted, evoked, described and analysed in novels like Zola's *Nana*, newspapers, studies and memoirs. As a professional of illusion and make-believe, she was a central figure in the new culture of appearances and surfaces. At bottom a prostitute, she was also in parts actress, fashion icon, celebrity and professional beauty. The very grandest courtesans lived in palaces, where they were maintained by a team of wealthy sponsors eager to pay vast sums in return for sexual favours. They lived on the margins of respectable society, but exercised considerable influence through their liaisons and their trend-setting role. At once vulgar and elegant, showy and fashionable, the courtesans captured the attention and occupied a place in the collective imaginary. According to art historian T.J. Clark, the courtesan was prominent because, by embracing luxury, she adopted a facade of respectability that at least partially concealed the uneasy intersection of money and sexuality that was such a widespread phenomenon in Paris.[31]

However, if the courtesan acted as the inspiration for a new language of allure, it took artists to give this language a concrete, reproducible form and develop it into a recognisable trademark style of modern celebrity. Several artists contributed to this enterprise, but none more than the Italian portrait painter Giovanni Boldini, who painted nearly all the prominent figures to pass through Paris between the late nineteenth century and the First World War. Boldini is not today regarded as an important painter, but in many ways he pioneered a type of edgy, fashionable portraiture that summed up the Paris of the Belle Époque. He forged a new pictorial language by combining the sensual atmosphere and bright colours of the worlds of prostitution and popular entertainment with the conventional society

30. On the mingling of theatre and consumerism in Paris, see Kracauer, Siegfried, *Jacques Offenbach and the Paris of His Times,* London: Constable, 1937. On London, see Rappaport, Erika, *Shopping for Pleasure: Women and the Making of London's West End*, Princeton: Princeton University Press, 2000.

31. Clark, T.J., *The Painting of Modern Life: Paris in the Art of Manet and his Followers,* London: Thames and Hudson, 1990, pp. 102, 109.

portrait.[32] Boldini painted many leading exponents of café society, as well as prominent artists and some aristocrats. His favourite subjects were mainly wealthy women, who revelled in the sexy, scandalous air he conferred on them and which they took to be quintessentially Parisian. He achieved this effect in part by elongating them and twisting their bodies as though they were rotating on an axis. Many of his subjects courted notoriety, like the eccentric Marquess Luisa Casati and Lady Colin Campbell, protagonist of one of the most controversial divorce cases of Victorian England. Being painted by Boldini conferred on them a theatrical kudos and turned them into icons of their era.

Boldini was not only a fashionable painter but also a painter of fashion. He was a master at conveying the effects of a variety of materials and accessories and he was careful to ensure his subjects were clothed in a flattering way. By working quickly and employing indefinite slapdash strokes, often sharply diagonal, he created an air of movement and frivolity. The result was a dazzling surface appearance that was extravagant and dramatic. Worth, Doucet and other designers were happy to lend him their creations because they knew that good publicity could derive from being incorporated into what Boldini's biographer describes as 'a highly potent pictorial *maison de beauté*'.[33] The flamboyance of Boldini's work owed much to fashion and to the creative collaboration he forged with the designers who produced the luxurious gowns women wore to society occasions. He was not interested in psychology or, in general, in character, but in image and effect. The concern with the exterior and artifice led some critics to label his work kitsch. Certainly, they owed more to popular taste than to any idea of refinement.

Many Boldini portraits were displayed publicly in salons, they were illustrated in newspapers and openly discussed. Just as, in later years, society photographers would contribute to the celebrity of their subjects, so too did a striking portrait by Boldini lend allure and status. Thus the painter may be said to have contributed to the birth of modern celebrity culture. Around the turn of the century, the interlocking spheres of high society, fashion, theatre and the *demi-monde* gave rise to figures who were the object of gossip and curiosity. Confirmation of this development is provided by the 1889 Paris Exposition, which featured a circular building holding a canvas entitled 'Le Tout Paris'. Customers paid in large, but not overwhelming, numbers, to see around 800 portraits of the rich and the beautiful. 'Like other panoramas,'

32. For a detailed analysis of Boldini, see Stephen Gundle, 'Mapping the Origins of Glamour: Giovanni Boldini, Paris and the Belle Epoque', *Journal of European Studies*, 29 (1999), pp. 269–95.

33. Cecchi, Dario, *Giovanni Boldini*, Turin: UTET, 1962, p. 274.

Charles Rearick observes, 'this one catered to a taste for skilfully wrought realism in illusion and a burgeoning touristic desire to see the most touted sites quickly and easily.'[34]

Boldini's work is interesting not just because many of his subjects featured in the press but because he developed a standardized and codified visual language of allure at the very beginning of the media age. Although the public that was interested in and familiar with his art was quite restricted, the related dynamics of celebrity and the popular press were contributing to a marked widening of the potential audience. The development of photographic reproduction and the illustrated press fuelled this trend. With the invention of *Vogue* in United States in the 1890s (and European editions in following years), the café society became a systematic phenomenon sustained by the media and commercial culture. In contrast to aloof and private members of the old social elite, actors, playboys, courtesans, financiers and young aristocrats were happy to disport themselves before the public gaze. They thus offered a facade of elite life that the public could relate to more easily because it was not based purely on class and inheritance.

This development coincided with the expansion of consumer culture. Department stores, the cosmetics industry and advertising drew on innovations in the arts but they also gave a new impulse to glamour. For marketing purposes, they cultivated royal and aristocratic patronage while also seeking to entice customers with a phantasmagoria of plenty. Bright colours, seductive atmospheres, exotic décor and theatrical razzamataz were employed as techniques to transport shoppers into a realm of fantasy where goods became symbols of values that were as much imaginative as utilitarian. Stores, like theatres, were open to the public, yet they also traded in exclusivity. Many were built like palaces, staff acted like servants and customers treated as honoured guests. From the 1920s, cinemas too presented themselves as people's palaces, where luxury was combined with democracy. The purpose of such techniques was to create appropriate spaces for the selling of luxury goods but also, crucially, to invest ordinary goods with associations of luxury and desirability. In this way they could be sold for premium prices. In fashion and cosmetics, glamour still serves precisely this purpose today.

Originally forged in the great capital cities of Europe, the commercial language of allure fed directly into Hollywood cinema. Between the 1910s and the 1930s, numerous cosmeticians, retail experts and window designers left a politically turbulent Europe for the United States. Several ended up in movie studio art departments. One of these was Ernest Dichter who, having

34. Rearick, Charles, *Pleasures of the Belle Epoque*, New Haven: Yale University Press, 1985, pp. 172–3.

designed stores and advertisements in Vienna, became an influential set and costume designer for Paramount. The most famous such emigré was Max Factor, cosmetic artist to the royal opera in St Petersburg and later to the Tsar's family, who migrated after the Russian revolution to the USA. Following a brief commercial experience in New York he moved to the West Coast where he quickly established himself as the leading purveyor of make-up to the movie industry. On the strength of this success, he developed lines of cosmetics bearing his name that were marketed to the general public through department stores. By buying products such as Max Factor's 'pancake' make-up, women were invited to buy into the world of glamour that they saw on the screen and in magazines. The commodification of aristocratic allure in this way completed its cycle.

Glamour and Modernity

In this chapter, we have shown that glamour is integral to capitalist modernity. It emerged at a specific point in history characterized by: the shift in terms of the general order of meanings and priorities from a society dominated by the aristocracy to one governed by the bourgeoisie; the extension of commodi-fication into ever wider public and private spheres; the development of a new urban system of life permeated by consumerism and the importance of fashion; the closer proximity of the theatre and high society; the creation of patterns of leisure shared by virtually all urban classes; an obsession with the feminine as the cultural codifier of modernity's tensions and promise.

Glamour became more important as modernity spread and the mass media developed. Popular magazines, cinema, radio and, later, television provided opportunities for staging, representing and inventing people, events and commodities. For this reason they were seized on by retail and cultural industries. Over time, a language of commercial seduction evolved and was codified. It may be suggested that, in recent times, the forms taken by this language have tended to be nostalgic or to employ pastiche. The fashion spreads that appeared in the leading magazines at the time of the glamour revival of 1994, for example, had a dull and familiar feel to them. Caprice, as a contemporary embodiment of glamour, seems more like a reminder of American television shows like *Dynasty* and *Baywatch* (which themselves were influenced by classical Hollywood cinema) than an original. There are several reasons for this. One is related to the sheer quantity of glamorous images that have been produced over the last century. Today we live in a complex, highly visual culture in which the iconic images of the past have, through repetition, acquired more resonance than everyday reality. Thus contemporary images of glamour tend to work off other images, creating a self-referential cycle that reinforces artificiality. The original social referents have become lost in time.

In the opening section, we offered our definition of glamour. In conclusion, it is appropriate to ask if it is possible to construct a theory. Any theory would have to take account of the imaginative appeal of glamour, its seductiveness and artificiality. It would also need to refer to persistent class divisions, the alienation of modern capitalism and the frustrations as well as the temptations of consumer culture. Although a great deal of work has been undertaken in recent years on consumerism, fashion, photography and the media, there is not as yet any theory of glamour. It may be suggested that early sociologists like Werner Sombart, Georg Simmel, Thorstein Veblen and Siegfried Kracauer still have much to offer. Their contribution is important because they were writing about luxury, fashion, conspicuous consumption and cinema towards the end of the moment that has been identified here as having witnessed the birth of glamour. Perhaps the most important starting point, however, is Walter Benjamin's concept of the decline of the aura of art in the age of mechanical reproduction.[35] Through reproduction, art may gain commercial potential, he argued, but it loses authenticity. Something similar can be sustained in relation to high society or fashion. Rita Felski argues that even woman loses her aura in an era of technical reproduction since femininity as nature is demystified and downgraded.[36] These ideas stem at root from Marx's theory of labour and value in capitalist society. The problem is that, without aura, imagination is impoverished and commercial potential is undermined. Glamour therefore is the manufactured aura of capitalist society, the dazzling illusion that compensates for inauthenticity and which reinforces consumerism as a way of life.

35. Walter Benjamin, 'The Work of Art in the Age of Mechanical Reproduction' in *Illuminations* London: Fontana, 1973.
36. Felski, Rita, *The Gender of Modernity*, Cambridge, Mass.: Harvard University Press, 1997.

4

Ethnic Minimalism: A Strand of 1990s British Fashion Identity Explored via a Contextual Analysis of Designs by Shirin Guild

Amy de la Haye

In 'The Cutting Edge: 50 Years of British Fashion' exhibition staged at the Victoria & Albert Museum in 1997, four key themes of post-war national fashion identity were identified: Romantic, Tailoring, Country and Bohemian. The latter category embraced the work of designers that drew upon classical and medieval revival styles and ethnographic sources. The striking, mainly exuberant exhibits included ensembles by Thea Porter, Yuki, Zandra Rhodes, Mr Fish, Charles & Patricia Lester and Georgina von Etzdorf. Remarkable for its understatement was a layered linen ensemble in a neutral palette consisting of an 'Abba coat', jacket and vest, teamed with linen trousers incorporating an apron front by Shirin Guild for Spring/Summer 1996. The coat was derived from the black gauze holy garment worn by Iranian men, whilst the trousers referred to the habit of peasant women to wear skirts and dresses over their trousers to obtain maximum protection from the harsh climate.

This article defines and sites Shirin Guild's work within the contexts of dress reform, avant-garde clothes, British fashion and minimal design in the twentieth century. It also analyses the designer's inspiration from her own clothing traditions in relation to the broader 1990s vogue for cross-cultural references within international fashion.

Figure 4.1. Portrait of Shirin Guild 1999. Photograph by Christian Cunningham.

The founding principles of the Rational Dress Society, established in 1881, were to: 'promote the adoption, according to individual taste and convenience, a style of dress based upon considerations of health, comfort, and beauty, and to deprecate constant changes of fashion that cannot be recommended on any of these grounds'.[1]

In many respects Shirin Guild's philosophy embodies these same objectives. Her signature look is oversized, square-shaped garments informed by the styles, flat cutting and layering characteristic of ethnographic dress, particularly Iranian menswear. These are interpreted with a modern, reductivist aesthetic and are made using the finest European fabrics and yarns.

Shirin Guild was born in 1946 and grew up in Iran. Before the revolution of 1978, she moved to Los Angeles and then to London. Her career in fashion, like that of many designers, took off when, unable to find clothes she wanted to wear, she started to design her own. Friends admired them, orders were placed and in 1991 she launched her own label collection. In common with many UK designer-level companies, Shirin Guild is in independent ownership and exclusively produces womenswear. With the support of her husband and business partner, the interior designer Robin Guild, the business supplies an

1. Newton, Stella Mary, *Health, Art and Reason*, London: John Murray, 1974, p. 117.

international market. Major outlets include Saks Fifth Avenue branches throughout America, Petra Teufel in Germany, and in London, Shirin Guild has been Liberty's top-selling fashion label since 1997. Nonetheless, few know her name.

Shirin Guild believes that certain styles of dress possess a time-honoured functionality and enduring beauty and thus her collections subtly evolve from season to season, whilst the basic square shaped silhouette and layered approach remains the same. Function and comfort are a priority. Styles are loose (many tops are made in just one size and skirts and trousers in small, medium and large), hang from the shoulders and engulf – but never shroud – the wearer. Unusual within the high-fashion industry, is the designer's pride in the fact that her clothes appeal to and flatter women of various ages, shapes and sizes. When worn in European or American urban contexts clothes bearing the Shirin Guild label can transcend distinctions between day and evening, formal and leisurewear. However a judicious variation in textiles and yarns can render garments of the same or similar cut ideal for specific purposes and occasions.

The most luxurious fabrics and yarns, often those associated with the masculine wardrobe – pinstripe wool, soft flannel, crisp cotton shirting, Scottish cashmere, grainy tweed and Irish linen – predominate in Shirin Guild's collections. However, she also actively embraces new developments in textiles: recent collections have featured a modernistic, gleaming yarn of steel encased within silk. Unusual materials accent the collections and include paper fabric and yarn and, since the decriminalization of hemp for textile purposes, the designer has made much use of this environmentally friendly and versatile fibre. The palette is predominantly dark and neutral, with injections of indigo, vibrant orange, yellow and muted spice tones. Where decoration appears it is geometric – printed and woven striped and checked designs and blocks of textured knit.

The ethnographic styling and practicality of Shirin Guild's designs can be assessed within the historical context of 'unconventional' (sometimes described as 'eccentric') dress – that is, styles selected by those who actively spurn high-fashion trends. In the post-war period fashions became increasingly diverse and open to individual interpretation, as well as a host of sub-cultural alternatives. Certainly before the 1950s, the evolution of fashionable style was strictly linear and to deviate from this was to risk ridicule and even social ostracism. Prior to the Second World War, it was therefore primarily the most daring members of the aristocracy, artists and intellectuals who dared to flaunt their rebellious attitudes via their mode of dress. Unconventional dress has an international context but has always found especially vocal expression in Britain.

Figure 4.2. Shirin Guild for Spring/Summer 1998. Oatmeal coloured linen gauze 'Abba coat' worn over Nehru collared, square-shaped jacket and apron-fronted pants in un-dyed, crinkled linen. Photograph by Robin Guild.

It is perhaps appropriate that in London Liberty is Shirin's major retail outlet: the store has consistently championed and supported original British clothing and fashion talents. Established as an emporium selling Japanese, Persian, Chinese and Indian textiles and household artefacts, Liberty was opened in Regent Street in 1875. From the outset the store attracted a progressive, literary and artistic clientele. Serving their unconventional predilections in dress it offered – alongside ultra-fashionable 'Gowns of the New Season' – 'Gowns Never Out of Style' – generally in the uncorseted, flowing medieval and classical styles favoured by the Aesthetes and Pre-Raphaelites. Whilst Shirin Guild also deviates from high-fashion trends, extolling comfort, the use of natural fibres and hand-crafted techniques, the cut of her work has more in common with the unconventional styles of dress reform.

The dress reform movement has been traced back to the late eighteenth century when it was associated with the political ideals of the French Revolution.[2] From this period through to the early twentieth century, organized debate focused upon trousered dress for women. Advocated on utilitarian grounds and for minimizing gender and class differences, bifurcated garments were appropriated by various communities of utopian socialists in Britain and America during the early nineteenth century.

By the 1850s the ideals of dress reform attracted public attention through the activities of Mrs Dexter C. Bloomer of New York. An active campaigner for women's emancipation, she devised and wore a style of dress that was to assume her name, "the bloomer". Rejecting fashionable full-skirted gowns, supported by cumbersome layers of heavy petticoats, she wore a loose knee-length tunic over baggy trousers that were gathered at the ankles. As Stella Mary Newton pointed out in her standard work *Health Art & Reason*, Mrs Bloomer was undoubtedly inspired by the engravings depicting seductive Turkish beauties, that were in vogue following the cult of Byron and the French conquest of Algeria.[3] More than a century later, Shirin Guild extols the functionality and aesthetic appeal of similarly cut 'Kurdish' style pants.

Although short lived (Amelia Bloomer abandoned the style following the introduction of the lightweight cage-frame crinoline) and very rarely worn, trousered dress for women prompted much debate about the unhygienic, irrational and ephemeral nature of women's high fashion, issues that were also to arouse concern within the medical profession. Under the umbrella of the International Health Exhibition, held in London in 1884, the ideals of

2. Wilson, Elizabeth and Taylor, Lou, *Through the Looking Glass*, London: BBC Books, 1989, p. 28.
3. Newton, Stella Mary, *Health, Art and Reason*, London: John Murray, 1974, p.117.

dress reform enjoyed renewed publicity. Exhibitors included the Rational Dress Society that was founded in Britain by Viscountess Harberton and counted several doctors on its committee. The RDS protested, 'against the introduction of any fashion in dress that either deforms the figure, impedes movement of the body, or in any way tends to injure health'.[4]

In spite of their pragmatic emphasis upon practicality, comfort, health and equality for women, dress reformers were often portrayed by the press as a ridiculous, eccentric bunch and were much lampooned by cartoonists. Women were victim to especially hostile caricature and feminists abandoned dress reform, concluding that it was damaging to their cause.

By the outbreak of the First World War, the dress reform movement was in abeyance, as changing lifestyles paved the way for more comfortable *sportif* styles in durable fabrics, such as knitted jersey as championed by Parisian couturiers Coco' Chanel and Jean Patou. Since the 1920s, fashion designers have presented a fast-moving series of fashionable silhouettes, some prioritizing function and comfort above others. By the twilight years of the twentieth century, fashion became pluralistic and women were granted more freedom in their choice of dress and adornment than ever before. Nonetheless, many could still identify with the objectives of dress reform. These women still cherish Shirin Guild's enduring designs derived from ethnographic styles, in preference to fashions that are skimpy, restricting and fleeting.

For almost a century, irrespective of prevailing trends, the designs of Mariano Fortuny (1871–1949) have retained their desirability. Coats and dresses bearing his label command high prices at auction and are purchased not only as museum pieces, but are still relished as luxurious, ethereal, wearable garments. The Venice-based designer-inventor's clothing simultaneously attracted an unconventional 'bohemian' and highly fashionable clientele, as Shirin Guild's work does today. In this and other respects, parallels can be drawn between the two designers work and working practice. Fortuny was a prolific and eminently successful creative talent, establishing himself as a fine artist, pioneer photographer and technical stage designer - he even patented designs for propelling boats. However, it was for his textiles and dress, produced from 1906 until his death, that he was to achieve greatest recognition. Fortuny was born in Granada into an artistic family. His father, a painter best known for his work on Arabic themes, was also a passionate collector of Eastern fine and decorative arts, including textiles, which were to inspire his son.

As a designer of textiles and dress, Fortuny was also self-taught. Critical of contemporary fashion trends, he researched and derived ideas from historical and ethnographic sources, looking in particular to Coptic, North

4. Ibid., p. 117.

African, Moorish, Indian, classical Greek and Italian Renaissance styles. His first professional garment design called *Knossos* – a rectangular cloth that wrapped around the body – was notable for its simplicity. In contrast to 1900s high-fashion trends for either corseted 'frou-frou' gowns or the exotic costumes promoted by revolutionary Parisian couturier Paul Poiret, it lacked construction and facilitated complete freedom of movement.

In 1907 Fortuny developed, and in 1909 patented, the design of his columnar *delphos* dress – a finely pleated silk sheath based on a Greek chiton – a style he made and sold for some forty years. Because it clung mercilessly to the body, the *delphos* was initially considered immodest and daring and attracted a 'bohemian' clientele, including the dancer Isadora Duncan. It also found favour amongst a coterie of international society women, with artistic leanings, who wore it within the confines of the home, in place of a tea gown to obtain temporary relief from corseting. Fortuny subsequently conceived variants of the sari, djellabah, kaftan and the Turkish dolman – which also permitted free movement – and which he dyed and printed according to his own (still secret) techniques.

Although sales of textiles and dress supported him financially for the rest of his life, Fortuny rarely commanded the attention of the fashion press (although his work was immortalized by Marcel Proust in *Remembrance of Things Past*). Generally, it is the very latest, most dramatic or shocking that entices fashion photographers, journalists and editors and, in turn, commands public attention – though, seldom are these items purchased to wear. Like Fortuny, Shirin Guild neither courts extensive media coverage nor does the enduring quality of her designs attract it. For the same reasons, she avoids the razzmatazz of catwalk shows. Shirin also eschews sensation and change for change's sake, by presenting timeless, elegant designs. However, unlike Fortuny, Shirin Guild does conform with the fashion calendar, presenting bi-annual collections and in 1999 introduced a 'mid-collection' (which many designers call 'cruise'). International buyers are invited as part of London Fashion Week to place their orders at the showroom, can do so at 'Tranoi', the Paris trade fair or via German and Italian agents.

Whilst Shirin has an international clientele, her clothes undoubtedly have a peculiarly British appeal. In 1954 Cecil Beaton stated that, 'At its truest the taste exhibited by the Englishwoman has a certain "literary" quality: almost one might say, a Virginia Woolf appreciation for clothes that possess the association is ideas . . . Old things have a certain romantic charm about them, and English women of sensibility appreciate this.'[5]

5. Beaton, Cecil, *Through the Looking Glass*, London: Weidenfeld & Nicolson, 1954 p. 244.

Almost fifty years later, this description still rings true. British women are renowned for skilfully combining high-fashion clothing with authentic ethnic and antique items and the UK fashion press is exceptional in its representation of this phenomenon. A cornucopia of period dress shops, ethnic emporia and auction houses fuel and serve this demand.

Fashion's appropriation of ethnographic sources is selective, often romanticized and irreverent in its application. Original garments, as well as paintings, engravings, sculpture and decorative ceramics are frequently used by designers as inspirational material. The stylistic appropriation of non-Western clothing and textiles into Western fashion can be dated to the late thirteenth century, when Marco Polo brought the first Chinese artefacts into Europe. Since then, the cut, patterning and colourings of Chinese, Indian, South East Asian and Japanese (and to a lesser degree Persian/Iranian) textiles and dress have recurrently fuelled the imagination of designers, dress reformers and entered fashion's forefront. This fascination and assimilation was the subject of an exhibition (and catalogue) 'Orientalism: Visions of the East in Western Dress', presented by Richard Martin and Harold Koda, at the Costume Institute at the Metropolitan Museum of Art in 1994.

The 'Orientalism' show presented a stunning range of beautifully displayed historical and contemporary fashions. In spite of the development of increasingly multi-cultural societies, most exhibits were conceived by designers inspired by the raiment of cultures that were not their own – works by Turkish-born Rifat Ozbek and Japanese designer Issey Miyake were among the exceptions. Predominant were fashions by designers working during the 1980s and 1990s, who were irreverent and eclectic in their employment of international references. A Gianni Versace design for Spring/Summer 1994 was inspired by the sari, fused with a punk aesthetic and re-presented as a glamorous evening dress. The clinging two-piece was made in neon bright synthetic jersey and featured a panel skirt provocatively fastened by eight large safety pins. During the latter half of the 1990s, the sari inspired countless designers and original sari fabrics were used to make fashion clothing, accessories and furnishings.

Fashion formed just part of a broader trend and obsession for Asian culture that permeated many areas of 1990s design and culture, including the vogue for henna tattoos, Asian fashion models and music. Perhaps not surprisingly these and similar developments prompted cynicism and even hostility within sections of the Asian community, who saw the rich fabric of their culture being reduced to little more than the latest lifestyle statement. Hettie Judah presented this argument in an article published in the *Independent on Sunday* called 'Hands off our Culture'. Condemning the 'pick and mix' attitude and consequent trivializing of Asian culture, the author

Figure 4.3. Shirin Guild for Spring/Summer 1999. White cotton tape sweater with
random slashes of seemingly dropped stitches, worn with white linen
'Kurdish' pants. Photograph by Robin Guild.

interpreted this Asia-mania as 'a panacea to the a-spirituality of Western capitalism'.[6]

In times of economic crises and social fragmentation 'advanced' industrialized societies often romanticize and make fashionable aspects of cultures that are – perhaps ironically – perceived as 'undeveloped'. Certainly, during the 1930s, late 1960s/early 1970s and again in the 1990s, fashions in dress have reflected this tendency, placing special emphasis upon the cut of non-Western clothing and hand-crafted textiles. However, whilst some designers have 'flirted' with ethnographic sources and could be criticized for indulging in parody and pastiche, Shirin Guild's ongoing inspiration and modern, minimalist interpretation of her own cultural clothing traditions is undertaken with cultural insight, dignity and integrity.

It is widely acknowledged that the most seemingly simple of designs can be the greatest testimony to a designer's talent: any fault or flaw in proportion, construction or material becomes glaringly apparent as it cannot be concealed or detracted from by extraneous ornamentation. John Pawson – master of modern-day minimal architecture – defines 'the minimum' as 'the perfection that an artifact achieves when it is no longer possible to improve it by subtraction. This is the quality that an object has when every component, every detail, and every junction has been reduced or condensed to the essentials. It is the result of the omission of the inessentials.'[7]

In the same way that British fashion is all too often perceived and characterized as outlandish, the nation's taste in interior design has often been associated with clutter and chintz. Yet, as in fashion, there exists a refined, minimalist strand within British design history in which Shirin Guild's work could be considered as part of a continuum – and similar parallels could also be drawn with fine art. Author of *London Minimum* (1996), Herbert Ypma celebrated the interior minimalism that was at its zenith in mid-1990s London. By presenting examples from Georgian architecture, Christopher Dresser's late nineteenth-century metalware designs, modernist architecture such as Berthold Lubetkin's penguin pool at London Zoo (1934) and the output of leading contemporary craftspeople, including Ray Key's carved wooden bowls and Edmund de Waal's porcelain vessels, Ypma highlighted Britain's history of utilitarian, pared-down design.

Minimalism embraces more than just style, it embodies an entire philosophy. Shirin Guild regularly commissions craftspeople to make refined, minimalist pieces for her home and workplace and is an intensely private

6. I am grateful to Professor Lou Taylor for drawing my attention to this article in the *Independent*, 6 December 1998, p. 2.

7. Pawson, John, *Minimum*, Phaidon: London, 1996, p. 7.

person who extols the virtues of modest living. The cult of simplicity is one advocated by many religions and spiritual sects as a route to inner peace and well-being. Drawing on a breadth of references, Bruce Chatwin states, 'Look at the "empty" churches of Sanraedam, the buildings of the Shakers, the piano music of Satie, or Cézanne's final watercolours. . . Emptiness in architecture – or empty space – is not empty, but full: yet to realize this fullness requires the most exacting standards.'[8]

Figure 4.4. Shirin Guild for Spring/Summer 2000. 'Coat Drop Back', 'Tribal Pants' and 'Top Tank' in dual tone linen, worn with knitted paper neckpiece. Photograph by Robin Guild.

8. As quoted in the frontispiece of Ypma, Herbert, *London Minimum*, Thames & Hudson: London, 1996.

Shirin Guild is fastidious about the design and high quality of her work, which is in perfect harmony within this context, as is the minimalist photographic representation of her collections. Models wearing her designs often assume contemplative poses and are photographed by Robin Guild against a plain white background, entirely devoid of stylistic props or cultural signifiers.

As it is primarily the ephemeral quality of high fashion that distinguishes it from other forms of dress (such as ceremonial and occupational), it could be argued that Shirin Guild operates outside its parameters. Because her designs are never really 'in' fashion, they never fall outside of it either. However, it is difficult to find nomenclature to accurately define her work. Joanne Eicher's useful definition of world fashion, that embraces garments such as tee-shirts, denim jeans, business suits and sports shoes that are worn across continents,[9] is inappropriate – and clearly, it is not ethnic. Her work has been defined as 'conceptual' which could imply that it is rooted in ideas rather than function, which is certainly not the case. Perhaps most suitable – although not without complexities – is the term avant-garde in its commonly accepted definition of being that which is in the forefront. Avoiding grandiose rhetoric, the designer simply states that she creates 'clothes' she wants to wear herself and is pleased that other women appreciate them too.

In 1997 Mark Leonard's perceptive report, *Britain – renewing our identity* was published by Demos (the independent think tank committed to radical thinking on the long-term problems facing the UK and other advanced industrial societies). The author highlighted the gulf that has opened between the reality of Britain as a creative and diverse society and the worldwide perception of Britain as ' a backward-looking island immersed in its heritage'.[10] A similar sentiment was expressed in the *New Statesman* (1997) by Yasmin Alibhai-Brown who wrote that 'The big project for the next century is to create a multi-ethnic British identity which is inclusive and not exclusive; progressive and not shrouded in pathos and longings for the past.'[11]

Arguably, Shirin Guild's designs contribute towards the achievement of this objective by utilizing cross-cultural references and drawing on the past, yet resolutely looking to the future.

9. Eicher, Joanne B., *Dress and Ethnicity,* Oxford: Berg, 1995, pp. 299–300.

10. Leonard, Mark, *Britain: renewing our identity,* Demos in association with the Design Council, London, 1997, p. 15.

11. Alibhai-Brown, Yasmin, 'Bring England in from the Cold,' *New Statesman,* 11 July 1997, p. 26.

Part 3

Design for Industry

5

The Invisible Man

Ian Griffiths

I have been told that I am a typical product of the British fashion-design education system, and to an extent this is true; I graduated from Manchester Polytechnic in 1985 and the Royal College of Art in 1987, and like many of my contemporaries became a designer working for one of the large Italian manufacturer retailers that flourished during the 1980s, in my case the MaxMara group. But my career took a more unusual turn in 1992 when I became Head of the School of Fashion, and Professor at Kingston University in tandem with my design role at MaxMara. With a foot in each camp, it was inevitable that I would be drawn to make the observations about the separateness of theory and practice which are the basis of this chapter.

As a student, my knowledge of the historical and theoretical aspects of fashion was informed largely by the linear chronologies and eulogistic biographies of Ernestine Carter, Prudence Glyn et al. Mildly soporific afternoons at the Platt Hall Gallery of Costume in Manchester reinforced the erroneous notion that the academy of fashion was a sleepy backwater largely concerned with 'hemline histories', not much connected to the more dynamic concerns of architectural and design history, and not entirely essential for the practice of fashion design. I think this was an opinion shared by many who were fashion students at the time, now fellow designers, and had I not returned to education as an academic, I might well have remained unaware that in the few years that had passed since I was at college, fashion had become the subject of such great and varied academic study.

I knew as well as anyone else that fashion had become a mass spectacle, its 'superstar' designers and models principal characters in the narratives of popular culture, but it was a surprise to discover that it had attracted equally frenzied interest from sociologists, psychologists, philosophers, cultural, social and economic historians and historians. Many of these develop arguments from studies which had existed long before I became a student, such as those of the nineteenth-century sociologist Veblen[1] and semiotician Barthes[2], but the volume of contemporary discourses has brought these formerly remote texts right to the heart of what now constitutes fashion's academy.

Inevitably, given the broad range of disciplines that have entered what Lou Taylor has described as the 'dress history ring',[3] there has been some quite heavyweight methodological pugilism. With the principal combatants now in a more conciliatory mood, the consensus seems to be for a multi-disciplinary approach. Yet the reconciliation of historical and theoretical approaches does not complete the debate; there is a voice whose absence is overlooked, but which is blindingly obvious. Amongst the entire body of academic work relating to fashion, there is scarcely a word written by a practising designer, or giving a designer's perspective. Designers like myself are as invisible in the academy of fashion as they are in the glamourized celebrity designer profiles manufactured by the press.

It is scarcely credible, but nonetheless true, that of the many thousands of graduates and postgraduates that have passed through our celebrated fashion-design education machine, with its more or less standard diet of 80 per cent practice and 20 per cent theory, none has published work which makes a significant contribution to the academic understanding of their field.

Just as fashion is sometimes regarded as occupying the lowest intellectual rung of the design ladder, architecture is regarded as occupying the highest. With this in mind, I compared the general 'theoretical and contextual studies' reading list issued to first-year students of the first degree course in Fashion,[4]

1. Veblen, T., *The theory of the leisure class: an economic study of institutions*, London: Allen and Unwin, 1970.

2. Barthes, R., *The fashion system* (translated from the French by Matthew Ward and Richard Howard) London: Cape, 1985.

3. Taylor, L., 'Doing the Laundry: A Reassessment of object based Dress History: *Fashion Theory*, vol. 2 issue 4, Oxford: Berg, 1998, pp. 337–58.

4. The 'general' reading list for first-year students of Fashion at Kingston contains the following:

Ash, J. and Wilson E. (eds), *Chic Thrills: A Fashion Reader*, 1992.
Barnard, M., *Fashion as Communication*, 1996.
Barnes, R., and J. Eicher J. B., (eds), *Dress and Gender: Making and Meaning*, 1992.
Barnes R., and Eicher J. B., (eds), *Dress and Gender: Making and Meaning*, 1993.
Barthes, R., *The Elements of Semiology*, 1967.
Barthes, R., *The Fashion System*, 1983.
Bordo, S., *Unbearable Weight: feminism, western culture and the body*, 1993.
Bourdieu, P., *Distinction*, 1986.
Boynton Arthur L., (ed.), *Religion, Dress and the Body*, 1999.
Breward, C., *The Culture of Fashion*, 1995.
Brydon A., and Niessen, S., *Consuming Fashion: Adorning the Transnational Body*, 1998.

at Kingston University to the equivalent list issued to first-year students of Architecture.[5] Of the thirty-nine titles listed in the Fashion School's bibliography

Butler, J., *Gender Trouble*, 1990.

Carter, E., *The Changing World of Fashion – 1900 to the present*, 1977.

Coleridge, N., *The Fashion Conspiracy*, 1989.

Craik, J., *The Face of Fashion*, 1993.

De la Haye, A., *A Fashion Source Book*, 1988.

Eicher, J., *Fashion and Ethnicity*, 1995.

Evans C., and Thornton, M., *Women and fashion: a new look*, 1989.

Fashion Theory: The Journal of Dress, Body and Culture

Featherstone, M., Hepworth M. and Turner, B. S., *The Body: Social Process and Cultural Theory*, 1991.

Finkelstein, J., *The Fashioned Self*, 1991.

Flügel, J., *The Psychology of Clothes*, 1930.

Gross, M., *Model*, 1995.

Johnson, K.P., Lennon, S.J., *Appearance and Power*, 1999.

Kidwell, C.B., and Steele, V., (eds.), *Men and Women: Dressing the Part*, 1989.

Konig, R., *The Restless Image: the Social Psychology of Fashion*, 1973.

Kunzle, D., *Fashion and Fetishism*, 1982.

Laver, J., *Style in Costume*, 1949.

Lipovetsky, G., *The Empire of Fashion: Dressing Modern Democracy*, 1994.

Lurie, A., *The Language of Clothes*, 1992.

Martin, R., *Fashion and Surrealism*, 1988.

McDowell, C., *McDowell's Directory of 20th Century Fashion*, 1984.

McDowell, C., *Dressed to Kill: power and clothes*, 1992.

McRobbie, A., *British Fashion Design: Rag Trade or Image Industry?*

Peacock, J., *Twentieth century Fashion - the complete source book*, 1993.

Roach, M. E., and Eicher, J., (eds.), *Dress, Adornment and Social Order*, 1965.

Rouse, E., *Understanding Fashion*, 1989.

Solomon, M. R., (ed.), *The Psychology of Fashion*, 1985.

Steele, V., *Fashion and Eroticism*, 1985.

5. The introductory reading list issued to first-year students of Architecture contains the following:

Furneaux Jordan, R., *Western Architecture.*

Jellicoe, G., *The Landscape of Man.* *

Kostof, S., *A History of Architecture.*

Nuttgens, P., *The Story of Architecture.* *

Crowe, S., *Garden Design.* *

Gombrich, E., *The Story of Art.*

Norberg-Schulz, C., *Meaning in Western Architecture.*

Pevsner, N., *An Outline of Western Architecture.*

Hellman, Louis, *Architecture for Beginners.* *

Riseboro, B., *The Story of Western Architecture.* *

Sutton, Ian, *Western Architecture.*

Pevsner, N., *The Sources of Modern Architecture and Design.*

only one author has ever practiced as a designer.[6] Of the fourteen titles listed in the School of Architecture's biography, seven were written by practising architects or landscape architects.

Fashion Theory was inaugurated in 1997, described by its editor as 'the first journal to look seriously at the intersection of dress, body, and culture'.[7] It has published contributions by distinguished academics in the fields to which it relates, its contribution to the understanding of the subject is undeniable and yet it has never to date featured an article written by a designer, nor indeed by anyone with an active role within the fashion industry or its related spheres. Architecture, by comparison, has a much longer tradition of refereed academic journals. Examination of a single issue of the AA Files, The Annals of the Architectural Association[8] reveals that of the fourteen contributors, eight are listed as having current practices or having been engaged on design projects within the last five years. Similarly, *Architectural Design's 'Millennium Architecture'* edition features contributions by Stephen Bayley, Nigel Coates, Zaha M. Hadid, Eva Jiricna, Nicholas Grimshaw and partners, Renzo Piano and Charles Jencks, who was co-editor of the issue.[9]

Of course, fashion designers produce books but although their publications are much consulted by students of fashion, they carry little or no academic gravitas. In the self-laudatory style established by Paul Poiret, with his claim to have single-handedly brought about the demise of the corset 'in the name of Liberty',[10] books by, or sponsored by designers do little to realistically describe the mechanisms of fashion. Colin McDowell refers to the endless designer picture books of the 1980s as 'the bimbos of the publishing world, beautiful but dumb'.[11] The literature of fashion has no counterpart to, say, the architect Steen Eiler Rasmussen's *Experiencing Architecture* which claims as its object 'to endeavour to explain the instrument the architect plays on, to show what a great range it has and thereby awaken the senses to its music' and does so by giving examples of work by other architects, rather than a promotion of the author's own.[12] Similarly, Bill Riseboro's *The Story of*

---

6. Colin McDowell.

7. Steele, V., 'Letter from the Editor' *Fashion Theory vol. 1*, issue 1, Oxford: Berg, 1997, p. 2.

8. AA Files 39, *The Annals of the Architectural, Association School of Architecture* (Autumn 1999) London: Architectural Association.

9. *Architectural Design vol. 69, Millenium Architecture*, London: Academy Editions, 2000.

10. Poiret, P., translated by Stephen Haden Guest, *My First Fifty years* London: Victor Gollancz, 1931, p. 73.

11. McDowell, C., *The Designer Scam*, London: Hutchinson, 1994, p. 52.

12. Rasmussen, S. E., *Experiencing Architecture*, Cambridge (Mass): M.I.T. Press, 1964, p. 8.

Western Architecture demonstrates the practitioner's insight and inside knowledge in exploring the social, industrial and ideological background to historical building.[13] It is quite usual for successful architects, not only to teach, but to publish books and articles giving perspectives on historical and contemporary design issues or outlining personal manifestos; the tradition stretches back through history from Robert Charles Venturi, Philip Johnson, Le Corbusier and Palladio to the Roman architect Vitruvius.

Fashion can never match architecture's long pedigree, but comparison of the two disciplines' relative theories leads to some interesting issues concerning their dominion. Whereas in architectural theory, practitioners hold a significant or predominant stake, in fashion theory it is the historians and academics who are the custodians, if not proprietors. This chapter aims to invert custom; this time, a practitioner scrutinizes the work of those who have scrutinized fashion. The purpose of doing so is not to disparage or decry, but to demonstrate where extant work disappoints the student and practitioner of fashion, to suggest how the designer's perspective might allow it to be reconstituted as a complete entity, how it may advance understanding of the subject, possibly remove some of the stigma attached to it and even elevate the lowly professional status of fashion and fashion design.

The next section presents a series of salient and interconnected themes drawn from consideration of what is regarded as the academy of fashion. It concentrates principally on those works which appear in the general reading list already referred to, which includes *Fashion Theory*. Some texts and references to exhibitions which are not named in the reading list have been used where they shed further light on themes of contemporary interest. The final part of the chapter is a short case study from my own experience as a fashion designer, intended to reinforce some of the points made in the second section and to illustrate the kind of text of which there is a paucity in the academy of fashion.

The Fashion Polyglott

Apart from the absence of any significant contribution by the practitioner, the most obvious observation on the body of academic discourses relating to fashion is the bewildering variety of its authors' disciplines. Students of fashion, so frequently labelled as shallow and frivolous, are required to be polyglotts, able to inform their understanding from texts using the language and ideas of anthropology, social, cultural, economic and art history,

13. Riseboro, B., *The Story of Western Architecture*, London: Herbert, 1979.

literature, sociology, psychoanalysis, psychology, semiotics, structuralism, Marxism, feminism and others. Malcolm Barnard insists that 'because fashion and clothing impinge on so many disciplines they must be studied in terms of those disciplines'.[14] Few writers recognize this as a problem. Elizabeth Wilson, for example, urges that the 'attempt to view fashion through several different pairs of spectacles simultaneously' is congruent with the postmodernist aesthetic to which fashion, with its 'obsession with surface, novelty and style for style's sale' is particularly well-suited.[15] For the student of fashion, the disadvantage with this fragmentary academic configuration is the uncertainty of obtaining the insight he or she seeks from a particular text. James Laver anticipated the problem with his reference to Carlyle's *Sartor Resartus* and its central character 'Teufelsdröck, Professor of things-in-general', author of the imaginary book 'Die Kleider, ihr Werden und Wirken' ('Clothes, their Origin and Influence'). The book is said to contain various anecdotes which hint tantalizingly at conclusions about the importance of clothing in society, but, Laver writes, 'it is soon clear that such fantasies as a naked House of Lords are no more than a jumping off place for meditations on the nature of man and his place in the universe. The truth is that Carlyle was not interested in clothes *as such*, indeed he despised them'.[16]

Students of fashion are accustomed to the sense of frustration deriving from texts which contain the word 'fashion' in their titles, but whose primary interest lies in the pursuit of another field of study. *Fashion, Culture and Identity*, for example, describes the aim of cultural scientists in looking at fashion as being 'to make sense of a phenomenon that has periodically intrigued them, less for its own sake, unfortunately, than for the light they thought it would shed on certain fundamental features of modern society'.[17] The author, Fred Davis, points out, quite correctly that 'each science purports to do some things and not others, and it is pointless to expect it to delve into areas lying outside its established boundaries'.[18] There is, of course, no reason why, say, a semiotician like Roland Barthes should wish to explore themes relating specifically to the design, production or diffusion of clothes. *The Fashion System* restricts itself rigorously to what the author describes as the 'written garment' using the texts accompanying illustrations in fashion

14. Barnard, M., *Fashion and Communication*, London: Routledge, 1996, p. 20.

15. Wilson, E., *Adorned in Dreams: fashion and modernity*, London: Virago, 1985, p. 11.

16. Laver, J., *Style in Costume*, London: Oxford University Press p. 5, 1949.

17. Davis, F., *Fashion, Culture and Identity*, Chicago: University of Chicago Press, 1994, p. 4.

18. Ibid., p. 114.

magazines to derive its influential ideas about communication. Barthes argues that systematic analysis of 'real garments' would necessitate working back to the actions governing their manufacture. Describing the structure of real clothing as 'technological' he correctly concedes that its study lies outside the scope of his theory.[19] And yet this is precisely what the student of fashion would like to know about.

Apologies

It is fairly safe to assume that a student or practitioner of fashion has selected the area because he or she believes it to be worthwhile and rewarding, if not in every aspect, at least in part. One might challenge the political, ethical or moral structure of the industry, but in continuing his or her study or practice, would presumably have a vision of some alternative model. No one working within the discipline in a practical capacity would expect to have to continually justify being there. But it seems that writers on fashion cannot, or at least have not, been able to enjoy such security. Elizabeth Wilson has explained that 'because fashion is constantly denigrated, the serious study of fashion has had to repeatedly justify itself. Almost every fashion writer, whether journalist or art historian, insists anew on the importance of fashion both as a cultural barometer and as an expressive art form'.[20]

In her introduction to the inaugural issue of *Fashion Theory* Valerie Steele refers to an article she had written several years previously, entitled the 'F word'. Describing the position of fashion within academia at that time she says, 'It was not a pretty picture.' Fashion was regarded as 'frivolous, sexist, bourgeois, "material" (not intellectual) and therefore beneath contempt'. Happily, she reports that by the time of the launch of *Fashion Theory*, the subject had begun to receive attention 'from artists and intellectuals alike'.[21] No matter how dramatic the change in attitude though, traces of the former ambivalence about fashion remain in extant tests still consulted by students. Many carry the defensive, quasi apologetic tone described by Wilson, some a loftiness which hints at the author's desire to be regarded as superior to the subject, and some the undisguised hostility described below.

The upturn in the academic fortunes of fashion welcomed by Steele, its newly acquired attractiveness to 'artists and intellectuals', has had a further

19. Barthes, R., translated from the French by Matthew Ward and Richard Howard, London: Cape, 1985, p. 5.

20. Wilson, E., *Adorned in Dreams: Fashion and Modernity*, London: Virago, 1985, p. 47.

21. Steele, V., 'Letter from the Editor', *Fashion Theory*, vol, issue 1, Oxford: Berg, 1997, p. 1.

effect, namely the sometimes bewildering and clumsy intellectualization of the subject, a tendency to depart from the real into the realm of the abstract, and a desire to reposition it in closer proximity to art.

Antipathy, Thinly Veiled and Undisguised Hostility

The reading list for first-year students of fashion design at Kingston University includes The Fashioned Self by the anthropologist and sociologist Joanne Finkelstein. It is my fervent hope that none but those students whose interest in the subject is unshakable should ever chance to get their hands on a copy; the book's arguments are presented with a devastatingly seductive logic and an authority that would persuade anyone else to abandon the profession without delay. In the author's words,

> It is the argument of this book that as long as we continue to value physical appearances, and sustain the enormous industries which trade on this value, namely, the consumer-orientated cosmetic, fashion and therapeutic industries, we authenticate a narrative of human character which is spurious.[22]

Finkelstein's numerous objections to fashion and its industries are founded in her theory that the origins of our interest in appearances lie in the discredited field of physiognomy, with its claim that individual moral character and intellect can be revealed by physical characteristics. She adheres to the view that fashion and 'fashionability' are devices whereby a complex modern society cynically regulates human exchange for economic motives, and argues that, by submitting ourselves to fashion with its claims to provide a means for self-expression, that we actually deny the self. The text returns several times to the idea that the manufactured or fashioned self invites appraisals which may be inaccurate, that fashion can be a disguise or pretence, that it can be ambiguous or even deceive. This is presented as an undisputed indictment, even though the possibility of things not quite being what they appear is the very thing which appeals to those who delight in fashion.

Like many who decry fashion, Finkelstein believes it to be a condition of capitalist societies. Those who are indisposed towards capitalist ideologies, must inevitably, it seems, take a similar stance on fashion. Writing in *Fashion Theory* Finkelstein concentrates specifically on the fashion industry, its

22. Finkelstein, J., *The Fashioned Self*, Cambridge: Polity Press and Oxford: Blackwell, 1991.

'troubling' economic consequences, and notes, as others have done, that in seeking to realize its profit-seeking aims, 'fashion is preservative of the status quo while appearing to make the claims of being the opposite'.[23] There does not appear to be a single aspect of the subject which pleases or excites Finkelstein. When first acquainted with her work, I could not quite believe the forcefulness of its antipathy towards the subject. I was not much reassured to read Palmer's review of Finkelstein's 'After a Fashion' in *Fashion Theory*. Having established that the book appears to have been written as an introductory text to fashion theory aimed primarily at undergraduate students, the reviewer notes that it 'seems as though Finkelstein is trying to convince herself as to the importance of studying fashion and leaves the reader with a sense that despite all her scholarship and wide reading she is still ambivalent on the subject'.[24]

Of course, any of Finkelstein's arguments can be countered by opposing views from other texts. Jennifer Craik, for example rejects the argument that ' "fashion" refers exclusively to clothing behaviour in capitalist economies'[25] and Malcolm Barnard points out that the 'possibility that fashion and clothing are deceptive in that they may be used to mislead, applies equally well to all other means of communication'.[26] The reason for citing Finkelstein's objections here though, is not primarily to counter them but to demonstrate the singularity of a subject that can be legitimately studied and practised, yet confronts the student with discourses which are innately hostile. Elizabeth Wilson has shown that even the works of Veblen and Barthes, so frequently referred to in academic texts on fashion, share a common view that fashion is 'morally absurd and in some way objectionable'.[27]

The Intellectual Assault Course

In his introduction to *The Fashion System* Barthes asks 'Can clothing signify without recourse to the speech which describes it, comments upon it, and provides it with a system of signifieds and signifiers abundant enough to

23. Finkelstein, J., 'Chic – a Look That's Hard to See', *Fashion Theory*, vol. 3 issue 3, Oxford: Berg, 1999, pp. 363–85.

24. Palmer, A., 'Book Review: After a Fashion', *Fashion Theory*, vol. 1, issue 1, Oxford: Berg, 1997, pp. 111–14.

25. Craik, J., *The Face of Fashion: Cultural Studies in Fashion*, London: Routledge, 1994, p. 5.

26. Barnard, M., *Fashion as Communication*, London: Routledge, 1996.

27. Wilson, E., *Adorned in Dreams: fashion and modernity*, London: Virago, 1985, p. 58.

constitute a system of meaning? Man is doomed to articulated language, and no semiological undertaking can ignore this fact'.[28] Perhaps so for a semiotician, but as a designer I am inclined to believe that 'real garments', as opposed to the 'image garments' or 'word garments' in which Barthes was interested can evoke responses without the mediation of words, if thoughts are not to be counted as words. On Saturday afternoons when people go shopping, they try something on and buy if it 'appeals' to them in some way, or in other words, has a 'meaning' for them, and as a person who is susceptible to clothes, I am aware that the 'meaning' is partly an emotional one, or one that often eludes articulation.

If I as a designer wish to communicate an idea, I usually, in common with most designers, find it most convenient to produce a sketch or a series of sketches. Sometimes, at MaxMara I am asked to clarify my idea. A technical description of the garment is usually fairly easy, but when I am asked to describe what the garment or collection is for, how it is intended to appeal, words are less useful. We find ourselves describing completely different sets of clothes using different permutations of the same frequently used words. So, one theme might be baptized 'sport-elegante-citá' whilst another might be 'sport-chic' and another 'elegante-giorno'. It would be quite impossible to recreate the clothes simply from the words used to describe them; the words we use act as an aid, but ultimately the meaning resides in the garments themselves, or at this stage the drawings.

Of course, we could be more ambitious in our attempts to describe the clothes. We could pore over our task until we were satisfied that what we had written fully described a particular garment and its intended significance to the customer, but what would be the point? The customer would expect to be able to understand the idea without the aid of our little essay, and although we use words and images to promote them, we ultimately sell clothes, not words. But those with an interest in fashion whose stock-in-trade is the word face a different problem. Writers on fashion understandably wish to rise to the challenge of translating the garment into the word, offers her sympathy to those 'whose brains have been taxed by over-modish and illiterate writing on art/dress, especially in the field of popular culture'.[29] Barthes describes how, once it passes into written communication, fashion becomes an 'autonomous cultural object' whose functions are more analogous

28. Barthes, R., *The Fashion System*, translated from the French by Matthew Ward and Richard Howard, London: Cape, 1985, p. xi.

29. Robiero, A., 'Re-fashioning Art: some visual approaches to the Study of the History of Dress', *Fashion Theory*, vol. 2, issue 4, Oxford: Berg, 1998, p. 319.

to those found in literature than to those of the vestimentary artefact.[30] When fashion is embraced by academic discourse, its meanings are subsumed into an intellectual framework with which they may or may not be congruent.

One designer whose work has been the subject of a great deal of academic analysis is Martin Margiela. He features in no fewer than four articles in *Fashion Theory* to date, and it is easy to see why: garments designed by Maison Margiela depart radically from, or even overturn, accepted conventions in the design, construction and presentation of fashionable clothes. Alison Gill for example associates Margiela's work with 'deconstruction fashion' and considers the parallels this style has with the 'influential French style of philosophical thought, deconstruction, associated with the writings of Jacques Derrida'.[31] The essay is an invigorating intellectual 'workout' but the author is not concerned with clothes, so much as words or ideas triggered by them. Gill states that:

> In that deconstruction has been defined *very* generally as a practice of 'undoing', deconstructionist fashion *liberates* the garment from functuality, by literally *undoing* it. Importantly here, through this association *dress becomes theoretical*, only by *exemplifying* a theoretical position developed in philosophical thought and brought to fashion in order to transform it. Yet, clothes are not liberated or released from functionality because of deconstruction as casual force coming from somewhere outside fashion, for the liberation of clothes from functionality is something realised as a complex interaction between bodies, clothing and the various settings in which they are worn.[32]

The text's deliberations lead to various conclusions of a philosophical kind, whose meanings lie in the words that have been used to compose the text. Without questioning the academic significance of such discourses, I would argue that the very wordiness of their arguments eclipses the extraordinary potential of their subjects to convey powerful meanings, without the use of words. Just as Derrida refused to define or translate the word 'deconstruction' on the grounds that to do so would alter or destroy its meaning, Margiela maintains a rigorous muteness about the meaning of his clothes, leaving them to "do the talking" through their use and wear, as Gill concedes in a footnote to her essay which claims to have been gathered around examples 'loosely

---

30. Barthehs, R., *The Fashion System* translated from the French by M. Ward and R. Howard, London: Cape, 1985, p. 8.

31. Gill, A., 'Deconstruction Fashion: the Making of Unfinished, Decomposing and Re-assembled Clothes' *Fashion Theory*, vol. 2, issue 1, Oxford: Berg, 1998, pp. 25–49.

32. Ibid.

compiled' from Margiela's ready to wear collections from 1989.[33] There are no illustrations, so it is not possible to relate individual garments to the meanings they are supposed by the author to convey.

I found it interesting that none of the articles in *Fashion Theory* dealing with or referring to Margiela include information or quotes directly from the designer. Margiela's refusal to 'explain' his clothes has been noted but when I approached Maison Margiela for some information for this chapter, my questions received useful and thoughtful answers, returned by fax and in the third person, which is the company's preferred way of conducting interviews. Maison Margiela revealed to me, first of all, that the company currently sells a total of 111,500 garments per season.[34] Since the total circulation of *Fashion Theory* is around 1,000 copies, we can assume that only a small fraction of those who buy Margiela's clothes do so armed with insight gleaned from theoretical analyses like Gill's; the clothes clearly communicate in a different way.

I also enquired how Maison Margiela thought its customers learned how to understand and interpret its products. I was informed that 'For those for whom this is a priority, the information on the collection tends to transfer to them through the sales teams of the shops as well as the video of the show at each shop.' The sales team is in turn said to be informed by the fashion show, or presentations of the collections at the company's showrooms in Paris, New York, Tokyo and Milan. The company's response emphasizes that there are a number of customers 'who react to the garments in a more *emotional way*, either to the piece itself or to a certain piece in relation to their existing wardrobe'.[35]

The great web of erudite discourses that has grown up around fashion may shed light on questions of a philosophical or intellectual nature, but from a practitioner's perspective, it is less able to explain the enormous power and occasional magic of which Margiela is an example.

33. Ibid.

34. Reply to written enquiry received by fax from M. Patrick Scallon, Director of Communications on behalf of Maison Margiela (February 2000) revealed the approx. number of pieces sold by the company per season to be 7,500 'artisanal production' for women, 31,400 'collection for women', 45,000 'basic garments for women', 25,000 'wardrobe for men' and 2,000 'artisanal production for men'. Artisanal production was described as 'the reworking by hand, at our ateliers in Paris, of vintage or new existing garments, fabrics and accessories'.

35. Ibid.

Fashion and Art

It is significant that the 1999 exhibition at the Hayward Gallery, 'Addressing the Century', took as its theme, not the almost unimaginable cultural and industrial prepotence which fashion has assumed over the last hundred years, but its relationships with art. This is not so surprising, though, when viewed against the recent spate of exhibitions and texts exploring the same theme, and it is easy to understand, when it has so long been denigrated as a frivolous and futile occupation, that fashion and its study should attempt to reposition itself in a more legitimate context. Having, at least until recently, no philosophy, critique or theory of its own, as Radford's recent essay describes, fashion has been inclined to appropriate those of others.[36]

There have, of course, always been relationships between art and fashion, as there have been between other fields in design, architecture, literature and music. Where such links have existed, it has often been in the economic interests of fashion to make them visible, and the original motives for such associations may occasionally or often have been calculated to this end. As Radford writes: 'Certainly a cadre of designers have had their work exhibited in specific contexts that identify their products as art rather than designed commodities . . . recent cases of using artists for modelling or engaging them to design the fashion show may be taken as instances of an attempt to procure the potency of status by this magical association'.[37] Despite the obvious and frequently cited arguments placing fashion in a different sphere from art on grounds of its economic motives and its persistent denial of recently past styles, there appears to be confusion in academic circles, amongst designers, and in style magazines, where art and fashion have become 'inextricably interfused', according to Radford.[38]

Martin Margiela has frequently exhibited work in art galleries and museums of modern art, contexts which invite art criticism.[39] Understandably, then, 'Addressing the Century' included no fewer than three pieces of work from Maison Margiela which were taken from a previous exhibition at the Museum Bojimans Van Beuningen, Rotterdam (1997) containing pieces from

36. Radford, R., 'Dangerous Liaison: Art, Fashion and Individualism', *Fashion Theory*, vol. 2, issue 2, Oxford: Berg, 1998, pp. 151–64.

37. Ibid.

38. Ibid.

39. A 'C.V.' supplied by Maison Margeila showed that the company has shown work at the Florence Biennale on Fashion and Art (1996), the Kyoto Museum of Modern Art (1999), Musee de L'Art Moderne (1993), Musee de l'Art Contemporain de Marseille (1996), Fri-Art Centre d'Art Contemporain, Kunsthalle, Friborg (1998), The Metropolitan Museum of Art, New York (1999 and 2000).

the ready-to-wear collection with specially made artisanal pieces. In 'Addressing the Century' the Margiela exhibits were included in the final section, 'Convergence', along with others by Issey Miyake, Roberto Capucci and Rei Kawakubo. According to Clare Coulson's review of the exhibition in *Fashion Theory*, 'These designers consciously resist categorisation. They want their work to exist where form and function are harmoniously fused and ideas flow freely. Their work is both art and fashion'.[40]

This illustrates a tendency which is currently very popular with students of fashion design. In the year of writing, there are a number of final-year students at Kingston University alone whose dissertations suggest that certain avant-garde designers' work might be regarded in a different context, and subjected to a different critique, namely that of art.[41] I have noticed that some students consider an elite of avant-garde designers such as Comme des Garcons, Yohji Yamamoto and Martin Margiela as being exempt from, or superior to the commercial considerations to which others are subject. There is a tendency to look at the word of these designers more as vehicles for self-expression than as products conceived, consciously or unconsciously to appeal to a group of people who are consumers. Like Luigi Maramotti, I believe that a designed garment becomes 'fashion' only when it has passed through some kind of system and became a product.[42] Those arresting pieces created solely for impact in a fashion show or exhibition, might possibly qualify as art, but are certainly not, in my opinion, fashion, and I am not alone in thinking so. When asked about this subject in a newspaper interview, Maison Margiela stated its view that fashion is 'a craft, technical know-how and not, in our opinion an art form'.[43] When I asked why it felt commentators have become so fixated by the fashion and art question, Maison Margiela explained to me that:

We live in a period in which we tend to prefer to over associate and interpret events, issues and movements in culture and taste rather than 'under-interpret' them. There are, in our opinion, two main ways of forcing a link between the worlds of art and fashion, firstly the artistic references of any one garment or group of garments, the second is the artistic quality of any one designer's approach to their work and their expression as a creator of clothing. The more individualistic

40. Coulson, C., 'Exhibition Review: Addressing the Century: 100 Years of Art & Fashion, the Hayward Gallery', *Fashion Theory*, vol. 3, issue 1, Oxford: Berg, 1999, pp. 121–6.

41. The students in the 1999-2000 academic year whose dissertations touch on relationships between art and fashion include Mallison, E. (an investigation of the relationship between Art, Craft and Fashion in late 20th century Britain) and Marin, L. (The discourse of veiling and the work of Zineb Sedira).

42. Maramotti, L., 'Connecting Creativity: chapter 6 of this book.

43. Frankel, S., 'Reality Check', *The Independent Magazine* 15 August, 1999, pp. 35–9.

the approach in relation to the current climate of the overall aesthetic referred to as 'in fashion' the more that approach may be linked to art.[44]

The turnover of Maison Martin Margiela in the 1998/99 financial year was 100 million French Francs.[45] The company supplies a total of 270 stores in Europe, the Americas, Japan and elsewhere.[46] Cursory examination of the labels in Margiela's clothes reveal that the company has licensing agreements with, for wovens, Staff International, a large Italian manufacturer and for knitwear, Miss Deanna. The sampling and production facilities, warehouse and administrative offices of Miss Deanna are located in Reggio Emilia, which is also where the headquarters of MaxMara are to be found. The company's proprietor is a personal friend and I have often visited her at work. Standing in the warehouse at S. Martino del Rio, surrounded by pile upon pile of carefully folded, bagged and boxed Margiela sweaters, labelled and boxed for despatch to Barneys, Bergdorf Goodman and Joseph, any ideas about art are dispelled; I am compelled to marvel at the creativity and intelligence of a design which can communicate so powerfully and widely. The most innovative and inspired clothes on earth are products to be bought and worn. They are not art, but no less worthy for not being so; if only there was an opposite critical structure in which to locate their triumph.

The Invisible Designer

I have already alluded to the frustration, from a practitioner's perspective, of reading texts which do not quite go to the heart of the reader's interest, which miss important points through not looking at clothes or considering their commercial context. This section deals more specifically with the paucity of texts, not just *by* contemporary designers, but even *about* contemporary designers. By this I do not mean the many glossy eulogies which people use to give their sitting rooms a fashionable feel, I mean texts which objectively consider the research, design process, realization and distribution of clothes in relation to their meaning. I am not the first to draw attention to this. Davis notes:

44. Reply to written questions received by fax from M. Patrick Scallon, Director of Communications on behalf of Maison Margiela (Feb 2000).
45. The faxed reply from Maison Margiela gave the 1998/99 annual turnover as 100,000,000 Francs for 'women's' and 'men's' ready to wear excluding footwear and mail order (for the moment with '3 SUISSE' a French-based catalogue company similar to Grattans or Empire stores) (Feb 2000).
46. Ibid.

changes in dress and fashion do not happen of their own accord. Human agency, in the form of fashion designers, a vast apparel industry, and a critically responsible consuming public, is necessary in order to bring them to pass. Obvious as this may seem, it is often lost sight of by the many writers who view the succession of fashion as somehow fated or ineluctably driven by the *Zeitgeist's* flux.[47]

Fashion, Culture and Identity promises to consider the 'labyrinthine passage whereby an idea in the designer's head is translated into the purchases and pleasures of the consumer'.[48] Following the largest section of the book, addressing the issues of identity, gender, status and sexuality, the final two chapters deal with the fashion's cycles and processes. The text does indeed include quotes from and references to some knowledgeable designers and journalists but despite some pithy observations, the picture created is rather wooden. Davis was a sociologist interested in the fashion industry from a sociological point of view, and his description rather recalls a Victorian ornithologist's study of the habits of a newly discovered species of bird. The description might edify the general reader but it would be of little use to young birds wishing to learn how to fly. The problem is not only that of the author's distance from his subjects, but also that of there being so few other texts of its type that might support it. Many use references to designers incidentally and sparsely to illustrate whatever point they are trying to make, which of course depends on the author's field of study.

Another criticism of those texts which attempt to portray the fashion industry is that they have rarely succeeded in scratching the surface of the glossy image presented by the industry itself. Very few have inquired further than the 'stars', 'the couturiers as display artists ... the members of the international personality circus'.[48] We read references to Armani, Valentino, Calvin Klein, Versace, Vivienne Westwood and the like, as if they were the sole creative agents within their respective organizations or within the fashion industry. Those who are not 'couturiers', on the other hand, are often lumped together as 'high street designers'. It is not uncommon to read comments regarding 'high street designers' such as 'although they follow the couture trend, their own collections are shaped by more pragmatic concerns'.[49] Such descriptions, with their air of having been written before the 1960s, indicate that the design explosion of the last three decades has passed unnoticed in

47. Davis, F., *Fashion, Culture and Identity*, Chicago: University of Chicago Press, 1994, p. 16.

48. McDowell, C., *The Designer Scam*, London: Hutchinson, 1994, p. 39.

49. Craik, J., *The Face of Fashion: Cultural Studies in Fashion*, London: Routledge, 1994, p. 60.

academic circles. Those thousands of graduates of fashion design have passed into oblivion.

As a final illustration of this, I refer to the chapter of Malcolm Barnard's *Fashion and Communication* entitled 'Fashion, Clothing and Meaning', in which the author debates the possible agents for the generation of meaning in clothes: the designer, the wearer or spectator, and authorities. He argues, logically, that because designers' views are so frequently sought in the popular media, it is clear that many believe the designers' intentions are the sole source of meaning in their work, but that if it were so, it would not be possible for the meaning of clothes to vary according to time or place. A similar argument concludes that the wearer cannot be responsible for the meaning of a garment either since, if it were so, no different interpretations could not exist. Thence, the argument proceeds into semiology, the arbitrary nature of signs and issues of denotation and connotation, syntagons and paradigms, myths and ideologies, without ever having given an example, illustration or without ever having named, quoted or studied a single stitch, sketch or without considering that there might be different 'realities' under the general heading of fashion.[50]

An Episode from the Life of a Designer

The final part of this essay is a short case study which is intended to demonstrate the kind of empirical analyses which might provide some answers to Davis' question:

> What does the shortened hemline or double breasted suit mean to those, who, cautiously, are among the first in their social circle to adopt them? How do these meanings, elusive or inchoate as they may be, relate to the meanings that proceeded and will follow them in the fashion cycle. Why do some new meanings (read fashion) 'click' while other 'fizzle'?[51]

Part of my work as a designer with the MaxMara group has been on the 'Weekend by MaxMara' range. Weekend is MaxMara's relaxed cousin, an informal collection which uses 'classic' inspiration, that is to say our research usually focuses on reinventing or modifying categories of garment which have recognizable generic features, such as aran sweaters, duffel coats or safari jackets. The customer prioritizes an essential aspect of 'correctness',

50. Barnard, M., *Fashion as Communication*, London: Routledge, 1996, pp. 69–95.

51. Davis, F., *Fashion, Culture and Identity*, Chicago: University of Chicago Press, 1994, p. 113.

even bourgeois respectability, but with a slightly progressive, 'modern' interpretation. The look is hard to define, but easy to recognize and very widely understood; the collection sells around 500,000 garments per season worldwide. I have chosen to give Weekend as an example of my work, in this instance, because I wish to highlight the 'sub-catwalk' products that do not figure largely in academic works in fashion, rather than to talk about the more glamorous MaxMara line. Weekend is clearly not an avant-garde or couture collection, its commerciality is plain to see, and yet with coats retailing at around £400 it is not High Street either. The example I have chosen is intended to illustrate the creative and rational processes which lead to the development of a relatively simple fashionable garment, to indicate the great subtleties of meaning and its derivations, in a way that academic work on fashion has not fully recognized.

An important area for Weekend, especially in winter collections, is outerwear, where customers look for an informal, innovative solution alternative or in addition to the more formal sartorially constructed coats in the MaxMara line. These are generally known in Italy as 'giaccone' which translates literally as 'big jackets', the word 'cappotto' or 'coat' usually signifying the more formal outerwear garment. Since there is no equivalent word in English to 'giaccone', I will use the term 'jacket'.

Figures 5.1a and 5.1b show two of the many thousands of jackets that we, the design team, have produced. Jacket A is from the Autumn/Winter 1997 collection and Jacket B from the Autumn/Winter 2000 collection. A sold over 3,000 which is regarded as a fairly good figure, whilst B was eliminated, that is to say, the sample was presented to the agents, merchandisers and clients who diffuse the collection but it was rejected by them and never went into production. Yet the two jackets look so similar, that many might mistake one for the other, so what happened?

Jacket A was designed in the winter of 1996 when we had noticed that certain fashion-conscious individuals in New York, London, Paris and Milan, those who might be said to be 'ahead' in the sense that they seemed to anticipate trends, had begun to mix garments which would not normally be worn together, or from different 'dress codes' – for example, second-hand evening dresses in velvet or silky fabrics with chunky sweaters, delicate feminine blouses with jeans. We concluded that this appropriation of the inappropriate was a way of creating a 'frisson' in the way that exotic motifs are often plundered to the same end.

The crumpled-evening-dress-with-a-chunky-sweater-and trainers look was too radical and yet at the same time obviously destined to go downmarket very quickly, since it could be reproduced so cheaply. We decided to interpret the look in a 'richer' way. Velvets and taffetas in 'jewel' colours would be

 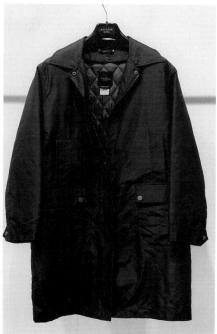

Figure 5.1a and b. Two 'giaccone' designed for by Weekend MaxMara ranges Autumn/Winter 1997 (Figure 5.1a) and Autumn/Winter 2000 (Figure 5.1b). Photo by Cesare di Liborio.

used to make garments with an authentic sportswear feel. The 'look' would be completed with white jeans in a fairly coarse cotton and sloppy mohair sweaters in the same jewel colours as the outerwear. Of course, one reason why velvet is not normally used for outerwear is that it is a delicate fabric which is easily crushed. One of our suppliers developed a cloth which looked exactly like velvet, which has a woven and cut pile, but was in fact a 'flock', i.e. the effect of a pile was recreated by bonding tiny particles of 'velvety' substance to a waterproof backing cloth. The jacket shown was one of three, which were designed to have more or less the same proportions, cut, details and constructional techniques as some authentic military garments from our archive. Some modifications were made for ease of movement, some details were simplified because they were too 'heavy' and the garment was given a quilted lining for warmth, but the impact was achieved by the faithfulness of the styling of the velvet garment to the military original. It was a *velvet parka*.

The garment was presented with a taffeta shirt showing beneath a mohair sweater and white jeans, as planned. No explanation was given, nor was any required by the agents, buyers and merchandisers to whom the collection was presented. The group of garments of which this was a part sold well in the stores, again, with no more information other than that the fabric was waterproof and would not crush. We know from information passed back to us from the sales teams that the garment was bought and worn in the way that we had intended. If, as Craik suggests, successful designers must 'compromise between showing something daring and new while at the same time ensuring that it is wearable (at least in a modified form) and recognisable (draws on previous fashion styles)', this was a success.[52]

Jacket B was designed in the winter of 1999, when the sleek 'urban sport' look had been a dominant theme for several seasons, using mostly synthetic fabrics with smooth surfaces, often in black. The look embraced slim silhouettes with detailing drawn from technical sportswear, such as zips and velcro fastenings. Although this look had been appropriated by the high-street, we speculated it would continue to be important at ready-to-wear level but using high-cost, high-performance, 'luxury' fabrics and finishes that would be beyond the reach of more downmarket collections, including the 'sub-designer' Weekend collection. In the meantime, though, we had observed that the same sort of young, fashionable people who had inspired Jacket A, had begun to wear recycled 'English' clothes – green quilted gilets, beaten-up waxed jackets, tweed trousers and skirts. The whole thing was done in an ironic way, but it was clearly a reaction to the clean minimalism of urban sportswear. This time, the whole collection took 'authenticity' as its theme, but to preserve the sense of irony, in order that the wearer would not be mistaken for someone who might *always* have worn those clothes, we played around with materials and the way things were put together. So, a tweed jacket might be presented with a pair of nylon trousers, a pleated tweed skirt with a hooded sweatshirt.

Jacket B was part of a series of three inspired by the 'authentic' English waxed jackets described, but since the 'real thing' was readily available, and having been in fashion relatively recently, many people already had one in the back of their wardrobe. We decided to 'move it on' by using a nylon canvas, instead of cotton, with a finish that had the effect of being waxed, but softer and without the smell or the tendency to mark. We took the features which characterized the 'original' and used them on garments with slightly different shapes and proportions. As I write, I cannot imagine how we ever

52. Craik, J., *The Face of Fashion: Cultural Studies in Fashion*, London: Routledge, 1994, p. 60.

really thought poor old Jacket B would work. The collection was a success happily, but when it came to this series, the reaction was always the same; the garment was too traditional. It was useless pointing to the subtle irony of using previously sleek black nylon in an 'authentic' English way; protestations of intended irony only served to condemn the garment further.

In this tiny episode from the life of a designer, it is important to note that the development of the product was the result of the designer's colloquy with other agencies, linking it to its various markets: supply base, technological development, means of diffusion and customer. It indicates that, in a sea of shifting meanings, fashion is successfully launched when there is a consensus about the meaning of a garment shared by the designer, the customer, and the various agencies that mediate between them (which, of course, would include the press). It would also appear to confirm Craik's theories about the relationship between a new fashion and previous ones although her choice of the word 'compromise' indicates that she does not recognise the creative challenge of achieving this delicate balance. It also indicates a positive answer to Davis' question, 'Can they (designers) somehow divine women's inchoate yearnings so as to fashion into cloth new symbolic arrangements that assuage or possibly even resolve the psychic tension?'.[53] In fact, apart from differences of nomenclature ('couture', 'high street' and so on), my anecdote contradicts none of the theories presented by the likes of Craik or Davis, but it does render their images of fashion as lacking in detail, perhaps slightly out of focus, and wooden. A body of work informed more closely by clearly understood empirical evidence, 'inside knowledge' of this type might enable writers on fashion to prove what Davis knew, but was unable to verify, when he wrote 'it seems altogether plausible to assume, albeit difficult to prove, the existence or non-verbal exchange between couturiers and their publics. The more difficult task is to specify what such communication consists of'.[54]

Conclusion

Fashion has become a suitable subject for academic treatment, but, it seems, only when viewed from the safe distance of the sociologically related fields or when dressed in garments borrowed from more exalted intellectual and artistic fields. The voices of practitioners, or indeed the practice of fashion do not figure large in its academy, and consequently a whole world of

53. Davis, F., *Fashion, Culture and Identity*, Chicago: University of Chicago Press, 1994, pp. 131–2.
54. Ibid.

information is hidden from view; unlike other fields in art and design, such as architecture, theory and practice remain disintegrated. The field which is commonly designated as the academy of fashion is the intersection of the various disciplines which have an interest in the subject. Yet it still has to establish its own identity; understanding of fashion per se is usually indicated to those studies which have examined it.

I have enjoyed nearly fifteen years as a fashion designer, and ten educating future generations of designers. I share the view of many that fashion is rich, complex and fascinating, but I have often been disturbed by the subject's lowly status, which derives from not having its own distinct academy or critical structure. When I delivered the lecture in the 'Perspective in Fashion' series which was the basis of this chapter, I reported my embarrassment at replying when asked what I do. Saying one is a fashion designer elicits a certain amount of disbelief; it is rather like saying you are a movie star. Fashion will always attempt to dazzle us with visions of stardom and mythical status, but a deeper understanding of the subject might enable one to say in the future that 'I am a fashion designer' in the same way as one might say 'I am an architect'. So, there is a very pragmatic reason for my wish to see the status of my profession raised but this is secondary to the feeling that fashion should be explored 'because it's there', and it is in that spirit which I write this chapter.

When I delivered my lecture in 1994, I had just been appointed a professor by my university. 'Professor of what?' I asked myself when the announcement was made. I think that I have come a great deal closer to being able to answer that question over the last six years. I am encouraged by the fact that the students who have gone through the fashion course at Kingston University, and elsewhere, during that time, with a much richer intellectual diet than the one I enjoyed as a student, to think that future practitioners will enter the academic debate and contribute to the establishment of the subject as a distinct theoretical entity.

6

Connecting Creativity

Luigi Maramotti

What is creativity? How are ideas generated? How do we define a creative person? Such questions have probably crossed our minds more than once, but rarely do we realise how much we depend on this very special output of human intelligence. If we look at the products around us, most of which today are manufactured industrially rather than handmade, we can appreciate how their design is related to creative thought and to the necessity for innovation and change. As the Chairman of the MaxMara group, with an annual turnover of £600 million, more than twenty separate collections and 600 stores situated around the globe, I have been confronted quite forcefully with this thought. I have devoted this chapter to discussing creativity, ideas of what it is, and how, in my experience it can be organized in order to originate some of the remarkable results that industry is capable of achieving, particularly in the world of fashion.

The first personal intuition I had about the importance of creativity was through the Disney character, Archimedes; the light bulb that appeared every time he had a good idea fascinated me. It may seem an unintellectual approach, but I have always liked the idea of invention as sudden intuition, and the magic behind it. The abstract concept of creativity can be linked to the selection, from thoughts and things, of those which lead to innovation, change or improvement. Creativity can be formatively defined as behaviour which includes such activities as origination, organisation, composition and planning. Any definition we may try will not be fully satisfying because, in order to make creativity distinguishable from mere arbitrariness, there must be a sort of legislation. We are perfectly aware, in the world of fashion, for instance, odd does not mean fashionable. There are plenty of examples, from the past and in the present. George Brummel was a fashionable trendsetter, while Liberace was an eccentric oddity; Chanel was a priestess of style whilst Mae West was provocative, amusing or comic.

Creativity is often associated with irrationality or pure intuition, but this, in my view, is an erroneous belief. I believe that creativity has to be part of a system or structure, if we want it to be a useful instrument in helping us to understand or improve our social and physical environment. That creativity flourishes through being subjected to constraint may sound like a contradiction in terms, but I believe that it is not. Perhaps as a consequence of an overall attitude to the world based on daily experience, many today regard creativity as being linked to disorder; abstract expressionism is evidence of this. Yet as recently as the eighteenth century, Pascal asserted that order was sufficient (and necessary) to define creativity,[1] though I find myself doubting this when I find myself in the chaos of our design department.

In my opinion we tend nowadays to rarely abstract the idea of creativity. We tend instead to regard it as an attribute of certain individuals. 'That is a creative person', we are used to saying. What do we mean? Do we judge outward appearance, the image we are offered, someone's behaviour or maybe new ideas, something done in a certain way, a project or performance with a particular style? Any of these would show us to perceive creativity as 'something different'. We tend to believe that normality does not favour a creative attitude, or if you like, that human beings are not 'normally' creative.

A great and fascinating debate on creativity and genius enlivened the psychoanalytical studies of Freud and Jung. The former thought creativity to be the artist's tool, by means of which he could express the contents of his unconscious. In the writings on Leonardo and Michelangelo he analysed the two great masterpieces St Anne and Moses in which he could see turned into art, the nature and the inner secrets of the artists' souls as individuals.[2] For Jung, on the contrary, the creative person was one, who, through his or her work, is able to emancipate the self from his or her own individuality to become an interpreter of the universal themes of mankind which he, unconsciously, activates.[3] Jung's model seems to be the one which most accurately defines creativity in the context of fashion,[4] where the creative challenge is to divine unconscious collective desires, as I shall discuss.

The Italian writer, Italo Calvino, in connection with some lectures he was to give at Harvard University within the prestigious Charles Elliot Norton Poetry Lecture Series, wrote some very interesting papers entitled 'Six Memos for the Next Millennium'.[5] They list the essential literary qualities for writers of the future as being lightness, quickness, exactitude, visibility, multiplicity and consistency. Unfortunately, his sudden death prevented him from giving

1. Pascale, B., *Pensieri*, Turin: Eindaudi, 1962.
2. Freud, S., *Writing on Art and Literature*, Stanford University Press, 1997.
3. Jung, C. G. *The Spirit in Man, Art and Literature,* Princeton University Press, 1971.
4. Arieti, S., *Creativity – The Magic Synthesis*, New York: Basic Books, 1976.
5. Calvino, I., *Lezioni Americane*, Milano: Garzanti, 1986.

the lectures, but his texts help us to identify some of the peculiarities of creative thought. When he writes about imagination, for instance, Calvino defines it as a list of potentialities, of hypotheses, of what was not and may never, but might have been. What is important to him is to draw from this gulf of possibilities, to recreate all the possible combinations, and to pick the ones which best fit the purpose.

As I have suggested, many who have dealt with the concept of creativity have used it as a label or accolade for individuals whose output is different in a striking, even obvious way. In my view, it is erroneous to make such evaluations without taking the context into consideration. Take, for example, Renaissance artists and their works. We would be obliged to regard their creative value as slight, to consider them as minor artists, if we did not judge their work in the context of the strict patronage; the political, social and religious reality they were commissioned to represent. By extension, products that vary only slightly from the established norm, contrary to their immediate appearance, may in fact be the result of great creative thought. In fashion, a 'commercial' product can be as much the result of creative 'genius' as an extravagant catwalk creation.

Creativity and Fashion

It is widely agreed that clothing is a language, but a very ambiguous one. Its vocabulary changes or evolves, and can express different meanings at different times according to the wearer and the observer.[6] We might say that clothing is a dynamic language open to endless resetting. Some adhere to the view that fashion follows a 'trickle down process'[7] whereby innovative ideas are transmitted from the elite top layers of the social pyramid to the bottom. Others consider it mainly a matter of points of view, where each style creates an anti-style that defines it, and stimulates further change.[8] In reality, it is difficult to frame the rules by which creative thought gives a shape to fashion and its changes, although it appears that a good many can be linked in some way to technological innovations in textiles, and there seem to be recurrent patterns such as the relaunch of historic items in different contexts.

6. Jullien, F., *Procès ou creation, Un Introduction á la Pensée des lettres Chinois*, Paris: Edition du Seuil, 1989.

7. After Veblen, T., *The Theory of the Leisure Class: an economic study of institutions*, London: Allen and Unwin, 1970.

8. Hollander, A., *Sex and Suits*, New York: Alfred A. Knopf, 1994.

For as long as it has existed, fashion, being a language, has always been used as a means of communication. This very peculiar kind of communication takes place on two levels: an open one, and a hidden one. There is in fact an underlying reading we might call a creative value left to each individual, which allows the transmission of ambiguous and equivocal messages; think of the eroticism of neglected lace, the hardness of riding boots or the provocativeness of some metal details.

If we agree that fashion is a language we should emphasize that it is a very sophisticated one and in a way complementary, a tool for articulating and supporting words rather than substituting them. And if we agree that fashion is distinct from style, we must admit that its acknowledged codes are variable. These changes can occur at different levels mainly, but not only, visually, often revamping outdated meanings. The system of constantly shifting meanings, codes and values is in fact fundamental to fashion as we understand it in our culture. Designers know this well and they are the first to perceive signs of instability, the trends pervading society. The instabilities, ambiguities and ambivalences, described by Fred Davis in his excellent book on the subject drive creativity to and fro between opposites such as young/old, male/female, work/play, simplicity/complexity, revelation/concealment, freedom/constraint, conformism/rebellion, eroticism/chastity, discretion/overstatement and so on.[9] The field where the game of change is played is framed within couples of constantly recurring antithetic meanings. Fashion delights us by playing on the tensions between these couples – we derive a frisson from the contradictions they suggest. We may tire of a look but whenever one of these themes returns, its freshness is restored; our fascination with them seems endless. James Carse, a professor of philosophy at New York University, and a friend of mine, in one of his books divides the world of human relations into 'finite and infinite games'.[10] What is the difference? In the former case the goal of the game is to select a winner, in the latter it is to play the game forever. Incidentally, the latter is typical of the games of children, which were in fact the author's chief source of inspiration. Without doubt, fashion is an infinite game, since nobody is interested in starting the ultimate trend, the final one.

Though changes in fashion correspond to macrochanges in cultures or societies, they nevertheless require human action, the work of creative people, of industry and the complicity of consumers. Fashion, after all, does not happen by accident.

9. Davis, F., *Fashion, Culture and Identity*, Chicago: Chicago University Press, 1992.
10. Carse, J., *Giochi finiti e infiniti*, Milano: Arnoldo Mondadore Editore, 1986.

The fashion industry purposefully identifies garments and accessories as indicators of social status. Historians have suggested that this has been so since the fourteenth century.[11] Nowadays, this identification has become a carefully planned and greatly accelerated activity. In the eternal ping-pong game between antithetical meanings, the motivating force for creativity within fashion is nearly always, or often, cultural. When Chanel urged her wealthy clients to dress like their maids,[12] she was playing on dialectics between rich and poor, high and low status, snobbery and inverted snobbery, but the reason for her attraction to these particular themes, and the reason for the fashion's success, was her ability to intuit the predominant social tensions of the moment (in this case ideas the uncertainties of wealth and power initiated by the economic unrest of the 1930s).

The potential of cultural models to drive creativity cannot be over-emphasized. Successful designers refer to as wide a variety as possible, drawing from history and going beyond it, they focus on conceived models of an ideal future life. No matter how successful though, designers cannot create the desire to possess or acquire a particular product, but they can create products which satisfy or arouse incipient or otherwise undetected desire. This, in my opinion, is usually achieved by the 'lifestyle' associations a product has for the consumer; designers and companies like ours devote themselves increasingly to formulating our identities from visions of an ideal existence.

The stimuli for creative ideas in fashion have always originated from the widest variety of sources. Even in the last few years, we have seen influences exerted by exhibitions, films, writers, geographical areas, traditional cultures and metropolitan phenomena. It seems that fashion can appropriate practically anything and turn it into a 'look', the success of the look depending of course on its resonance with the cultural/social concerns of the day. Many enjoy the challenge of 'unpicking' fashion to reveal the influences which shaped it, but to me, what really matters is not to identify fashion's sources, but to examine how they generate innovative product ideas, the design process and the marketing of the product.

I have compared fashion to a language, and to a game, and there are sufficient similarities to justify both analogies. But where fashion differs is in its scant regard for rules. In a field which prioritizes innovation and change, practices are swept aside before they become established. Rules have a very short life indeed, and this is what I appreciate most about my work. Successful strategies inevitably become harder and harder to forecast, since the elements

11. Breward, C., *The Culture of Fashion*, Manchester and New York: Manchester University Press, 1995, pp. 22–9.

12. Charlie-Roux, E. Trans Amphoux, N., *Chanel*, London: The Harrill Press, 1995.

to be considered, from the creative and marketing point of view, have multiplied, and everything is subject to change. And yet we must attempt to devise strategies for innovation, since the successful inauguration of new fashions is increasingly likely to be the result of such planned approaches and less the result of the almost accidental fashionableness that was the case with the mini skirt in the 1960s, or Timberland shoes. In noting the necessity for a strategic approach I refute the widely held view that fashion is 'change for change's sake'; Craik has described how the current fashion acts as a determinant for the future one.[13] We who work in the industry are acutely aware that not everything is possible, and have learned by experience that new ideas must usually relate to what already exists if they are to succeed. At the same time we are conscious that the evolution of fashion is punctuated by spasmodic flashes of revolutionary genius, such as Chanel's, which radically change its course before it becomes too predictable. If we are to be successful, therefore, we must keep an ear to the ground ready to detect the first signs of such.

A company producing fashion is the utmost example of forced innovation. It is absolutely necessary to relaunch, recreate, rethink and to discuss things over and over again. Despite what one might think, this does not only apply to the design team, but the whole organization. To be successful, each element in the process of developing and marketing the product must be innovative and everybody should have a creative attitude. I must emphasize that I consider a designed garment 'fashion' only when it is marketed and worn by someone. I have a high opinion of the 'idea' but I believe we should consider it developed and embodied only when it has passed through some kind of process and become a 'product', no matter how small the market. Original ideas are only the first step of a long journey towards a desired success.

Before examining how the creative process develops in a company I should observe that companies, being human organizations, have many similarities with living organisms. Each possesses its own original 'genetic code' which is normally connected to the figure of its founder, but during its life its character may evolve in consequence of the external stimuli it is subjected to. A company possesses its own culture, which will become stronger over the years, transmitting itself through the inevitable conditioning of the individuals entering its ranks. But company culture is not necessarily positive, in fact, it is sometimes so deeply rooted that it hinders that renewal which is so critical to its survival. Company culture is like an enormous database from which can be read the company's life, experience, skills, individuals' contributions over the years but also its limitations and handicaps.

13. Craik, J., *Cultural Studies in Fashion*, London: Routledge, 1994, p. 60.

If we consider the product as being at the core of a manufacturing company's culture, and all the related activities of development, production, marketing and promotion arranged around it, we can appreciate how the company's internal activities, through reciprocal flows, engender a distinctive texture in the image of the product itself. Connecting creativity means, to me, positive interaction between different functions. The designer's creativity must be linked to a project; the company itself cannot exist without one. A well-delineated project multiplies the opportunities for the application of creative ideas, just as the artists and craftspeople who symbolized creativity in the past worked freely, yet to precise briefs. At the same time, we must recognize that creativity cannot be strictly planned, and especially in such a complex organization as ours, we must be flexible and ready to modify, at least partially, our project. A simple but frequent example of that need for flexibility is evident in the process of selecting materials. We may happen, in the course of our work, to discover fabrics and colours we find interesting, and wish to include them in a project, where they had not been foreseen. This might appear straightforward but the introduction of something new in to a collection can have enormous implications for supply, production, workability and quality control. Even the smallest of variations can cause a chain reaction, which must be assimilated. The potential dangers of creativity are undoubtedly a factor in industry's ambivalence towards it, yet to cut it out of the company culture is to risk stagnation and decline.

How, then, does MaxMara handle creativity? Our firm has a singular history. It was founded by my father, Achille Maramotti, more than fifty years ago and its roofs are to be found in the tradition linking my family to dressmaking on one side and to education on the other. My great-great-grandmother was the head of a well-known local couturier in the middle of the last century, whilst my grandmother was a true pedagogue. Experimental by nature, she not only taught the techniques of design, pattern cutting and sewing, she also invented new methods, offering at the same time moral and practical guidance to the girls attending the 'Scuole Maramotti' which she established in the 1930s.

There is no doubt that this history has greatly spurred love of experimentation and innovation at every level in our company. But as I have argued, creativity is of little purpose unchecked or unsupported. We have over the years established a sequence of critical mechanisms by which creative energy is directed to the most effective ends. These are outlined in the paragraphs that follow.

Market Research

Despite the importance of market information, I happily confess that our group has no dedicated research department, and rarely uses the services of research consultants. We have discovered that the most effective strategy is to conduct this kind of research through those members of the group who are operative (namely the design, sales and marketing areas). We base our work on a very simple method: observation. Those who are involved with the development and marketing of the product know it well enough, and are sufficiently armed with the history of the company to know where to look for the most relevant material, and how to interpret information.

The fashion market is so segmented that it is not uncommon for a manufacturer to obtain results quite different from the ones foreseen by the macrotrend. In 1996, for instance, the sales of our coats increased by 15 per cent yet this outcome contradicted the general survey of the market that had predicted a negative trend for this item. Trends in spending, social behaviour and lifestyle, gained through macroanalysis therefore must be regarded as background information.

It is of course essential that the company applies its creativity to developing the right products for real market needs. With awareness of our capabilities, our potential and our position in the market we must be alert to new opportunities. Again, we at MaxMara believe that the most attentive and intuitive lookouts are likely to be those that work within the company. Nobody from outside, however well qualified, could produce a piece of market research which says that if you product jacket x in cloth y and at z price you will sell 10,000 of them, but with a healthy company culture we can expect our project to evolve and develop along the right lines.

Data Processing

This kind of work is concerned less with broad intuition and more with minutely detailed knowledge. We are in a position to check daily precisely how the market is reacting to our products with reference to style, size and colour. This can be done thanks to a data-processing system we developed independently, to our specific requirements many years ago. Our sales information is supplemented by interviews with the managers of our stores, who can give us reasons for the success or failure of a particular model.

The importance of change in the fashion industry might tempt us to conclude that we should not be too greatly influenced by information on the market's reaction to a particular product; after all the market is bound to change and the product will be superseded. I have found that designers especially are sometimes particularly reluctant to confront this kind of information; it is unnerving to discover that the market does not affirm one's convictions. But a cumulative knowledge of how our customers' taste develops and what influences their choice, besides being deeply interesting, is an invaluable tool in predicting the chances of success for the next season's product, and in forming future strategies.

Technological and Technical Innovation

I have acknowledged the role of textile developments in launching new fashions. Fabric research is of fundamental importance to MaxMara. Innovative textiles, offering for instance enhanced comfort, practicality, fluidity, lightness, stability, or which allow new techniques of construction, for example the new generation of 'double face' fabric, or can engender new modes of dressing, for example the recent 'urban sportswear' phenomenon based on luxurious interpretations of high-performance fabrics. Innovative solutions can and should extend to the entire process of the development and even the marketing of a product, and we should consider this a critical aspect of research. Innovation can be the primary reason for a product's success.

Design

The market research, retail, information, fabric and technical research, the social tensions, ambivalences and ambiguities, the projections of future life, all that I have mentioned in this essay are transformed first into a drawing, then a form. This is the core of our work, and it has for me a magic and mysterious appeal. The sketches, patterns, phototypes, the styling and accessories are all equally important steps which require great investment. It is in the transition from bidimensional to tridimensional that we encounter the crucial artisanal aspect of our business. There is no substitute for the accumulated experience and craftsmanship of those pattern cutters and technicians in achieving the delicate balance that validates, authenticates or qualifies a designed garment. The designer must have an eye for these subtleties, and an appreciation of the crafts that enables his/her ideas to come into being.

Figure 6.1. MaxMara campaign Autumn/Winter 92/93.

Cost Analysis

If a seam in the back of a jacket can save 20 per cent in the fabric lay, is it worth doing? Questions of this type represent the difficult but necessary mediation between the defining characteristics of the original idea and the demands of reality. Cost analysis is a challenge to the designer since it requires him/her to devise ingenious solutions and should be regarded as a spur to the creative process, not an impediment.

Production Opportunities

Although most of our products are manufactured in Italy, we are conscious that in the future there will be a proliferation of opportunities for high-quality production in other parts of the world. Information on new manufacturing and finishing techniques and special processes is part of the research described above, and can stimulate new products, but we must be circumspect regarding, for example potential bottlenecks and other damaging production problems. When we embark on new projects in production, we must verify our willingness and ability to train, and the investment which that entails.

Marketing

Creating for sale is different from creating for creation's sake. At MaxMara, the product is rigorously defined in relation to the retail concept. There are over 600 MaxMara stores and our organization regards the selling phase as integral to the project. The visual merchandizing and display of proposed products, their coordination and communication are a vital part of the design activity.

Advertising

The importance of creating in this field is obvious, but more than anywhere else it must be exercised with a view to consistency since our objective is that the product should be immediately recognizable and associated with an absolute, possibly unique, identity. In my experience, the most successful advertising campaigns are those resulting from a very close collaboration between designers, photographers, and those such as stylists who, from an external perspective can add to this a story, an element of conceived reality.

Advertising in the fashion field is, in my opinion, more conventional than in others. Whilst we require it to be new and innovative, conveying an important element of fantasy, imagination and feeling, fashion advertising must also be relatively representative and explicative. To the question 'do advertised garments sell better?' I simply answer: Yes, but mainly if they are original and unusual.

Promotion

In the field of fashion, promotion means documentation, through the press in general and through the branch of the press that serves it specifically. I recently debated with some American journalists the ideal contents of a fashion publication. Their opinions were, predictably, very different and our discussion returned to the familiar dilemma between dream and reality, between the desire to report extreme and fascinating trends and the need to give useful advice and information to the readership. Everyone agreed on one point: the apparently 'objective' documentation of a product acts as a kind of endorsement or legislation which augments its chances of commercial success. It is therefore critical that an organization such as ours invests in effective communication with the media.

When these elements are synchronized, a circle is completed where creativity can flow freely. Since the creative thought represented by Archimede's light bulb has always fascinated me, it has been a pleasure to have worked in a field where one can experiment with its deployment. Where these experiments are successful, the results are tangible and I attribute our company's success, in no small part, to the way in which creativity is embedded at the heart of its culture. Further satisfaction is to be gained from the certainty that our experiments will never reach a conclusion. The game will last for ever.

7

The Chain Store Challenge

Brian Godbold

This chapter takes the form, initially, of an autobiography. Its story is not only that of my own life, but that of British fashion since the 1960s; I was fortunate to find myself right at the centre of the art school culture of that period, which as I hope to show, sparked off the design-conscious mass-market phenomenon by which I, as the Divisional Director of Design at Marks & Spencer was ranked as number 8 in *The Face* magazine's 100 most powerful people in fashion,[1] and at number 15 by *Elle*.[2] This chapter aims to describe the developments, challenges and opportunities for contemporary designers and retailers with reference to radical changes in consumer attitudes, redefinition of age profiles, the revolution in how and where we shop, and the advent of 'lifestyle' consumerism. But to place my analysis and projections for the future into context, I must refer to the past.

I cannot talk about my career without mentioning Walthamstow School of Art. As a schoolboy I had always been good at art, and my father had always encouraged me in the hope that I would eventually study graphics and enter the family's printing business. In 1961, he took me to the local art school for an interview. When the Head saw my work, he immediately suggested that I join the fashion course. My father nearly fell off his chair but I was delighted; it was something I had always wanted to do but never dared mention. I must emphasize that I was embarking on a journey into the unknown; at the time there were no existing high-profile, art school trained designers whom I could regard as role models. Part of the exhilaration of those days was the feeling that we were pioneers. As it turned out, I was well advised; the graphics department was good but fashion was excellent. The legendary, and even then influential Daphne Brooker[3] was head and

---

1. '100 most powerful people in Fashion', *The Face* September 1994 pp. 74–80.
2. 'Elle's hottest 100 names in fashion', *Elle*, April 1998, p. 115.
3. Not a great deal has been written about Daphne Brooker, but when the definitive history of post-war industrial fashion is compiled, she undoubtedly deserves a prominent position. As

Figure 7.1. Brian Godbold. Photograph by Norman Watson.

current students included Sally Tuffin, Marian Foale[4] and Ken Russell.[5] For two years I studied for the National Design Diploma with fashion as my principal subject. Our painting classes were often taken by Peter Blake[6] and Quentin Crisp[7] was the life model. He was very popular because of his ability to remain perfectly still for hour after hour, and because he never took breaks as other models did. Amongst my fellow students, the two who seemed least likely to succeed at the time, were Ian Drury[8] and Peter Greenaway.[9] After my first year, Daphne Brooker left to become Head of Fashion at what was then Kingston School of Art and I continued my studies at the Royal College of Art.

head of the Fashion School at Kingston School of Art, later Kingston Polytechnic and later still, Kingston University, from 1962 until her retirement in 1992, she was very largely responsible for establishing a prototypical model for design education in the UK, and there are several generations of designers at all levels within the industry who acknowledge her as their principal mentor.

4. Marian Foale and Sally Tuffin. 'Students of fashion at Walthamstow School of Art, Foale and Tuffin both studied at the Royal College of Art, which they left in 1961. They set up as partners in a private dressmaking business and their chance came in 1962 when their clothes were bought by the London store, Woollands. Their looks aimed at the young ready-to-wear market and Foale and Tuffin were at the heart of the London fashion revolution. Based on Carnaby Street, they and their designs reflected the fashion influences of the 1960s. Beginning with Pop Art, especially that of Hockney, then Op, they moved through an Art Deco phase towards the romanticism of old lace.' McDowell, C. (1984) *McDowell's Directory of Twentieth Century Fashion*, London: Muller p. 142.

5. Russell, Ken. 'British director Ken Russell was 42 when his film of D.H. Lawrence's *Women in Love* placed him in the ranks of movie directors of international stature. For more than a decade before that, however, British television viewers had been treated to a succession of his skilled TV biographies of great artists like Frederick Delius and Isadora Duncan ... he is the only British director in history ever to have three films playing first-run engagements in London simultaneously: *The Music Lovers, The Devils* and *The Boyfriend*. Lyon, C. and Doll, S. (1984) *The MacMillan Dictionary of Films and Film makers*, London: MacMillan, p. 472.

6. Blake, Peter, painter and graphic artist, London since 1956. 'In style and manner, Blake had a culture break-through to population millions and was able to speak in visual terms in a voice that was at once direct, without art complications, and "popular".' Williams, S. (1996) in J. Cerrito (ed.) *Contemporary Artists*, Detroit: St James Press pp. 130–1.

7. Crisp, Quentin. Commercial artist, artist's model, broadcaster, wit and gay campaigner, author of *The Naked Civil Servant*, London: Cape, 1968.

8. Drury, Ian. 'The Zenith of Drury's musical career, *New Boots and Panties*, came in 1977, when youth was being celebrated amid power chords and bondage trousers – he was 35 at the time. Lead singer of the 'Blockheads', television and film actor and late-night television show presenter. Larkin, C. (1995) *The Guinness Encyclopedia of Popular Music*, London: Guinness Publishing Ltd., pp. 1274–75.

9. Greenaway, Peter, film director, painter and writer. Films include *Zandra Rhodes*, 1981, *The Draughtsman's Contract*, 1982, *A Zed and Two Noughts*, 1985, *The Belly of an Architect*, 1986, *Fear of Drowning*, 1988, *Drowning by Numbers*, 1988, *The Cook, The Thief, His*

My main recollection of the two-year period at the Royal College of Art from 1963 to 1965 is one of working extremely hard. Once again, I found myself amongst formidable colleagues, this time Ossie Clarke,[10] Zandra Rhodes[11] and Bill Gibb.[12] Walthamshow had taught me how to draw, and had shaped my appreciation of things creative whilst the Royal College developed a competitive edge, an ability to deal with the highs and lows of life in fashion. Something about being a student in the Royal College of Art fashion school under the headship of Janey Ironside made one incredibly tough. Then, as now, a great deal of the projects of which the course was comprised, were actually competitions and our work was the object of a great deal of media attention. I was successful in a swimwear project, where my bullseye swimsuit received coverage in a large number of magazines, and in a second-year project where my 1940s inspired coat was featured on the front page of the *Evening Standard*. During the first year, Ernestine Carter[13] had sketched one of my garments for the *Sunday Times*, which caused great consternation amongst second- and third-year students, but I was not always so successful. I can still recall my feelings when, after working for weeks on a garment for a competition, Ossie Clarke arrived the evening before the deadline, cut out a dress and made it in half an hour. It looked as if it had never been touched by human hand.

Wife and Her Lover, 1989, *Prospero's Books*, 1998, *The Baby or Macon*, 1993, *The Pillow Book*, 1996.

10. Clark, Ossie. Raymond Clark, known professionally as Ossie, studied at Manchester School of Art from 1957 to 1961. He went to the Royal College of Art on a scholarship and graduated in 1964. His design career began with Alice Pollock's Quorum in the 1960s heyday of London fashion . . . His clothes had everything for those heady days when the *jeunesse de vie* of the Royal College seemed able to break all the rules and canons of taste, secure in the knowledge that they would receive ever-increasing praise from the press. McDowell, C. (1984), *McDowell's Directory of Twentieth Century Fashion*, London: Muller p. 108.

11. Rhodes, Zandra. 'Zandra Rhodes designs romantic and fantastic clothes which cannot be mistaken for the work of any other designer . . . . Her fabrics – chiffons, silks, tulles – are hand-printed with squiggles, zig zags and stars and float like butterfly wings. She has given us ruffled tulle crinolines, glamorised punk, uneven hems, bubble dresses – all with the strong Rhodes signature'. McDowell, C., (1984), *McDowell's Directory of Twentieth Century Design*, London: Muller p. 229.

12. Gibb, Bill. 'Educated at the Fraserborough Academy, Gibb enrolled at St. Martins' School of Art in 1962 and then went on a scholarship to the Royal College of Art in 1996. He soon became the golden boy, Fashion's Hockney, adored by all for his talent and charm.' McDowell, C., (1984), *McDowell's Directory of Twentieth Century Design*, London: Muller p. 147.

13. Ernestine Carter entered fashion via the post-war exhibition, 'Britain Can Make It', which lead to her fashion editorship of *Harper's Bazaar*, then Women's Editor and Associate Editor of the *Sunday Times*. She received an OBE in 1964 and published several books on fashion including *With Tongue in Chic* (1974), *20th Century Fashion: A Scrapbook 1900 to Today* (1975), *The Changing World of Fashion* (1977) and *Magic Names of Fashion* (1980).

During vacations, I worked in the design department of Marks & Spencer, where Hans Schneider had been head since 1936 and at the end of my second year of the, then, three-year course, he offered me a permanent position. This did not appeal to me at all; like many of my contemporaries I was convinced that you had to be a star by the time you were thirty, otherwise you really had not made it. I did feel ready, though, to venture out into the world, so, with some scholarship money I had won, I bought a three-month return ticket to New York.

With little more than ten dollars a day, I had to find a job quickly, so I bought a copy of *Womenswear Daily* and answered an advertisement for a designer at a company called Jovi. I got the job and although the company was very small to begin with, it became an overnight success and I found myself designing a range of clothes bearing my name, Brian G for Jovi. The exhilarating thing about working for the newly discovered junior sportswear market was producing a completely new collection every six weeks, for clients such as Macys, the New York department store. Never particularly interested in 'one-off', or elite products, I derived enormous satisfaction from seeing racks and racks of my designs in different colourways, ready for dispatch and I was fascinated by the idea that vast quantities of people would be able to enjoy well-designed clothes – this was something quite new, particularly in the United Kingdom. Within a few months buyers were queuing for the collection and scarcely a day went by when it was not featured in *Womenswear Daily*. The experience of Brian G for Jovi opened my eyes to the huge potential of the mass market and the revolution that was about to occur in fashion.

With the success of Brian G for Jovi I felt fairly confident that my education was complete and I decided not to finish my degree at the Royal College of Art, but I did return to London and in 1967 I became head of the coat and suit design room at Wallis. Jeffrey Wallis was the great high-street entrepreneur of the late 1960s and it was a privilege to work with him. One of Wallis's greatest successes was the Pick of Paris range, which featured inexpensive couture copies and it fell upon me to go to Paris to select coats from the Autumn 1969 collections. This was a widespread and quite legitimate design practice; we attended the shows as buyers and developed the garments we chose back in London, modifying the cut, fit and finish to suit our market and price. This we had to achieve in three or four weeks in order to get the garments in store for the release date and to secure newspaper coverage. Most of the 1969 coat collections were short. Every other manufacturer dutifully complied with the general trend, but I put a few long coats into the Wallis collection. There was a huge amount of publicity and within days they sold out. Jeffrey Wallis demonstrated his great entrepreneurial skills by halting production on everything short and turning it over to the longer styles. Wallis had never experienced such a successful season; we put every fabric we had into Maxi coats, as they were christened, and they all sold out. What lead me to go against the grain, and how did I know that long would beat short that season? The answer is that the prediction of future trends is an instinct and the career of a designer is made or broken on a hunch about the length of a coat.

In 1969, I left Wallis, to go to an American company manufacturing in the UK but my instinct served me less well on that occasion, and they went out of business within a year. After a few months spent teaching with Daphne Brooker at Kingston, I went to Cojana, an upmarket tailoring manufacturer whose biggest customer was Harrods where I stayed for four years until I heard that Monty Black,[14] the entrepreneur who had built Baccarat from nothing in three years, had purchased the moribund reversible coat manufacturer Weatherall. I was immediately struck by the idea of revamping this old-fashioned company which had, for years, been selling blue and brown reversible coats, so I wrote to Monty Black who then offered me the job. By updating the fabric and style, we produced a new classic, the camel and white reversible which was still worn twenty years later.

Cojana and Baccarat made excellent products but no longer exist. This, I believe, is because they did not fully understand how design could differentiate them from the competition. I have always felt this is an English disease and one of the reasons we have been unable to grow great brands like the Italians.

This brings us to 1976, when for the second time in my career, I was offered a position at Marks & Spencer, but this time as head of the Design Department, since Hans Schneider had retired. At the time, Marks & Spencer was certainly not noted for design innovation, and most of my contemporaries were horrified that I should work for a volume chain store. But my career up to that point had done everything to strengthen my belief in the future importance of the mass market, and I was convinced that at Marks & Spencer there was huge, but as yet untapped potential. It is at this point in my story, then, that the extraordinary creativity, the appetite for innovation and originality unleashed during the 1960s feeds directly into national culture, via Britain's biggest retailer. Not only had the 1960s created the art school culture which, I believe, revolutionized attitudes to design, they spawned a

14. Monty Black worked with Jeffrey Wallis at Wallis shops and then went on to start his own business, Baccarat, where he hired designers like Bill Gibb, John Bates, Gina Frattini to design collections (a very new practice at the time). The company made beautiful tailored garments with high work content, like leather trims. Following the success of this, he bought Weatherall, the reversible coat manufacturer, which was in the doldrums.

generation with levels of disposable income sufficiently high to sustain an unprecedented market for products.

However, it would be misleading to suggest that when I joined Marks & Spencer, the Design Group was poised to capture the new market. The team I inherited consisted of around a hundred pattern cutters, machinists and so-called designers, but the level of creativity and competence was modest. The practice was to promote machinists to pattern cutters and thence to designers. My first objective was to reform the department and to raise the level of design competence. In this, thankfully, I had the support of the board of directors, which was at the time telling the suppliers to improve their own design facilities in order to improve their products and meet our quality standards. The Design Group's method of working would inevitably have to change if this was to happen; we became less concerned with designing in detail on behalf of the suppliers, and more concerned with fashion prediction, colour and product coordination. The move to a more strategic role for design meant the building of a more concentrated team of higher calibre designers. In 1980, a joint ladieswear project heralded our long collaboration with the Royal College of Art, and we also undertook projects with Kingston and Brighton Universities and Shenkar College in Israel.

In 1985 Peter Salisbury, later Chief Executive, recommended greater concentration on research and development, separating pattern technology from design and moving it to the Technical Executive. In the same year, with the addition of menswear to my portfolio, I appointed the celebrated designer Paul Smith as a consultant. By this time, each area of the design department (Ladieswear, Childrenswear, Menswear and Lingerie) had a small but qualified team of designers, with a high level of experience in industry and forecasting. From 1986 a mode of operation was established whereby each area produced a seasonal design brief, a 'bible' to be used by the buying groups to give direction to the suppliers, covering colour fabric, print, pattern and styling. The buying groups were concerned with product areas such as ladies' knitwear or mens' trousers, not with 'lifestyle' areas such as casualwear, formalwear and so on. Since a buying group's annual turnover could be well in excess of £100m, the coordinating function of the design group was, and is, critical.

Throughout the 1980s and most of the 1990s the success of Marks & Spencer, and the Design Group seemed unstoppable. We acquired homeware in 1990, packaging and graphics in 1995, launched the Marks & Spencer magazine in 1987, were the first chain store to shoot promotional campaigns using supermodels in 1994; we became accustomed to nominations in the British Fashion Awards and won the 'classic' section twice, in 1994 and 1995. The dedication of the April 1996 issue of *Vogue* to high street fashion and the cover the following month showing our £21 shantung skirt photographed by Mario Testino and styled by Lucinda Chambers signalled that mass-market design had come of age. By 1994 we had 610 stores worldwide and a group turnover of £5.9 billion. As Divisional Director of Design, my portfolio represented a business worth £3.5 billion pounds.

The downturn throughout 1999 in Marks & Spencer's business has led to massive and continuing change, not just cosmetic but reaching deep into fundamental attitudes and approaches. In the second part of this chapter I will give my view of the issues challenges and opportunities, which I consider to be key to the volume retailer today and in the coming years.

Age Profile

With the 'cultural flip' of the 1960s, instead of values passing from age to youth, they began to flow the other way. Although we thought at the time that you were either young and part of it or old and out of it, it seems that our generation has yet to reach its sell-by date. The post-war 'baby boomers' are now beginning to grow old, and are confounding marketeers in the process. Unlike their parents, whose lives were shaped by depression and war, this generation has in truth never had it bad. The first to enjoy significant levels of disposable income, everything throughout their adult lives has been targeted at them; the new 'third agers', as the 50–75 age group is often called, insist it should remain so, and have the financial might to ensure that it does. No longer faced with slipping into obscurity or striving to feign youthfulness, the generation of which I am part aims for continuing style and there are plenty of role models to inspire us: Calvin Klein, Paul McCartney, Catherine Deneuve and Mick Jagger are in their mid to late fifties. What will be the impact of this marketing phenomenon on product? In my opinion, the 'third-agers' will lead the demand for products which are 'modern' but will eschew ridiculousness and excess, they will prioritize ease of care, practicality and comfort appropriate to their relaxed lifestyles. In other words, they will effect a fundamental shift away from faddish or dictatorial 'fashion' towards enduring, interpretable 'style' and genuinely high-quality design.

How We Shop

We have not stopped spending our money, but it seems we are more reluctant to spend it in public. Whether it is a matter of embarrassment about appearing extravagant, or whether it is a matter of convenience I cannot say, but it is certain that home shopping is transforming the retail landscape.

The first indication of this was in the United States, during the 1980s. Industrial analysts suggest that the introduction of zip codes and toll-free telephone numbers, increasing subscription to credit cards and the development of computer networks that could cross-check individual spending habits, enabled the meteoric rise of mail order. Mail order business grew at three times the rate of store business throughout the decade and according to the Direct Marketing Association, in 1993 alone, in the United States, more than 10,000 mail order companies issued 13.5 billion catalogues and 55 per cent of the adult population bought $51.5 billion worth of goods by mail.

Moreover, as Matthew De Bord noted in his essay on the J. Crew phenomenon 'mail order used to mean dowdy, as in Sears-Roebuck stylessness and industrial-strength presentation. It now means *reliably* stylish. It used to mean cheap; it now competes with the pricier designers for customers'.[15] The real impact of the mail order revolution is the mass dissemination of style consciousness. The product, improved editions of standard sportswear, seems calculated to be instantly familiar, ready to take its place in our wardrobes besides those favourite items that have the status of old friends. The 'barn jackets' are 'pre-aged' and ideally battered, the twill work shirts are dyed to look as though they have faded over the course of several years' wear. Most items are just like something we already own, except for some small detail, some slight improvement that makes us feel that the version we have at home is inferior; the gym shorts are in vivid colours they never come in at school, the espadrilles are in gingham, denim jackets have tartan linings. The appeal of these clothes is subtle novelty, rather than any kind of flamboyant fashion, but it is communicated with breathtaking clarity. J. Crew, Racing Green et al stimulate the desire to buy using the printed image; confident, relaxed models looking like the kind of people we would like to be or to know, idyllic locations, carefully studied styling and photography lend a kind of aspirational 'added value'. Borrowing the devices long used by fashion magazines, they have, in my view, the potential to beat the magazines at their own game. Whilst the magazines struggle to offer something to satisfy their various advertisers and disparate readers, relaying the designers' runway proclamations, they are in any case preaching to the converted. The mail order catalogues, however, insinuate themselves into the homes of the indifferent and the disaffected and they are in a position to give a distinct and coherent editorial point of view which seems to speak directly to the reader.

The next great contribution to home shopping has been the television shopping channels that, again, originated from the United States. If you had

15. De Bord, M., (1997) 'Texture and Taboo: The Tyranny of Texture and Ease in the J. Crew Catalogue', *Fashion Theory* vol. 1, issue 3, pp. 261–78.

a telephone and a credit card QVC, standing for Quality, Value and Convenience, 'the-mall-you-call' allowed you to shop for everything from clothes to cookware, day or night, from your sofa or bed. In 1993, the midst of recession, 44 million Americans eagerly dialled QVC and its sister QVC Fashion Channel and parted with $1.1 billion. Its rival, the Home Shopping Network also did business of over $1 billion. QVC combined entertainment with shopping, giving viewers the opportunity to talk to programme hosts and celebrity guests on the air, participate in games show and win prizes.

QVC's merchandise and appeal has been largely downmarket, kitsch or downright cheap and cheerful. Q.1, described itself in the press release announcing its launch as the 'combination of a great speciality store and a great lifestyle magazine'. The service was designed to reach a contemporary audience whose needs were not addressed by existing home-shopping media. The various promises of its press release read like a prescription for the cure of the ills and anxieties of urban life:

> How to look great without living in a gym, buying and cooking healthy foods, gardening – even if you live in a city, cheap three-day getaways, great coffees and teas of the world, cards and stationery for the lost art of letter writing, shopping for your girlfriend, gifts grandkids will love, camping for beginners, great presents shipped anywhere fast, housewares from the Italian countryside, creating a bachelor's kitchen, redecorating your apartment in a weekend, 50 ways to work a little black dress, sweatwear for show-offs, clothes for men who hate to shop and great trash reading for the beach.

After television shopping channels came virtual retail, e-commerce as it is known, which also began in the United States, where in 1994 Apple teamed up with a group of mail order companies to distribute 30,000 electronic versions of their catalogues on compact disc. With access to merchandise from retailers such as L L Bean, Landsend and Tiffany & Co., users could browse through catalogues on screen, or ask their computer to search specific items such as mens' trousers or dinner sets, they could even change the colour of garments to assess different combinations. They were also given access to supporting editorial material such as guides to fashion and financial planning supplied by publications like *Elle Décor* and the *Wall Street Journal*.

In 1999 with millions worth of goods purchased on the Internet in the UK alone it seems certain that home shopping will become a greater and greater feature of retail, and the clothing business. At Marks & Spencer we recognized this fact with the launch of Marks & Spencer Direct, our clothing catalogue in 1998, and the Marks & Spencer online shop in 1999. We offered an initial batch of 200 products, with the ambition of reaching 3,000, of which approximately one third was anticipated to be clothing, within two years of operation. This would represent the equivalent of a 5,600 square metre department store; in other words, a range of products only represented in the largest ten of the group's outlets.

But I do not suggest that home shopping will wipe out the need for shops and stores. On the contrary, this is one of the greatest challenges that we currently face.

Retail Environments

My story returns yet again to the United States, where in the 1980s and early 1990s, the department stores took quite a knock caused by the impact of home shopping. It would be naïve to conclude, however, that home shopping must inevitably wipe out the stores. The pleasures of going shopping, experiencing the physical environment of the store itself, the element of social interaction, being able to touch merchandise are an important aspect of urban life that will not be eradicated by the convenience of shopping from home. I believe that department stores have a future, and that those which survive will be the ones that turn shopping into an entertaining, exciting or in some way distinctive experience, in other words, those that have the confidence to look different and separate themselves from the mainstream. In the United States, this was pioneered by Barney's, who, with Japanese finance, formulated a new concept. Rather than follow the fail-safe blanket-buying policies of other stores, Barney's dared to buy selectively from designer collections, which gave its merchandise a particular flavour enhanced by its own brand, or 'private label' collections. In the United Kingdom, first Harvey Nichols and then Selfridges reinvented themselves along similar lines. Harvey Nichols turned itself into a fashion lifestyle experience with a series of dedicated designer 'boutiques', both clothing and homewear, top-of-the-range specialist food retail in the stylishly designed food hall, ambitious private label clothing and food products and restaurants. The refurbishment of Selfridges trans-formed it from a 'safe' department store stocking the same kind or products in the same kind of visually uninspired or indistinctive environment as any other department store, into a fashion pantheon, where the most current collections are enticingly displayed in a showcase environment. A Saturday or Sunday afternoon visit to the store confirms that shopping is as much a fashionable social activity today as it was when the store was established by Gordon Selfridge.

Alongside the innovative department stores, the generation of new specialist retailers is playing its part in the reassertion of shopping. My personal list of visionaries in this field would include Joseph Ettelgui, whose stores in London,

Paris and New York carry his distinctive personal style and reflect his aim to turn shopping into a social experience, and Terence Conran, whose stores in London and Paris emphasize furniture, homewear and food as fashionable products. These retailers, as do Selma Weisser of the, sadly defunct, Chiaravari in New York, Joyce Ma of Hong Kong, Colette in Paris and Jeffrey in New York, address the concept of what I would term 'lifestyle retailing'. They have a strong point of view, their selections of merchandise have an editorial quality, which extends from clothes to food to furniture and is asserted through the interior of the store itself. The secret of their success appears to be in their refusal to attempt to be all things to all people. Maureen Doherty and Asha Sarabhai's London store, Egg, for example carries a distinctive mix of clothes and *objects* which reflect the proprietors' taste for high quality artisanal products which stand outside the usual dictates of fashion. The store is situated in a quiet Knightsbridge mews and is characterized by a low-tech simplicity harmonious with the product. Shopping there is a leisurely social event, with frequent special events and private views for the well-defined intellectually and artistically inclined clientele.

Egg is clearly very different from Marks & Spencer but there is no doubt in my mind that volume retailers will have to take their cue from the small-scale specialists and department stores who have restored the pleasure of the act of shopping, and have re-established it as a defining social activity. The increasing 'visual literacy' which fuelled the mass demand for well-designed or fashionable products in the first instance will, or has extended to the retail environment itself. High-street retailers must pay as much attention to the design of their stores and their visual merchandising as to the design of their products, and it is no coincidence that so many have, over the last few years, opened in-store coffee bars, crèches, delivery services and home shoppers.

Product

My career bears witness to the mass-market fashion explosion of the last thirty or so years. The recent downturn in business reflects the resulting worldwide over-capacity, which I believe will be a significant factor in the industry's future. This is especially true in the area we describe as 'core casual', that is to say, the pivotal items which define generic leisure/weekend wear. In the late 1980s the American retailer Gap built a huge business on the demand, amongst all age groups and social classes, for a more relaxed and practical approach to dressing. Their hugely successful advertising campaigns offered us stylish black and white images of icons of all ages, and from all fields, wearing anonymous casual basics. The trend systematically moved performance fabrics from the active sportswear market to being an acceptable and essential part of everyone's wardrobe. At the same time, the market learned to accept casualwear classics such as chinos and jeans as staple items. For years, we at Marks & Spencer had believed that we could never move into the jeans market, that it was a business best left to the brands. But when we did introduce them in the early 1990s we discovered that the trend was so powerful that by 1994 we had developed a £60 million annual jeanswear business across mens', women's and children's wear.

Our market research during the 1990s revealed that our customers, particularly the influential baby boomers, were and are continuing to enjoy more leisure time, taking more and longer holidays throughout the year, and participating in more sports and fitness activities. Changing lifestyle dictated changing spending patterns. We found that customers were becoming less interested in carefully coordinated looks. The emerging market was motivated by the acquisition of versatile pieces, either basics or 'hot' items that would update the wardrobe. We christened the trend 'item shopping' and in terms of design we fed the demand by addressing subtle changes in core items. So, the white cotton shirt would become longer and french-cuffed, then collarless and more fitted, deconstructed then refabricated. The black polo neck would become a tunic, lose its rib, become small-shouldered and shrunken, sleek and layered, soft and felted. We discovered that customers responded to pieces that could be interpreted in a variety of ways, according to taste and allowed the gradual evolution of their wardrobes. This of course represented a radical shift from the approach that prevailed at the beginning of my design career, where I had responded to the market for complete new looks every six weeks.

Item shopping is still very much part of our lives, but market saturation has taken its toll and replacement purchases of core product continue to decline. Added to this is the changing profile of the customer, who, through constant exposure, is becoming wiser, more astute, more confident in mixing products and consequently, likely to be less brand loyal. This has not only intensified the necessity to maintain demand through technological developments which provide greater comfort, functionality and practicality (supportive stretch 'footglove' shoes and non-iron shirts are just two examples) but also highlights the need for new, exciting products that stimulate the desire to buy on impulse. Alongside the 'sensible' purchases, we have discovered that the customer responds well to the aspirational, luxurious appeal of, for example, the pashminas and cashmeres that we introduced in 1999.

Predictably, the demand for anonymous basics in its turn spawned a renewed interest in conspicuous 'design'. We responded to this with the launch of our Autograph range in Spring 2000. For the first time Marks & Spencer worked directly with independent designers such as Betty Jackson, Julien

MacDonald and Katherine Hamnett to produce small collections for sale in stylishly decorated dedicated areas within top stores. It seems that the demand was well met; in its first week Autograph generated £1m worth of sales. I am keenly aware that it is the interest of volume retailers to support the emergent designers and small-scale craft operations that can feed this demand. Back in 1994, when I gave the lecture at Kingston University that was the basis of this chapter, I warned that the consumer would tire of the volume-priced quality and machine-made consistency of mass production if there were no alternative to provide the occasional intoxicating treat. I suggested then that we should be investing in small-scale niche operations that we ourselves were too big to provide for. Autograph is one example of this, but the tradition stretches back to 1994, when our suppliers started, for the first time, to work with independent designers to produce ranges for Marks & Spencer. The relationship between the then small-scale niche designer operation Ghost, our supplier Coats Viyella and ourselves not only helped to raise design for the High Street to a completely new level, but enabled Ghost's Tanya Sarne to increase her business dramatically. Ghost have joined Paul Smith as the first United Kingdom based designer brands and I, as Deputy Chairman of the British Fashion Council since 1998, have a vision that others such as Hussein Chalayan and Clements Ribeiro could achieve similar success, supported by the volume retailers. Another example of Marks & Spencer's support for independent design is our sponsorship, from 1994 onwards, of New Generation, which, operated by the British Fashion Council funds emergent designers to show their collections during British Fashion Week. Recipients of New Generation funding include Hussein Chalayan in 1993, Clements Ribeiro in 1994 and 1995, Julien MacDonald in 1997 and 1998, Matthew Williamson in 1998 and 1999 and Anthony Symonds in 1999 and 2000.

So, in reality, the beginnings of the new approach to design which I believe is the way forward were already in place before the downturn in business occurred. Our objective since 1998 has been to accelerate the rate of change. Opportunities still exist, but as I have described, the market is more knowledgeable and more fickle than it was, and we have to be more agile in order to spot and meet new demands. As a result, we now work in smaller teams with fewer people involved in developing a product. This way decisions are made by those working closest to the product, and the process is much speedier, enabling us to get the right products to the market more quickly. Marks & Spencer's designers maintain their strategic 'forecasting' role but they also work directly with suppliers on putting ranges together, ensuring high-quality definitive products which are not diluted by a drawn-out decision-making process. We have begun to assemble our products, clothes, homewears and even food, into coordinated lifestyle themes that have aspirational appeal. We have embarked on big changes in the design of our stores, the presentation of products, and the quality of supporting items such as packaging and promotional material.

I have been fortunate to be part of an influential generation, one that turned design from a minority to a mass interest. The extent of this increasing visual literacy is now so great that the way forward is without doubt greater, better and swifter design. From the art school culture of the 1960s, through the volume retail revolutions of the 1970s and 1980s to the nurturing of a new generation of art school talent in the 1990s and beyond, my story has come full circle.

Part 4

Image and Marketing

8

The Hilfiger Factor and the Flexible Commercial World of Couture[1]

Lou Taylor

Introduction

All 'things' carry within them a weight of cultural complexities, including the products of the couture industry, whose meanings are centred specifically on overt notions of elitism. The cultural power of couture clothing and accessories remains so strong that it now impacts on the style of clothing at more market levels than ever before. All around the world, a shoe is just a shoe, a perfume just a perfume, until magically transformed by a 'designer' logo or house style into a symbol of global sophistication. The business of couture is now so successful that it penetrates right through the global fashion market place.

Business and couture have always been twinned in close partnership, though the economics behind the great couture salons have always been carefully secreted behind the presentational glamour of seasonal fashion shows. Indeed our knowledge of the past and present of the haute couture industry, with some notable exceptions,[2] is largely based on a fiction of consisting only of the story of the designing and making of glorious garments. This revisionist history of couture is manipulative, strategic and cynical. It deliberately leaves

---

1. All translations from French are by the author. Thanks for advice from Claire Wilcox and Amy de la Haye.
2. Steele, V., *Paris Fashions – a cultural history*, Oxford: Oxford University Press, 1988; Coleman, E.A., *The Opulent Era, fashions of Worth, Doucert and Pingat*, London: Thames and Hudson,1989; Bertin, C., *Paris 'a la Mode – a voyage of discovery*, London: Gollancz,1956.

out far more than it leaves in, with a sense of bravado which would astonish even the most bold professional confidence trickster. These accounts are awesome traps for the innocent and gullible reader. Aided by many fashion journalists and by a range of professional acolytes, these books promote and hype only the notion of couture fashion as high art, as beyond-reality dreams. The designer is placed centrally as 'genius' and the clothes become miracles of creative invention.

Until the mid-1990s there was little debate which explained that since the 1970s nearly every couture house in Paris had run at a financial loss. There was little public acknowledgement that the main function of a couturier over the last thirty years has been to create the glamorously seductive house image used to launch the million-dollar global manufacture of over-priced 'designer' products. You will find in the glossy books no end-of-year financial reports, no details of prices of the garments and certainly no listing of profits or losses – in fact nothing that indicates the real function of haute couture and elite fashion companies. This is quite simply the need to make decent, preferably very large, profits.

Certainly, the glorious clothes of this *industrie de luxe* exist, as they have since the eighteenth century, the clothes eulogized over in the glossy books. We all respect, admire and acknowledge the creativity of designers, the perfectly cut tailoring, the astonishingly high levels of needle craft and the artisan skills of weaving, knitting, embroidery and so on. Yet, as every effort is made to maintain the glamorous image of the couture world, we hear little about the serious problems that have beset the trade since the inter-war period. Revisionist history has ensured avoidance of debate about failures of companies or collections, or the subsidies poured in to keep companies running. The fact that the couture trade has lurched from one economic crisis to another since the late 1920s has not been properly acknowledged. As a result, one of the main strengths of the Paris couture industry has not been fully recognized – its business flexibility.

The trade's design flexibility, has, by contrast, long been admired. We know all about Worth and Doucet and the socially correct clothing they designed for the international elite in the 1900 period. We are all aware that Chanel's alertness in recognizing the 'new poor' client in the inter-war period led couture into innovative, new, creative directions. Jean Paul Gaultier is admired today for pulling in younger clients through the freshness of his new range of couture garments launched in 1998. But the trade's brilliance in commercial flexibility has been hidden from history. It is knowing, manipulative and clever, building with vast success on the uniqueness of couture's sartorial elitism. By avoiding any discussion of business activities, these glossy books successfully obscure the fact that successful business is the driving factor which ensures the continuation of couture companies. It is this issue which forms the focus of this chapter.

The Function of Couture Clothing

As Alexandra Palmer, has so well explained, the basic function of the making of individual couture clothing is, and always was, to provide the etiquette-correct 'social uniform' for its private clients.[3] The basic financial problem within couture is the inevitability that it will only ever be bought by the tiniest minority of women and that in times of economic trauma, they too balk at spending cash on luxury clothing. Thus this *industrie de luxe* can never run securely and smoothly. It never has. It is always subject to vicissitudes caused by international economic crisis and has only survived over the last 150 years because of its sensitive commercial flexibility.

Where the money is, couture clients will be found and then educated into the specific consumption etiquettes of the trade. Up to 1914, the focus was exclusively on the private European and US plutocratic rich. In 1900, the *Syndicat de la Couture Parisienne* with its elite twenty-one members, already exported 65 per cent of its products to the international elite circles of royalty and plutocratic rich all around the world.[4] In truth, it was only in this 1890–1914 period, in the first thirty or so years of *Syndicat*'s existence, that the industry of couture was relatively crisis free. Unrivalled, Paris had no challengers. It could produce and sell clothes at any price it chose to its eager, captive, international clientele. With astute business acumen even then, the couturiers were already selling to elegant department stores from New York to Berlin. The *Syndicat* launched itself into public view for first time at the Paris International Exhibition of 1900. The success of their pavilion was so huge that the police had to be called in to hold back the crowds pressing to see the staged scenes of wax dummies posed as if at grand soirées or at the races. By this time, according to Anny Latour, the top six or seven couture houses, such as Doucet, Worth, and Drécoll, were each employing 400–900 workers, at the Rue de la Paix or Place Vendome, with a turnover of 30 million francs.[5] Wealthy clients were to be found, often royal and aristocratic, from St Petersburg, Stockholm, Madrid, London, Buenos Aires, Chicago and

3. A. Palmer, 'The Myth and Reality of Haute Couture, Consumption, Social Function and Taste in Toronto, 1945–1963', PhD thesis, University of Brighton, 1994, Vol. 1: Royal Ontario Museum no. 1986. p. 165.

4. Latour, A., *Kings of Fashion*, London: Weidenfeld and Nicolson, 1958, p. 164.

5. Ibid., pp. 64-165.

Tokyo and production of garments was high. The London couturier Lucile, showed a collection before leaving for the USA on a marketing trip in 1910 for example. A thousand guests packed her Hanover Square showroom in London. 'When the parade was ended the saleswomen found that they had booked orders for over 1000 gowns.'[6]

These clothes represented the social and economic power of the circles in which they were worn. Stuart Ewen recognizes that 'the relationship of style and social power is not a creation of twentieth-century consumer culture. This alliance has a long history.' Specifically the dress of the nobility provided 'excessive images [which] connoted a power over others: the employment of enormous forces of detailed labour for the purpose of body decoration; the enjoyment of waste and leisure in a context where most lives were spent in arduous squalor'.[7]

The wealthy had no sense of guilt in wearing their luxurious clothes. They saw this as their natural due and as the right of their social class. They firmly believed that it was also their social duty to look superbly and expensively dressed in order to uphold the visual public image of their rank. They were convinced that it was their duty, too, to provide employment for the workers who made the clothes in the luxury trades. When the vogue for heavyweight brocaded silks went out of fashion in the 1860s the specialist silk weavers in Lyons went hungry. Worth begged the French Empress, Eugenie, to wear evening gowns of heavy silk brocade, woven with complex jacquard patterns, a fabric which had been the mainstay of the town's industry. She much preferred the new fashion fabrics of plain, lightweight silk but agreed reluctantly. She hated the resulting dresses, calling them her 'robes politiques', but they did indeed get the looms working again.[8]

Overall the couture industry flourished in the 1880–1914 period. The consumer base widened. Paul Nystrom noted that Jeanne Lanvin was finding clients in Argentina through a successful branch outlet in Buenos Aires, whilst the house of Paquin was already selling 'to masses of wealthy women formerly not participating in the main currents . . . [through] developing sales outlets in a big way to department stores and to wholesalers for resale to dealers'. Illegal copying by private dressmaking salons was already a problem. Callot Soeurs took pirate companies to court, (they were usually private fashion houses till 1915) and then permitted buyers the right to reproduce, for a

6. Gordon, Lady Duff, *Discretions and Indescretions*, London: Jarrolds, 1932, p.70.

7. S. Ewen, 'Marketing Dreams – the Political Elements of Style', in Tomlinson, A., *Consumption, Identity and Style*, London: Routledge, 1990, pp. 43–8.

8. Latour, A., *Kings of Fashion*, London: Weidenfeld and Nicolson, 1958, p. 85.

Figure 8.1. Front Cover of Les Modes, Paris, 13 January 1918. Half-mourning day dress. Author's collection.

large fee.[9] Thus as the First World War broke out, a pattern of successful style and manufacturing dominance in the world of elite dressing at an international level had been maintained and enhanced in Paris.

Whilst the industry did not close in the 1914–1918 period it did not flourish and ever since has been hit time after time by a series of commercial blows. It has only survived through the development of highly flexible design and commercial responses to its shifting consumer base. As the First World War

9. Nystrom, P., *The Economics of Fashion*, New York: Ronald Press, 1928, pp. 215–16 and pp. 20–210.

ended and both Europe and then America entered periods of economic depression, very direct problems faced the couture world which are rarely mentioned in the glossy books. The industry had lost much of its male labour force during the War, such as specialist weavers. Silk was in short supply because at this point Japan began exporting and manufacturing fashion silks herself to a much larger degree. There was such a shortage of quality silk available that the Lyons luxury silk trade seriously contemplated moving production over entirely to rayon. In 1913 the textile industry in Lyons used only four million francs worth of artificial silk fibre. As the yarn improved somewhat in quality and silk became less and less available, by 1921 this figure had risen to eighty million francs. By 1938 the town was using 72.2 per cent rayon yarn and only 8.1 per cent of silk.[10]

The cultural mood had changed too and designers, including Lucile, who could not adapt, went bankrupt, merged or closed. Lucile wrote in 1931 that in the 1920s the salons could only make 50 per cent of the profit they had before the War. The old extravagant dressing style-beyond-price had gone for ever. 'It passed away with the hey day of the great courtesans . . . even the women who were noted as the best dressed in Europe had cut down their dressmakers bills to half the previous amounts. There was consternation in the Rue de La Paix. World famous houses were faced with the prospect of closing down.'[11] Russian aristocracy no longer bought the clothes. After the Revolution they were in fact more likely to be found working as *vendeuses* in the salons of Paris than purchasing garments. However, with flexible design and business acumen at play, a new generation of designers responded to the economic and cultural challenges of the 1920s. Lucile was left far behind complaining bitterly that couturiers had 'decided to cut down on cost to the lowest possible limit . . . no more picture dresses – no waste of fabric on linings, no lace, cheaper embroideries, every yard saved must be looked upon as a yard to the good'.

The boyish look was the perfect solution. Rather than seeing the new *garçonne* style as a creative, flexible response to a new mood of feminine modernity sweeping through the world of fine and applied arts, Lucile condemned it dismissively. 'No woman . . . could cost less to clothe.' She saw the style not as 'the result of emancipation or modernity' but as 'a creation

10. L. Taylor, 'Dufy, the Lyons Silk Industry and the Role of Artists', The Textile Society Newsletter No. 2, Summer 1984, p. 6, quoting C. Roupiez, 'Reconstructions et Crises dans la Soieries Lyonnaise de 1850-1940', Programmes de Recherches en Sciences Humaines dans la region Rhone-Alpes, Conservation du Patrimonie, CNRS, Centre Regional de Publication de Lyon, Paris, 1980, pp. 48-9.

11. Gordon, Lady Duff, *Discretions and Indescretions*, London: Jarrolds, 1932, p. 159.

of the dressmakers – clothes set to the new life style of the post war period'.[12] The industry as it continued consistently to do thereafter also responded with far-sighted business acumen to shifts in its post-1920 consumer base. The fashion salons profited more and more from selling to less well-off consumers through widening their department store and official copyhouse sales. Commercial retailing methods grew more competitive. Lucien Lelong, who ran his salon with the aid of a young design team and was not a major designer himself, launched into elite ready-to-wear production,[13] whilst at the same time encouraging private couture sales by staging his evening collections as if in a theatre, 'blocking out the real daylight with heavy curtains'.[14] Patou, the supreme modernist, just like Chanel, sold franchised perfume products and successful lines of chic leisure, travel and sportswear clothes and accessories, as well as the most elegant of avant-garde haute couture. The war crisis had been dealt with, but only as another financial agony reared its head in the shape of the Wall Street crash.

The Crisis of the Early 1930s

After the 1929 Wall Street crash, panic ensued in 1930 following the US imposition of a 90 per cent import tax on Paris haute couture garments under the new Hawley-Smooth bill. Paris lost its entire fleet of US buyers over the 1930–2 period and costs simply had to be cut. Thus in 1931, Chanel designed the first range of couture evening dress in cotton to bring costs down as her company was hit badly when both commercial and private US consumers stayed away. What on earth was to be done? It was at this exact point, in 1932, that Chanel turned briefly to Hollywood as a source of income and vitally needed international publicity. She accepted a lucrative invitation to work for Samuel Goldwyn, a project that met with signal failure. However, by 1935, as her couture business picked up again, she was employing 4,000 workers, making 28,000 model garments a year and no longer had any need for Hollywood approval or publicity.[15]

The designer Paul Iribe proposed his own solution to the 1932 crisis in sales. He published a furious and passionate polemic, *Défense de Luxe*, to persuade wealthy clients, in the name of French patriotism, to keep up their levels of luxury spending on elite French consumer products. 'Defend, as we

12. Ibid. p. 159–60.
13. Nystrom, P., *The Economics of Fashion*, New York: Ronald Press, 1928, pp. 167–8.
14. Wilson, R., *Fashion on Parade*, Indianapolis: Bobbs-Merrill, 1925, p. 74.
15. Grumbach, D., *Histoires de la Mode*, Paris: Seuil, 1993, pp. 35–6.

would the flag, these supreme industries,' he declared, listing specifically French architecture, decorative arts, silk and other luxury textile production, fabric and the manufacture of French carpets, fashion, jewellery and perfume, 'which are our glory and our wealth.' He warned that *'les industries Françaises du luxe sont en peril de mort'*. Seeing *le luxe* as sacredly embedded in the definition of the word 'France', he wrote: 'we must defend *le Luxe* with pride'. He saw it as a bulwark against standardization and mechanization within the design and manufacture of fashion, the decorative arts and perfume. Iribe, who had been well trained by Paul Poiret in such matters in the 1910s, saw these luxury levels of manufacture as 'the symbol of the creative genius of France, her prestige, her strength, her capital and her guarantee'.[16]

In fact, the economic crisis of the early 1930s forced the great fashion houses into an even closer financial relationship with the ready-to-wear trade, which thereafter became the basis of their business success right through to the 1960s, through the direct selling of *toiles* to ready-wear manufacturers. Little detail is given on this type of business in the eulogistic accounts of the work of the great Paris couture salons. By the end of the 1930s the reoriented couture trade was once again flourishing. Schiaparelli for example was selling her gloves, jewellery, perfume and scarves from her new boutique and all the major fashion houses had their own perfume lines. In 1938, the Paris couture industry had a financial turnover of at least 25 billion francs. So prestigious was the reputation of France in the international fashion world that spin-off ready-to-wear and accessory manufactured flourished mightily. The *Geneva Tribune* estimated the total number of pre-war workers in fashion-related areas in France to be as high as 300,000.[17] The business situation for Paris couture was therefore promising by 1939 as Paris still dominated international style and exports were strong.

The Development of Franchised, Branded 'Designer' Products in the 1950s

The behaviour of much of the Paris couture industry during the Nazi occupation of the city unravelled all this commercial success. The industry was left in a truly dire moral and economic position in the 1944–7 period, only overcome with the help of foreign buyers, the international fashion press and the vitality of the designs of the couturiers themselves with the success

---

16. Iribe, P., *Défense de Luxe*, Montrouge: Draeger Freres, 1932 (no page numbers).
17. 'Bulletin des Soies et de Soieries', no. 3362, Lyons, 1942, p. 3 and pp. 127–44.

of the New Look. The processes of elite social dressing had however changed irrevocably. Faced with a severe drop in private clients, the commercial imagination of the couture houses was once again called into play. Dior had clothes made up in London, New York and Australia as well as France. Balmain put shows on in Argentina and Thailand, and Fath together with many others in Brazil. Dior's was the supreme success, still with 3,000 private clients in the 1950s. His turnover of couture garment production vastly overshadowed all of his rivals. Alexandra Palmer's research shows that between spring 1954 and autumn 1955, his workshops produced 5,154 garments. His nearest rival over the same period was Jacques Fath at 4,140, Balmain at 3,112 and the House of Nina Ricci at 2,800. Chanel, just reopening in Paris after her dubious wartime activities, had a turnover of only 300 garments.[18] Dior was the master of the franchise agreement and thus his perfume company was established in 1947, his prêt-à-porter de luxe opened in New York in 1948, his 'Dior New York' franchised stocking line made by Kayser began in 1949, as did Dior jewellery manufactured by Pforzheim, in Germany. Dior capitalized too on menswear retailing, developing a franchised range of silk ties in partnership with a US twill silk manufacturer, Benjamin Theise. These ties were first marketed through the department store, B. Altman, in New York in 1949. By 1984, couture fur and fashions represented only 1.5 per cent of the business of the House of Dior.[19]

Pierre Cardin, inspired by Dior's commercial success, became the couturier with the largest number of franchised licensed products. Already by 1958 he was selling a prêt-à-porter line in the Paris department store, *Le Printemps*.[20] *Women's Wear Daily* announced on 9 February 1982 that his company had 540 licensed contracts worth 50 millions dollars annually.[21] Cardin was denied membership of the *Chambre Syndical de la Couture* for a while as a result of this vast commercial expansion. Didier Grumbach confirms that in 1930 Paris couture kept 6,799 workers directly employed in fifty-nine major fashion houses. This number included 33 apprentices, 1,735 workers, 118 'second' hands, 135 cutters, and 116 fashion models. By 1990 this had dropped to 928 workers.[22]

18. A. Palmer, 'The Myth and Reality of Haute Couture, Consumption, Social Function and Taste in Toronto, 1945–1963', PhD thesis, University of Brighton, 1994, Vol. 1: Royal Ontario Museum no. 1986. p. 208, quoting f12/10.504, Paris Couture production, Spring 1954-Fall 1955, Archives Nationale, Paris.

19. Grumbach, D., Histoires de la Mode, Paris, Seuil, 1993, p. 77, p. 80 and p. 57.

20. Vincent-Ricard, F., *La Mode*, Paris: Segliers, 1987, p. 64.

21. Ibid., p. 97.

22. Grumbach, D., *Histoires de la Mode*, Paris: Seuil, 1993, pp. 35–6 and p. 57, the Fédération Française de la Couture, note de novembre, 1974.

London couture blossomed briefly in the 1950s period but simply did not, could not, and would not cope with the radical drop in private clients. It had neither the international standing, nor the financial resources, nor even the wish to emulate Paris in this way. As a consequence, with the exception of Hardy Amies' company for example, the old pre-war style of elegant London couture had virtually died by the late 1960s.

The 1960s, 1970s and 1980s

Paris couture had by contrast responded instantly as we have seen, to international cultural and economic shifts during the 1950s and 1960s, through a continuous transformation of both its style and business. Elitism in couture manufacture was retained but Yves Saint Laurent by 1966 was designing and producing a specific prêt-à-porter line not related to his haute couture collection. From around 1970, tie-ups with ready-to-wear and franchised accessory production expanded and became essential. The truth was that with only one or two exceptions (such as the house of Chanel), from that date, couture has been by running its salons at a loss. G.Y. Dryansky verified on 3 February, 1972 in *Women's Wear Daily* that the '$40 million yearly volume done by 20 couture houses in Paris is far and away a deficit operation . . . a small price to pay for the reputation couture makes for a name'. He reported that after only four years of ready-to-wear operations, the House of Givenchy had already reached sales figures of nearly $2 million. In the same year, the salon of Yves Saint Laurent was 'losing $700,000 a year on its couture operation', but was 'grossing $24 million retail sales world wide on ready-to-wear' after less than six years of production.[23] By 1980, according to Françoise Vincent-Ricard, there were only 2,000 private clients remaining amongst the Paris couture houses.[24]

The Economist reported on 17 March. 1984 that Cardin had allowed his logo to go on 150 products from telephones to jet aircraft and was raking in annually 1 billion dollars. Even that, *The Economist* reported, was dwarfed by St. Laurent, with a turnover of 2 billion dollars from his licenses in 1982, $400 million from perfume sales licensed to *Charles of the Ritz*. Couture accounted for only 0.15 per cent of the financial turnover but in 1983 that was 40 million francs. St. Laurent was selling $30 million dollars worth of products at one Tokyo department store Seibu.

23. Taylor, L., *Romantic Fashions*, p. 82 in de la Haye, A., *The Cutting Edge, 50 years of British Fashion, 1947–97*, London: Victoria and Albert Museum, 1997.

24. Vincent-Ricard, F., *La Mode*, Paris: Segliers, 1987, p. 61.

Commercial Competition

By the 1980s Paris was, however, being seriously and successfully rivalled for international designer leadership by New York designers such as Calvin Klein, Ralph Lauren and Donna Karan, all of whom were also widely selling franchised products. Rivalry steadily grew also from the great Italian fashion companies in Milan of Versace, Armani, Gucci et al and from Issey Miyake and others in Tokyo. Below these in status but not business terms, however, lay another layer of commercial threat to elite fashion manufacture. This was competition from the US-driven leisure and sportswear markets such as Levis, Adidas, Nike, Reebok, Nautica, Guess, Gap, Hilfiger and many others. Through the 1990s the extent of the product retailing of these companies reached global proportions never before known in the garment and accessory industries.

That the products of these specific mass production companies are literally in every way thousands of miles apart from those of the couture world in cultural terms goes without saying. Yet the great design houses had much to learn from leisurewear marketing methods. Specifically, they quickly came to terms with the vast commercial harvest to be reaped from attaching their own elite names to very ordinary clothing. Thus by the 1990s they too added their own jeans and even trainers on to their list of branded spin-off products. The *Guardian Weekend* of 3 April 1999, for example, featured as a high-fashion item, '"Quick trainers" from Hermes' at £290. By adding on a few feathers, a logo and some machine embroidery ordinary jeans became 'designer' jeans and could be sold at highly inflated prices.

Thus, the worlds of elite couture and mass casual wear clashed for the first time in direct commercial competition for the same mass consumers. Profits to the parent retailing companies, who now own the couture salons, were unprecedented. The French retail group *Pinault-Printemps Redoute* paid '$3bn (£1.85bn) for 40% of Gucci', in 1999, for example, whilst the next day its takeover rival, LVMH, 'tabled an $8 billion offer'.[25]

The Hilfiger Factor

By the late 1990s, as the success of Tommy Hilfiger's company reached global proportions, the Hilfiger Factor reared its head as a serious commercial challenge to the couture world. This Hilfiger crisis stemmed from the massive popular success of the products of these casual leisurewear companies. Success

25. *Independent*, 22 March 1999.

Figure 8.2. Advertisement for Versace jeans couture on the back of a number 24 London Transport bus, March 1999.

flourishes on the international popularity of the American way of dressing – jeans, trainers, leisure jackets, and T-shirts and for both sexes. Diffused all around the world through US music videos, movies and MTV, target consumers cover an increasingly global market of under thirty year olds.

Tommy Hilfiger's company makes a particularly interesting case study. His success up to 1999 was phenomenal, following massive growth in the 1990s. At first selling a wide range of male leisure and 'athletic' wear such as jeans and chinos, the company expanded into womenswear. Net income for 1996–97 increased 38.4 per cent to $661,688,000 over 1996 figures. The fourth quarter net revenue in 1997 alone reached $170,453,000, with

Figure 8.3. Dreaming of 'designer' trainers, a young boy shopping in Brighton, UK, July 1999.

joint venture and buying agency agreements firmly established in Japan.[26] That same year licensing income increased by 136 per cent.[27] Hilfiger is a Hong Kong based corporation, with manufacturing undertaken in China, including the £85 jerseys available from the flagstore outlet in Knightsbridge in 1998. Reuters reported on 2 February 1998 that Hilfiger had bought out Pepe Jeans for $1.1 billion.

Through expert marketing, Hilfiger has been able to market his mass-produced casual clothes as 'designer' products and even as high fashion. By reworking the elite marketing ploys of the couture industry, used by houses such as Givenchy, Dior, Chanel and Lacroix, by Christmas of 1998, Hilfiger was selling his perfume 'Tommy Girl' at British department stores, typified by Debenham's in Cheltenham, at £35 for 100 milligrams, whilst St Laurent's 'Kouros' was sold for less at £25 for the same amount. Dior's 'Eau Sauvage' was priced at only £3 dearer.[28] Hilfiger's fragrances are made under licence by the Aramis division of Estée Lauder. Since the grand salons are now utterly

26. Tommy Hilfiger Corporation 1997 Annual Report, New York, p. 17 and 28.
27. *DNR*, 31 October 1997.
28. With thanks to Patrica Whitehead for this information.

Figure 8.4. Young shoppers wearing logoed leisurewear, Churchill Square Shopping Precinct, Brighton, UK, July 1999.

dependent on their franchised accessory and perfume retail for survival, there was a real and obvious commercial problem here. Hilfiger on the other hand had no couture salon to subsidize.

'The future is limitless,' he told *DNR*, 17 October 1997, 'The challenge is to maintain your credibility with the youth market. The secret to longevity is truly to be a lifestyle brand.' What has been astonishing has been the extent of Hilfiger's successful marketing of basic but expensively priced leisurewear garments, such a baseball caps, puffa jackets and jeans, as highly desirable 'designer' fashion items.

A marketing technique which served Hilfiger well for a while was to pump up the advertising hype. Through glamour advertising geared to specific international youth markets and to the young black US market, Hilfiger's sales figures rocketed, based on appropriating marketing methods long understood by the old couture salons in Paris. Thus Hilfiger and others launch seasonal 'collections', as if they were couture shows, winning almost as much press coverage as if they were. Just like the great couturiers, Hilfiger too uses superstars at his collection launches, with Naomi Campbell and Kate Moss strutting their stuff in his T-shirts at the London launch of his new Sloane Street, London flagship store in 1997. Hilfiger firmly established his

Figure 8.5. Promotional advertising form Tommy Hilfiger Corporation, 1998.

US success when rap stars, such as Snoop Doggy Dogg wore his clothes in 1994. Like a couture house, Hilfiger too places advertisements in the elite fashion magazines right alongside those of Dior, Gucci and Chanel. Just like the famous design houses, Hilfiger expanded his business and boundaries in the late 1990s by opening new international branches and retailing in thirty countries. 'I am inspired by Europeans and their sense of style,' he declared in *DNR*, 17 October 1997 when he was first launching his products upon an unsuspecting Europe. Exactly how his designs festooned in the red, white and blue stars and stripes of the American flag are European inspired seems unclear, but these were launched like couture products at celebrity parties in Hamburg, Madrid and London, with Sheryl Crow providing the musical backing.

Hilfiger has understood his market well. It is not the safely well-off, middle-class, middle-aged rich but the international, mass, multi-racial youth market. The best-selling Hilfiger jacket in Europe is the 'Admont' puffa jacket in cotton sateen with a nylon lining and large HILFIGER logo – at £295 each. His company mission statement for 1998 read: 'The spirit of youth is our greatest inspiration. Resourcefulness is the key to value and excellence. In making quality a priority in our lives and products. By respecting one another we can reach all cultures and communities. By being bold in our vision we continually expand our boundaries.'[29]

Hilfiger understood the need for 'glamour' in his new retail stores. Couturiers have always understood the necessity for impressively expensive retail establishments, hence the vast amounts spent on the interiors of elegant salons in the Rue St Honoré, for example. Hilfiger's new 1998 London 'International Speciality Store' in Sloane Street, London, was situated next to those of Lacroix, Chanel and Harvey Nichols.

Above all, in terms of marketing techniques, Hilfiger understood the commercial power of a successful brand logo. Many of his garments became little more than advertising billboards, swathed and striped with his brand colours and patterns with the name HILFIGER or TOMMY featuring very largely. Thus Hilfiger sells his middle-market leisurewear and perfumes as if they were the golden goodies of a top Paris couture house. As long as his customers can be persuaded that his products are touched with the same elite 'designer' quality as those of the couture houses, he will have made a major and fascinating cultural and economic breakthrough. He will have broken into the sacred portals of the elite fashion world without carrying the financial burden of elite manufacture. He will have turned his TOMMY logo into a gold mine. Without the brand logo Hilfiger products could in many ways just as well be those of a sports/leisurewear company such as Millets. With it, they are seen on the backs of stars such as the footballer, David Beckham, who, wearing a white Hilfiger waterproof jacket, was featured all over the press pushing his baby in a pram in March 2000.

Ever intent on upmarketing his design image, Hilfiger's Internet publicity in 1998 declared that 'Tommy Hilfiger is THE American designer – he, along with Ralph Lauren, Calvin Klein, and Perry Ellis are considered the four top American designers.' Unlike couture salons which move downmarket in their launch of mass-franchised products, Hilfiger has tried to move up-market to find credibility and therein may lie his Achilles heel. He opened an exclusive store in the late 1990s at 466, North Rodeo Drive in Beverley Hills selling cashmere goods at very high prices. Designed by Allen Greenberg with a vast white neoclassical portico at the cost of $25, 000,000, this glass fibre reinforced concrete building won the PCI Precast/Prestressed Concrete Award for the best US commercial building of 1999.[30] In 1999 he launched his Red Label line. With his new womenswear designer, Daryl Kerrigan as creative

29. Tommy Hilfiger Corporation, Annual Report, New York, 1997.
30. http.//www.pre-cast.org/complete1.html

consultant,[31] Hilfiger commented that his new line was created for celebrities such as rock stars. Aping couture's own in-house trickle-down processes, he launched his own elite designer range of red, white and blue, leather jackets, Texas boots and jeans, which are to be copied in the cheaper lines. As the year 2000 commenced, the London Red Label outlet was to be found at Tommy Hilfiger, 51 New Bond Street.

Like every other 'designer' product, the logo is essential to Hilfiger's success as it is with other 'designer' companies. Every franchised designer product bears this badge of official status (or a faked version, but that is another story), which enables these goods to be sold far beyond their actual value. Brand logos have become talismanic symbols of glamour and desirability which lift products to heights of desirability unattainable by Marks & Spencers, as the company has recently learned to its cost and as Hilfiger is very clearly aware.

Couture Reaction

What we are looking at here in the 'value' of designer logos is designer goods as magical symbols of the glamour world of international fame, beauty, success and style. The world of couture and top prêt-à-porter offers the public a tantalizingly beyond-reach image of the fabulous and the elegant – a magical aspiration. Grant McCracken in his book *Culture and Consumption* calls it a process of displaced meaning – namely that top designer objects act as a bridge to the ideal luxury world.[32] The perfume bottle by Jean Paul Gaultier at £30 is attainable whilst the Gaultier dress at £1,300 is not. We can buy Dior perfume instead of the beaded fantasy dress by Galliano at Dior worth many thousands of pounds. These purchases attach us directly through product ownership to the couture world and through that we enter our world of dreams. It is almost a process of sympathetic magic. We can never own a £1,000 McQueen dress from Givenchy but we can make ourselves believe that we 'own' the Givenchy glamour through one squirt of a Givenchy 'Fleur Interdit' vaporisateur (£9.95, Harrods sale, 1997). It is this process that the big designer houses have long understood and exploited so cleverly. Since the 1950s and even as the great fashion monopoly conglomerates of Prada, Gucci, LVMH and Louis Vuitton gobble up ownership of one great couture salon after another, enormous care is taken to guard the individual sacred

31. Rebecca Lowthorpe, *Independent,* 16 February, 2000, with thanks to Amy de la Haye.
32. McCracken, G., *Culture and Consumption: new approaches to the symbolic character of consumption*, Indiana Univ. Press, 1988.

logos of each company. Stuart Ewen, a sociologist, describes the couture world as 'beyond the real', believing that this notion of beyond reality is an 'essential element to the magic of style, its fascination and enchantment. . . . Part of the promise of style is to lift us out of the dreariness of necessity.'[33]

The brand logo holds the magic of style. As long as Hilfiger, through astute marketing, can succeed in creating an élite image for his mass-produced leisurewear and fragrances and as long as he can successfully market them as 'designer' products, he represents a serious commercial threat to the elite designer fashion world. As long as Hilfiger can successfully attach this element of magical desirability to his very ordinary leisurewear products and continue to launch his products to a generation of international young consumers, he presents a most serious economic threat to the world of Paris couture and designer prêt-à-porter, a threat as serious as the consequences of the Wall Street crash of 1929.

It seems however, that the established Paris fashion houses were aware of the Hilfiger threat as soon as it reared its head. Their astute commercial flexibility and response to challenge, once again came into play. By the mid-1990s plans were in place in Paris to deal with the threat of commercial rivalry from global leisure/lifestyle clothing companies such as Hilfiger (and indeed the increasing commercial rivalry from Italy.) Hence the employment of the avant-garde young London designers, John Galliano at Givenchy and Dior, Alexander McQueen at Givenchy and Stella McCartney at Chloe from the the mid-1990s. These companies recognized the urgent need both to rapidly lower their consumer age appeal and to modernize their image of glamorous elitism. Even as they were chewed up by the great financial companies LVMH, Gucci and Louis Vuitton, the commercial need to retain a cutting-edge, innovative house style remained paramount. If the sale of branded products was to continue to flourish, the need for this sharp, young image was essential. This outweighed the need to satisfy their few hundred private clients, who can always be serviced with watered-down versions of outrageous catwalk styles. The retention of an image of seductive glamour, however, remains vital for the continuation of the million-dollar international selling of branded perfume, maquillage, handbags, jewellery, stockings, watches, shoes, tee-shirts, luggage, underwear, sunglasses, scarves and now interior design too.

As Tommy Hilfiger and other similar brands have expanded the extent of their marketing hype, so too have the great couture salons of Paris. By the late 1990s their advertisements featured more and more seductive images

---

33. S. Ewen, 'Marketing Dreams – the Political Elements of Style', in Tomlinson, A., *Consumption, Identity and Style*, London: Routledge, 1990, p. 43–8.

that the likes of Hilfiger could never possibly achieve. Elite advertisements featured very young, bejewelled, gilded, beautiful, fantasy women next to elegant glass bottles, or peering into logoed handbags or wearing elegant branded shoes. What we are seeing here again is the classic flexibility of the trade. Let no consumers escape the magical lure, from Saudi princesses, to opulent Russian mafiosi new rich, to Hollywood stars given free couture clothes to wear to the Oscar Awards nights. Above all, the appeal must be to the cross-channel ferry passenger or the package tourist waiting for hours in the airport lounge. Tamsin Blanchard headlined her Paris report on the 21st January 1998 for the *Independent* with the line 'What Lagerfeld Knows and Galliano Knows Not'. She slated Galliano's collection for being too fantastic and romantic. 'If the sole purpose of a couture show is to sell perfume and be a glorified advertisement, then the entire concept of haute couture is indeed a wonderful poetic and fantastic sham.' But, perhaps the existence of companies, such as Dior, does indeed depend on creating precisely this image of poetry and fantasy. The Dior company very deliberately and evidently with careful commercial forethought, uses Galliano's couture fantasy in all its glossy advertisements for its franchised products. A survey of Dior advertisements (and Chanel, Gucci, Versace, etc.) taken out in Vogue's international editions for Poland, Singapore, Paris, Milan, London, New York, Moscow and Tokyo, reveals the very same fantasy images across the world.

Couture Victory?

And it seems that the famous salons may have successfully already seen off any serious commercial threat from the Hilfiger factor. To much surprise, by February of the year 2000, Hilfiger shares were slipping badly. 'So what has gone wrong?, asked John Harris in the *Independent* on 8 February. 'The company is in deep trouble – the share price . . . has fallen by two thirds in the last six months, wiping £1.5 bn off its market value.'

Part of the problem had been caused by the new, supposedly elite Red Label line which had failed to impress and was described by Rebecca Lowthorpe in the *Independent* of 24 February 2000 as 'something of a disaster'. Despite the logic that lay behind the launch of the Red Tab line and despite the huge marketing efforts thrown into launching the clothes, Hilfiger has been quite unable to reproduce the carefully honed 'beyond reality' design elitism of couture garments. Unlike a couture salon which starts from a position of cultural elitism and then downmarkets its mass-franchised products, Hilfiger has not yet been able to make a financial success

Figure 8.6. Elite globalized fashion magazines, from Japan, Canada, Poland, Singapore and the UK, 1999–2000.

of the reverse process. He has not been able to upmarket his mid-market image and that seems to have been his downfall – so far.

Thus, Hilfiger and his peers have not yet destroyed the couture world after all. Instead, by totally transforming its business activities since the last war, the *industrie de luxe* may be 'seeing off' the upstart rivalry of Hilfiger et al. These leisure/sportswear companies will, without doubt, continue to expand and flourish but it does not look as if they will overwhelm the elitist 'magic' of the couture product. It is true, however, that increasingly the 'success' of a design house is judged not only on its catwalk collections but on the sales figures of its franchised products and the billions of dollars of shares attached to its parent company.

The Globalized Product?

Exactly the same 'designer' products are now sold all around the entire world. The press is full of terms such as the 'globalisation' of style, 'global retailing' and 'global consumption'. International editions of *Vogue* and *Elle* verify that you can buy exactly the same Chanel watch, bag, lipstick or sunglasses

Figure 8.7. Two young Chakma women crossing a river on a ferry boat, Rangamati, the Chittagong Hill Tracts, Bangladesh, February 2000, with one wearing a Tommy Hilfiger T-shirt. With thanks to Polly Jones.

in Singapore, Sydney, Warsaw, Rio, Abu Dhabi, Seoul, Tokyo, Nicosia, Johannesburg, or Moscow. Adidas, Nike and Hilfiger and the products of their sportswear rivals also make appearances in youth magazines the world over. Travel the world as we will, we come across the same logos everywhere. So Chanel, Dior, Nike and Hilfiger rule one world of 'designer' consumption?

Perhaps, before all sense of reality is entirely lost in this analysis of the consumption of 'designer' goods, we should remind ourselves of quite another globalized reality – the 'consumption' of poverty. In early March 2000, a BBC Radio 4 reporter described the plight of a victim of the Mozambique floods. On returning to what remained of her devastated home, all the victim of the deluge found was one chair and one drawer. These she placed for safety in a tree. Her other belongings consisted of one pair of shoes. These were drying out on the top of two poles stuck firmly in the mud for safe keeping.[34] This tale serves to remind us that as a means of examining the realities of the world we live in, with all its tensions, horrors, aspirations and dreams, assessment of the cultural meanings of clothing is perhaps one of the very best tools of analysis. For millions, as the magical style element of couture touches our lives through the consumption of mass-produced 'designer' goods, the dream is of a pair of "Quick trainers" from Hermes at £290. For yet more millions, the dream is of a pair of dry shoes.

34. BBC Radio 4, 1.00pm News Bulletin, 5 March, 2000.

9

John Galliano:
Modernity and Spectacle

Caroline Evans*

This chapter starts by contrasting two sets of imagery: from the 1990s, the luxurious, opulent and theatrical fashion shows of the fashion designer John Galliano and, from the second half of the nineteenth century, the fantasy displays, rides and optical illusions of the Parisian department store and world fair. Walter Benjamin described this technique as 'literary montage', and he wrote, perhaps disingenuously, 'I have nothing to say, only to show.'[1] His intention was, however, that the images would do the talking, not singly but by virtue of their juxtaposition and arrangement. Benjamin's ideas offer art and design historians a complex and sophisticated model of how visual seduction works, because his ideas are predicated on an understanding of how visual similes function, something which other historians have not privileged. His method allows us to perceive similarities across periods apparently separated by rupture and discontinuity, and to plot historical time not as something that flows smoothly from past to present but as a more complex relay of turns and returns in which the past is activated by injecting the present into it.[2]

* This is an expanded version of the lecture given at Kingston University and I would like to thank the Arts & Humanities Research Board of Great Britain whose funding in 1999–2000 of the 'Fashion & Modernity' Research Group at Central Saint Martins College of Art and Design, London, enabled the further development of this paper.
  1. Quoted in Buck-Morss, Susan, *The Dialectics of Seeing: Walter Benjamin and the Arcades Project*, Cambridge, Mass. & London , England: MIT Press, 1989. References in this chapter are to the paperback edition, 1991, pp. 73 & 222.
  2. For a discussion of fashion and Benjamin's historical method, see Ulrich Lehmann, '*Tigersprung*: Fashioning History', *Fashion Theory*, vol. 3, issue 3, September 1999, pp. 297–322.

My own purpose in this chapter, in juxtaposing images over a hundred years apart, is neither to pinpoint superficial stylistic similarities for their own sake, nor to make facile fin-de-siècle comparisons but, rather, to situate both sets of imagery within the context and tradition of modernity. In particular, I wonder whether it is possible to 'activate' the excess and opulence of nineteenth-century Parisian consumer culture by 'injecting' it with the excess and opulence of Galliano's contemporary designs. Both are visually similar, and both are dominated by the idea of woman as spectacle. Yet the considerable differences between their historical contexts suggest that the term 'modernity' might no longer apply to both, and that Galliano's designs should be analysed in the context of 'postmodernity'. Insofar as both moments encapsulate rapid technological change and social instability, parallels can be drawn; yet there are fundamental differences in the type of change and instability between both periods which also differentiate the effects of one from the other. Thus contemporary fashion is on the edge – of centuries, and of its own margins. Janus-headed, it looks simultaneously back (with nostalgia) and forward (with anxiety). Galliano is one of the former tendency whose work brilliantly sums up its paradoxes and contradictions; as such, his work is a significant marker of a wider cultural trend.

Galliano: 1990s

Figure 9.1 shows a moment in the Christian Dior Autumn-Winter 1998/9 couture collection designed by John Galliano. Entitled 'A Voyage on the Diorient Express, or the Story of the Princess Pocahontas', it was shown in the Gare d'Austerlitz in Paris, where the models arrived on a steam train while the audience were seated on sand-covered platforms decorated with huge bronze platters of spices to look like an oriental spice market or souk. As the visitors sat surrounded by canopies, potted palms, antique Louis Vuitton suitcases and Moroccan lanterns, consuming champagne and Turkish delight, the train chuffed into the station and a model dressed as the Princess Pocahontas burst through a wall of orange paper at the front of the train. Only then did the train come to a halt and disgorge its cargo of models, dressed in a jumble of native American and sixteenth-century European dress. The presentation and the majority of the garments were pure spectacle, such that the consequent press coverage was in fact rather critical of the designer for having substituted showmanship and pantomime for fashion design itself.[3]

3. For example, see Susannah Frankel, 'Galliano Steams Ahead with Any Old Irony', *Guardian*, 21 July 1998, pp. 10.

Figure 9.1. John Galliano for Christian Dior, Autumn-Winter 1998–9 couture collection, shown at the Gare d'Austerlitz in Paris. The audience was seated on sand-covered platforms decorated like an oriental souk; the models arrived on a steam train with a wall of orange paper at the front through which a model dressed as the Princess Pochahontas burst as the train pulled into the station. Photograph: Niall McInerney

The name 'Diorient Express' stencilled onto the side of the train aptly suggested both Galliano's orientalism, which eclectically combined cultures, continents and centuries, and the disorienting effects of his showmanship. Although the 'Diorient Express' show was, perhaps, his most excessive in terms of spectacular presentation it was far from the only one. Other shows were staged in a suburban sports stadium transformed into a forest scene with forty-foot high spruce trees, the Paris Opéra converted into an English garden where the fashion photographers were given straw hats on entry, and the Carousel du Louvre, the official venue for the Paris collections, made over as a Manhattan rooftop scene, complete with battered chimney stacks, designed, like most of his shows, by the set designer Jean-Luc Ardouin. In every case, Galliano's transformation of a space involved effacing its real characteristics in the interests of imposing his fantasy vision on the space.

In keeping with the spectacular mis-en-scène of his shows of this period, each collection was based on a fantastical narrative. For example, in an earlier collection than the one illustrated here, Pocahontas met Wallace Simpson in Paris, designed her own couture collection (which included beaded flapper dresses) and took it back to her tribe (the Galliano Autumn-Winter 1996 collection); or, in the 'Suzy Sphinx' show a punk schoolgirl who dreamt of cinema and ancient Egypt was taken from her English girl's school through Egypt to Hollywood where she starred as Cleopatra in a film, seated on a golden throne wearing a dress made entirely of golden safety pins (the Galliano Autumn-Winter 1997 collection).

Galliano's first collection for Dior had juxtaposed Masai beading and couture historicism in full-blown evening gowns that required 410 metres of fabric. In his designs of this period, Galliano's historical research ranged far and wide. Galliano himself said, 'It's a very impressionistic approach. It's a dialogue between past and present. The starting point is usually factual, but we allow our imaginations to run riot. The story happens differently each time. Certain things begin to go around in my head and then we start to embroider on them.'[4] Sometimes his designs collaged together motifs from different cultures, juxtaposing them against each other, mixing maharaja jewels and an aigrette with Burmese neck jewellery and Afro-Caribbean braids, while styling the model to look spookily uptight and Parisian. At other times he morphed references and motifs from different periods and cultures into single fusions. His collections eclectically mix images of japonisme with those of the Weimar Republic, early cinema and the belle époque, images of Empire and Masai beading.

4. McDowell, Colin, *Galliano,* London: Weidenfeld & Nicolson, 1997, pp. 51.

To his mixes of cultures and history were added a significantly different ingredient, the image and inspiration of real historical figures. He was drawn in particular to Edwardian actresses, demi-mondaines and women of independent means, all of whom were identifiable by their striking, outré or 'exotic' appearances. Flamboyant women of wealth such as Nancy Cunard and the Marchesa Casati rubbed shoulders in his collections with bohemians like Misia Sert, the artists' model and sexual libertine Kiki de Montparnasse, the actress and demi-mondaine Gaby Deslys, and the great courtesan Liane de Pougy. These real women were mingled with images from art and cinema: society women from the paintings of Boldoni, Sargent and Tissot, cinema actresses like Claudette Colbert, Theda Bara, Gloria Swanson, Marlene Dietrich and Elizabeth Taylor, and, from Britain, the aristocratic women photographed by Madame Yevonde in the 1930s. These moneyed images were mixed with references from popular culture of the past: pearly kings and queens, Hells Angels, migrant southern Italian circus folk from the 1930s. Then there were couture influences, from Madeline Vionnet's bias-cut tea gowns of the teens and 1920s and the Dior archive from the 1940s and 1950s. These too were intercut with imagery of tattooed Samoan women, Asian jewellery, African beading and native American patterned blankets, or woven with 'Europeanised' images of the orient, in figures like Suzie Wong and Madame Butterfly. Galliano's historical and cultural promiscuity can be tracked in his diaries, or sketchbooks of his collections, kept by Amanda Harlech, his right-hand woman from 1984 until his move to Dior as principal designer in 1996, and in his sketchbooks from 1997 onwards, some of which are reproduced in Colin McDowell's book *Galliano*.[5] So acute and wide-ranging is Galliano's eye for the visual detail of the past, and so inventive the way he juxtaposes histories, styles and cultures, that it is hard to imagine a Galliano design which is not a visual quotation from a pre-existent source. What is unique, however, is the way he kaleidoscopically fuses a range of references into a single figure.

In keeping with the spectacular quality of his designs, his fashion presentations were highly theatrical during the 1990s, both in his own name and as principal designer for Givenchy and then Dior. Although the spectacle was conceived on a grander scale in the late 1990s, all Galliano's shows had been characterized by highly developed sense of theatre. In 1984, his graduate collection from St Martin's in London, 'Les Incroyables', was heavily influenced by a contemporary production of *Danton* at the National Theatre in London where Galliano worked as a dresser while a final-year student.

5. Ibid. McDowell reproduces several interesting pages from Galliano's sketchbooks which show the breadth of his eclecticism.

The theatricality of this and all his subsequent collections may also have been informed by Galliano's immersion in the London club scene of the early to mid-1980s in which the relentless reinvention of the self through costume and make-up was the currency which guaranteed entry to the clubs.

In 1990 Galliano moved to Paris where he existed in a hand-to-mouth way; in 1993 he showed a small but very influential collection in the eighteenth-century house of the Portuguese socialite São Schlumberger. Capitalizing on the fact that the empty house was up for sale, he created an atmosphere of romantic decrepitude by scattering it with dead leaves and rose petals, unmade beds and upturned chairs, and filling the air with dry ice. In July 1995 he was appointed principal designer at the couture house of Givenchy for which he produced his first couture show in January 1996 and two subsequent ready-to-wear collections before being appointed principal designer at Dior. In his couture show for Givenchy Galliano created a Princess and the Pea scenario in which two models sat twenty feet in the air preening themselves on top of a pile of mattresses. A year later, in January 1997, he produced his first couture show for Dior, audaciously staged in a fake *maison de couture*: in the Grand Hotel in Paris Galliano created a scaled-up facsimile of the original Dior showroom, including the famous staircase on which Cocteau and Dietrich had sat in the 1950s to watch Dior's shows.[6] In this, as in the 1993 show sponsored by São Schlumberger, Galliano wove instant mythologies, creating something evocative out of nothing.

With the substantial backing of a major couture house Galliano was able to create his shows on a far bigger scale than previously. Increasingly he began to use more theatrical techniques, for example replacing runway lighting with theatre lighting and minutely choreographing each section of the show three days before. Each model had only one outfit per show, thus avoiding the hectic series of rapid costume changes which characterized other fashion shows. The more conventional parade down a catwalk was replaced by a walk through a series of connecting rooms dressed like film sets through which the story was told, reminiscent of the 1993 show in São Schlumberger's house when, in Galliano's words, 'the girls worked the whole house from the top floor down. It was like an old salon presentation.'[7] The audience, far smaller than the usual fashion show audience, was seated in small groups in these rooms, far closer to the clothes than usual. The models, each of whom had been rehearsed like an actress by Galliano before the show, were encouraged to feel their way into, and act, the part of their characters as

6. Ibid., p. 38.
7. Ibid., p. 169.

they paraded through the rooms, striking attitudes and poses, staging tableaux vivants as they went.

Dream Worlds: 1852–1900

From the opening of the Bon Marché in Paris in 1852, the Louvre in 1855, Au Printemps in 1865, and La Samaritaine in 1869, department stores, with their radical new techniques of retail and display, rapidly became theatres of consumption. Shop windows became astounding sources of display, as did the goods inside the store, where everyday objects were rearranged by repetition into sculptural forms of flowers, castles and boats. Displays included out-of-season flowers, caged live birds and, later in the century, splashing electric fountains. Electric lighting further galvanized some of these displays into fairytale scenes. In addition, department stores often drew on the conventions of theatre and exhibitions to produce orientalist scenes, including living tableaux of Turkish harems, Cairo markets or Hindu temples, with live dancers, music and oriental products.[8]

In *Dream Worlds* Rosalind Williams describes how, in nineteenth-century department stores and world fares, the real commercial nature of the transaction was disguised by the creation of seductive 'dream worlds' in which the consumer lost him or herself in fantasy and reverie. In these displays, the department stores' orientalist scenarios promiscuously mingled goods from different cultures and communities in a fantasy bazaar.[9] Throughout the second half of the nineteenth century department stores also mobilized the newest scientific techniques from optics and photography to create 'cinéoramas, maréoramas and dioramas to create the illusion not only of travel in exotic places but also by balloon, above the sea, and to the surface of the moon'.[10]

In the same period, Paris hosted a number of International Exhibitions, in 1855, 1867, 1878, 1889 and 1900. As in department store display, these world fairs created the illusion of exotic locations. At the 1900 exhibition in

8. Williams, Rosalind H., *Dream Worlds: Mass Consumption in Late Nineteenth-Century France*, Berkeley, Los Angeles & Oxford, England: University of California Press, 1982. For a review of the literature on the nineteenth-century French department store see Mica Nava, 'Modernity's Disavowal: Women, the City and the Department Store' in Pasi Falk & Colin Campbell (eds), *The Shopping Experience*, Thousand Oaks, New Delhi: Sage Publications, London, 1997, pp. 56-91.

9. Williams, ibid., pp. 66-72.

10. Nava, Mica, 'Modernity's Disavowal: Women, the City and the Department Store' in Pasi Falk & Colin Campbell (eds), *The Shopping Experience*, Thousand Oaks, New Delhi: Sage Publications, London, 1997, p. 67.

particular twenty-one out of the thirty-three main attractions involved taking a fantasy journey to 'distant visions'.[11] The World Tour traversed the length of an enormous circular canvas panorama representing, in the words of a contemporary journalist, 'without solution or continuity, Spain, Athens, Constantinople, Suez, India, China and Japan . . . the Acropolis next door to the Golden Horn and the Suez Canal almost bathing the Hindu forests'.[12] In front of each country 'natives' danced or charmed snakes before the painting of their homeland. Having made the tour of the world, visitors to the diorama could enjoy a simulated voyage to the moon. Voyagers in the Cinéorama could make an imaginary journey in cinematic techniques to the floor of the sea or up in a balloon, standing in a stationary basket while the pictures moved before their eyes. The Maréorama reproduced a sea-voyage from France to Constantinople and involved a canvas panorama, the smell of salt air, gentle swaying motions and music from each of the regions visited. A contemporary described the music 'which takes on the colour of the country at which the ship is calling; melancholy at departure, it . . . becomes Arabic in Africa, and ends up Turkish after having been Venetian'.[13] At night visitors to the 1900 exhibition could be dazzled by displays of electrically lit fountains or watch the belly dancers in a reproduction of a Cairo night spot.

Dialectical images

In the nineteenth century it was through the spectacles and dreamy scenarios staged in the department store that female consumption was nurtured, trained and encouraged, as well as in the great exhibitions which granted a vision of luxury consumption to a mass audience. Many of these visions have striking parallels in the staging of Galliano's shows in the 1990s, which drew on illusion, drama and theatre for their effects. Just as in the nineteenth-century 'reveries were passed off as reality',[14] so Galliano's Spring-Summer 1995 presentation, in which a photo studio was made over as a private set and dressed with vintage cars against which the models posed as 'divas' from 1910 to the 1950s, 'was like a dream and not a show'.[15] Galliano's spectacular

11. Williams, Rosalind H., *Dream Worlds: Mass Consumption in Late Nineteenth-Century France*, Berkeley, Los Angeles & Oxford, England: University of California Press, 1982, p. 73.

12. Michel Corday, 'À l'Éxposition - Visions lointaines', *Revue de Paris,* 15 March 1900. Quoted in ibid., p. 74.

13. Ibid., p. 75.

14. Ibid., P. 65.

15. Joseph Ettegui, owner of Joseph: from *Videofashion News*, vol. 19, no. 20, 'Paris Reflections', Spring-Summer 1995.

runway shows, simultaneously enticement and advertisement, were highly innovative, but the link between spectacle and commodity culture was first made in the nineteenth century. In his designs, Galliano piled up cultural references like the goods on display in nineteenth-century Parisian department stores and world fares, evoking Paris's reputation as a city of luxury goods in the luxury of his contemporary designs. Émile Zola's novel about a Paris department store in the 1860s, *The Ladies' Paradise,* describes a window display of female dummies dressed in the most sumptuous and elaborate fashion which suggests the textiles used by Galliano in his designs for Dior – snowfalls of costly lace, velvet rimmed with fox fur, silk with Siberian squirrel, cashmere and cocks' feathers, quilting, swansdown and chenille.[16]

The rest rooms and roof gardens of nineteenth-century department stores, fitted with pergolas, zoos and ice rinks, strikingly resemble some Galliano show settings. Department stores were fantasy palaces through which the customers moved. The modern fashion show fulfils something of the same role, with the difference that the audience remains seated while the spectacle unfolds before them like a panorama. Perhaps the show itself, in which the stationary spectator is dazzled by lights, effects and rapid-fire presentation, has more in common with the fantasy journeys of the world fairs. In the spectacles of the 1900 exhibition colours, cultures and sounds were fused in a way very similar to the design fusions of a Galliano show; the 'Cairo belly-dancers' and 'Andalusian gypsies' of the world fair are not dissimilar to Galliano's performing models. The piling up of historical and cross-cultural references in a Galliano collection differ only in specific detail, rather than general effect, for his techniques of historical pastiche and cultural collage fuse disparate cultures and places, much as the World Tour did in the 1900 Paris Universal Exhibition by abutting a Hindu pagoda, a Chinese temple and a Muslim mosque, enlivened by live jugglers and geishas.[17] And the effect both of a Galliano show and of the displays in the 1900 exhibition is to normalize, contain and manage non-European cultures through the very process of creating them as spectacle.

The 1900 exhibition had been the first to feature contemporary fashion, brightly lit by electricity, in glass cages containing couturier-clad wax dummies. In the 'Pavillon de la Mode' were displayed thirty examples of the history of costume, including the Empress Theodora on her throne, Queen Isabelle of Bavaria waiting in a tournament, the Field of the Cloth of Gold,

16. Émile Zola, *The Ladies Paradise*, trans. with an introduction by Nelson, Brian, Oxford & New York: Oxford University Press, 1995, p. 6.

17. Jullian, Philippe, *The Triumph of Art Nouveau: the Paris Exhibition of 1900*, London: Phaidon Press, 1974, p. 169.

and Marie Antoinette at the Trianon. These historical displays of fashion randomly juxtaposed Byzantine empresses, medieval ladies and eighteenth-century queens side by side, creating continuity solely through the splendour of their costume, erasing significant historical difference. Galliano's eclectic historical pastiche has something of this quality. In the 1900 exhibition twenty couture houses were represented, including Worth, Rouff (established in 1884), Paquin (established 1891) and Callot Soeurs (1896). Modern society was represented by scenes of society life, such as 'the departure for the opera', or 'a fitting at Worth'. The style of these displays resurfaced, particularly, in the staging of the Dior Spring-Summer ready-to-wear 1998 show, in a series of classical rooms dressed with period furniture and a harpsichord, around which the models draped themselves like Hollywood starlets from the 1930s. The tableaux vivants they formed recalled the wax tableaux behind glass of the 1900 exhibition, with their simulations of the luxury and extravagance of haute couture.

For the Dior couture show that same season Galliano created a giant crowd scene, a fantasy carnival of confetti and human figures in apparently endless celebration. Yet it would be wrong to confuse this fantasy crowd with the actual crowd of a Parisian international exhibition of the late nineteenth century. The crowds at such world fairs consisted essentially of middle, lower-middle and sometimes working-class people; the displays made luxury and excess available as a spectacle to the many who, while they could afford the entrance ticket, could never aspire to owning the exclusive and expensive consumer goods on display. The exclusivity of the couture show has more in common, perhaps, in its studied artifice and minute attention to detail, with Huysmans novel *À Rebours* of 1888. Its dandyish and fastidious hero Des Esseintes constructs a dream world as a counterpoint to what he sees as the nightmare of mass consumption. Rosalind Williams argues that *À Rebours* 'makes a powerful case for the seductiveness of a dream world – the fascination of artifice, the beauty of the imagination, the pleasure of self-deception, the flattering sense of initiation into mysteries'.[18] All these could equally describe the allure of the couture show, and couture has always been at pains to differentiate itself from the mass market. Yet, Williams goes on to argue, decadence is never free from mass consumption because it shares the same desire to be ahead of the rest, and condemns its followers to the same restless pursuit of novelty. They are doomed to the same disappointment because they have invested too many expectations in the world of goods.

18. Williams, Rosalind H., *Dream Worlds: Mass Consumption in Late Nineteenth-Century France*, Berkeley, Los Angeles & Oxford, England: University of California Press, 1982, p. 145. Williams argues that dandyism, and Huysman's *À Rebours*, were an élitist challenge to mass consumption.

For Georg Simmel, the aesthetics of world exhibitions conferred a feeling of presentness so that fashion's intensified pace 'increases our time-consciousness, and our simultaneous pleasure in newness and oldness give us a strong sense of presentness'.[19] It is this same sense of 'presentness' in a late twentieth-century fashion show, with its brevity and drama (it lasts no more than thirty minutes) that is created precisely through the mingling and telescoping of historical themes and pastiches. Mike Featherstone argues that the writing of both Simmel and Benjamin can

> direct us towards the ways in which the urban landscape has become aestheticized and enchanted through the architecture, billboards, shop displays, advertisements, packages, street signs, and through the embodied persons who move through these spaces: the individuals who wear . . . fashionable clothing, hairstyles and make-up, or who move or hold their bodies in particular stylised ways'.[20]

This enchantment and stylization were replayed in the hyperreal space of the late twentieth-century catwalk.

Walter Benjamin wrote that 'every image of the past that is not recognized by the present as one of its own concerns threatens to disappear irretrievably'.[21] In contrasting these images of the late twentieth century with others from the mid to late nineteenth, I have tried to construct a set of what Benjamin called 'dialectical images', images which were not based on simple comparisons but which created a more complex historical relay of themes running between past and present. For Benjamin, the relationship between images of the past and the present worked like the montage technique of cinema.[22] The principle of montage is that a third meaning is created by the juxtaposition of two images, rather than any immutable meaning inhering in each image. Benjamin conceived of this relationship as a dialectical one: the motifs of the past and the present functioned as thesis and antithesis. The flash of recognition, between past and present images, was the dialectical image that transformed both.[23]

19. Featherstone, Mike, *Consumer Culture and Postmodernism*, Thousand Oaks, New Delhi: Sage Publications, London, 1991, p. 74.

20. Ibid., p. 76.

21. Benjamin, Walter, 'Theses on the Philosophy of History', *Illuminations*, London: trans, Harry Zohn, Fontana/Collins, 1973, p. 257.

22. Buck-Morss, Susan, *The Dialectics of Seeing: Walter Benjamin and the Arcades Project*, Cambridge, Mass. & London , England: MIT Press, 1989. References in this chapter are to the paperback edition, 1991, p. 250.

23. Ibid.

Jolted out of the context of the past, the dialectical image could be read in the present as a 'truth'. But it was not an absolute truth, rather a truth which was fleeting and temporal, existing only at the moment of perception, characterized by 'shock' or vivid recognition.[24] It was not that the past simply illuminated the present, or that the present illuminated the past; rather, the two images came together in a 'critical constellation', tracing a previously concealed connection.[25] Benjamin identified some key figures – one might say key tropes – of nineteenth-century Paris as 'dialectical images': the prostitute, fashion itself, commodities, the arcades. It is as just such an image that I now turn to the question of the coincidence of woman as spectacle and modernity in this period.

Modernity and The Spectacle of Women

The wholesale rebuilding of Paris in the second half of the century, in the grand scheme concocted between Napoleon III and the Baron Haussmann, transformed it into the city we know today and allowed the development of the 'society of the spectacle' which, I have tried to indicate, still resonates in the imagery of the contemporary fashion show. [26] In the rebuilding of Paris the old, medieval *quartiers* were broken up and replaced with wide boulevards, open spaces and parks. With industrialization came urbanization and massively increased consumption. Paris became a city for the production and sale of luxury goods, and its parks and squares became new sites of

24. Ibid., pp. 185, 221, 250 & 290.

25. Ibid., pp. 290–1.

26. My use of the term 'spectacle' derives from Guy Debord's *The Society of the Spectacle*, trans. Malcolm Imrie, London: Verso, 1888 (first published 1967) in which Debord argues that everyday life is colonized by a new phase of commodity production. Debord, however, situates this phase in the 1920s, whereas others locate it as far back as the court of Louis XIV: Williams, Rosalind H., *Dream Worlds: Mass Consumption in Late Nineteenth-Century France*, Berkeley, Los Angeles & Oxford, England: University of California Press, 1982 and Jay, Martin, *Downcast Eyes: The Denigration of Vision in Twentieth Century French Thought*, Los Angeles & London, England: University of California Press, Berkeley, 1993, p. 432. I have discussed modernity in the context of nineteenth-century Paris, following both Walter Benjamin and, more recently, Clark, T.J., *The Painting of Modern Life: Paris in the Art of Manet and his Followers*, London: Princeton UP, Princeton, & Thames & Hudson, 1984. Thomas Richards provides a useful model of the application of Debord's ideas to nineteenth-century Britain in *The Commodity Culture of Victorian England: Advertising and Spectacle, 1851-1914*, London & New York: Verso, 1991. A very useful consideration of the convergence of spectacle and modernity, in relation to late nineteenth-century woman, is Heather McPhearson's 'Sarah Bernhardt: Portrait of the Actress as Spectacle', *Nineteenth-Century Contexts*, vol. 20, no. 4, 1999, pp. 409-54. Thanks to Carol Tulloch for bringing this invaluable article to my attention.

display and parade. While Haussmann's rebuilding had broken up the old Parisian working-class communities, who were henceforth pushed out towards the newer, industrial suburbs, new inhabitants continued to flood into Paris. New service industries flourished, providing jobs for women as waitresses, shop assistants, seamstresses, laundresses, hairdressers, servants, and milliners. Many of these women were new to Paris, without the support of friends or family. In the absence of the old certainties of class and community, in this new space of uncertainty, anyone could pretend to be anything if they had the money to buy clothes.[27] Surface was full of meaning; fashion and dress became vitally important as a way of signalling an identity, but also of reading one.

The Parisian arcades on which Walter Benjamin based his study date from the first half of the nineteenth century, [28] and housed a variety of luxury shops, clubs and, later, brothels which created a model of consumption later in the century for the Paris of the Second Empire. In the second half of the century the department store in particular played a vital role in offering middle-class women the possibility of mapping out an identity through their patterns of consumption. Shopping became a leisure activity, as the department store gave middle-class women new opportunities to stroll, to enjoy, to contemplate, to observe, come and go, the same opportunities afforded in the city space to the Baudelairean figure of the male *flâneur*. Janet Wolff has argued that they opened up a space for the woman as *flâneuse*.[29] Mica Nava has argued that modernity gave female consumers a way of being 'at home' in the chaos, the maelstrom, of city life, and becoming the subjects as well as the objects of modernization.[30] Nava argues that middle-class women were not so much left out of the spaces of modernity, as Janet Wolff had claimed, as excluded from the story by historians of modernity. For Nava fashion, men's and women's, presumably, was important in modernity precisely because of the emphasis of both on the instability of the sign. Dress signified 'rank' but also 'choice' and 'identity' – and she contends that 'women played a crucial part in the development of these taxonomies of signification'.[31]

27. T.J. Clark, ibid., p. 47.

28. Benjamin, Walter, *The Arcades Project*, Cambridge Mass & London England: trans. Howard Eiland & Kevin McLauchlin, The Belknap Press of Harvard University Press, 1999.

29. Wolff, Janet, 'The invisible *flâneuse*: women and the literature of modernity' in *Feminine Sentences: Essays on Women and Culture*, Cambridge England: Polity Press, 1990.

30. Nava, Mica, 'Modernity's Disavowal: Women, the City and the Department Store' in Pasi Falk & Colin Campbell (eds), *The Shopping Experience*, Thousand Oaks, New Delhi: Sage Publications, London, 1997, p. 66.

31. Nava, Mica, 'Modernity's Disavowal: Women, the City and the Department Store' in Pasi Falk & Colin Campbell (eds), *The Shopping Experience*, Thousand Oaks, New Delhi: Sage Publications, London, 1997, p. 66.

While nineteenth-century Paris gave middle-class women new opportunities for consumption of fashionable goods, it also saw the origins of a more elite form of contemporary fashion, haute couture. This was, and still is, the only branch of fashion to be exclusively female (there is no couture for men), and although it was available to comparatively few women it gradually set the tone for fashionable consumption across a broader spectrum of consumers.[32] In the process, however, of fashionable consumption, be it in the department store or the couture house, women of all classes were themselves spectacularized; caught up in the web of images they sought to consume, they themselves became image. Increasingly the nineteenth-century 'dream world' became epitomized in the spectacle of woman, with her links to fashion and the city, in the figures of the Parisian woman of fashion, the shop girl, waitress or milliner, the prostitute, even the dummies in shop windows, and the allegorical figures of sculpture.[33] The main entrance to the 1900 exhibition, at the Porte Binet, a monumental gateway on the Place de la Concorde, was surmounted by a 15-foot tall polychrome plaster statue of *La Parisienne*, whose robe was designed by the couturier Paquin. The sculptor, Moreau-Vauthier, subsequently specialized in small bronze figurines of Parisian ladies of fashion, generally dressed in Paquin gowns, which would be exhibited in the ladies' salons. However at the time the original statue was unveiled in 1900 it attracted both ridicule and harsh criticism for the connotations of prostitution which contemporaries saw in its dress and demeanour. Their response highlighted the ambiguous and uneasy relationship of woman to spectacle in this period, particularly the slippage between the woman of fashion, the prostitute and the actress, confirming Mica Nava's point that spectacular fashion is an unstable sign. One could also make a connection here to Andreas Huyssen's formulation of mass culture as feminine at a later period in the twentieth century, the inter-war years.[34]

For women, in particular, modernity was a double-coded experience, in which euphoria was juxtaposed with alienation, autonomy with objectification. While the middle-class woman was relatively safe in the department store the working woman was prey to any importunity, and the instability of fashion as a sign could work equally to her disadvantage as to her

32. Marly, Diana de, *Worth: Father of Haute Couture*, New York: Holmes & Meier, 1980. De Marly argues that Worth had, by the 1870s, initiated many of the business and bureaucratic practices which would, in the twentieth century, define a couture house.

33. For example, see Jullian, Philippe, *The Triumph of Art Nouveau: the Paris Exhibition of 1900*, London: Phaidon Press, 1974, p. 169, for a discussion of the allegorical figure of electricity at the 1900 Paris exhibition.

34. Huyssen, Andreas, *After the Great Divide: Modernism, Mass Culture, Postmodernism*, Basingstoke: Macmillan, 1986. See chapter on 'Mass Culture as Woman: Modernism's Other'.

Figure 9.2. Monumental figure of 'la Parisienne' on top of the Porte Binet, the main entrance to the Paris International Exhibition of 1900, made from polychrome plaster, with a robe designed by the couturier Paquin. Sculptor: Moreau-Vauthier. From: 'The Paris Exhibition 1990: An Illustrated Record of Its Art, Architecture and Industries', The Art Journal Office, London, 1900. Photograph: Syd Shelton

advantage. Added to this, the salaries of working women were so meagre that, without family support in the city, many were driven to support themselves through prostitution.[35] Anton Corbin argues that with the Haussmannization of Paris the prostitute emerged from the shadows and circulated tirelessly in the city of spectacle. Alongside the world exhibitions and the shop windows of the new department stores the prostitute in turn came to show herself, as the commodity form was indissolubly linked to its image.[36] In the 1900 Paris Exhibition this connection was explicit in the section devoted to theatre which was in the Rue de Paris and which became the main centre for soliciting at the exhibition.[37] Already by the 1880s, Corbin argues, 'the prostitute . . . had become woman as spectacle. She paraded or exhibited herself on the terraces of high-class cafes, in the brasseries, in the *café-concerts*, and on the sidewalk . . . in this way . . . the primacy of the visual in sexual solicitation originated.[38]

Corbin has also described how, within the brothels, sexual practices became more elaborate, and more staged. Spectacles and tableaux vivants were enacted on gigantic revolving turntables, simple peepholes were replaced by draperies, mirrors, binoculars and acoustic horns hidden in the wall; prostitutes were required to perform a greater range of activities. What had previously been perceived as aristocratic tastes were now lower- and middle-class spectacles. Contemporary descriptions of brothels reveal fantasy settings not dissimilar to those of department stores, and it was not uncommon for brothels to renovate their establishments for each universal exhibition: opera settings, oriental scenes, Louis XV salons, and 'electric fairylands'.[39] For Baudelaire the prostitute was the key figure of modernity because she was, in Benjamin's phrase, 'commodity and seller in one'.[40] 'As a dialectical image, she "synthesises" the form of the commodity and the content',[41] and although Benjamin's comments about women in general may reveal his own ambival-

35. Wilson, Elizabeth, *the Sphinx in the City: Urban Life, the Control of Disorder, and Women*, London: Virago, 1991, pp. 49–50.

36. Corbin, Alain, *Women for Hire: Prostitution and Sexuality in France After 1850*, Cambridge Mass: trans. Alan Sheridan, Harvard University Press, 1990.

37. Jullian, Philippe, *The Triumph of Art Nouveau: the Paris Exhibition of 1900*, London: Phaidon Press, 1974, p. 175.

38. Corbin, Alain, *Women for Hire: Prostitution and Sexuality in France After 1850*, Cambridge Mass: trans. Alan Sheridan, Harvard University Press, 1990, p. 205.

39. Ibid., pp. 123–5.

40. Buck-Morss, Susan, *The Dialectics of Seeing: Walter Benjamin and the Arcades Project*, Cambridge, Mass. & London , England: MIT Press, 1989. References in this article are to the paperback edition, 1991, pp. 184.

41. Ibid.

ence they also echo a certain nineteenth-century ambivalence about women, commodities and consumption.[42]

This ambivalence spilled out in the avant-garde painting of the time. In paintings of the femme fatale of the period, the Salomés and Judiths of the Decadence, where the image of desire was tinged with dread, the spectacular displays of consumer capitalism were transposed from the world of goods to the woman herself. Colin McDowell has suggested that Galliano's work from the mid-1990s exhibited the same ambivalence in his projection of a libidinous female image, 'bringing echoes of hookers, geishas, hostesses in opium dens'.[43] In this context, his fascination with spectacular historical figures of the late-nineteenth and early-twentieth centuries echoes the ambivalence of that period. His couture collection for Dior Autumn-Winter 1997 reconfigured the belle époque and, specifically, Colette as a showgirl. His own label collection for Autumn-Winter 1998 referred to the vampish and ambiguous sexuality of German cabaret in the Weimar period. These shows evoked pre-war Paris as a city of spectacle and luxury, and post-war Berlin as a city of modernist experimentation and decadence. Whether his references were to real historical figures or images from cinema and art, his particular fascination with women who used their sexuality spectacularly to make their way in the world harked back to the ambiguous relation of sexuality, commerce and fashion in the modernist period.

Modernity into Postmodernity

There are many competing usages of the terms modernity, modernization and modernism, particularly between the social sciences and the humanities traditions. A number of historians, for whom the idea of modernity is bound up with an analysis of industrial capitalist society as a form of rupture from

42. Nava, Mica, 'Modernity's Disavowal: Women, the City and the Department Store' in Pasi Falk & Colin Campbell (eds), *The Shopping Experience*, Thousand Oaks, New Delhi: Sage Publications, London, 1997, p. 81. Yet he also suggests fashion can be emblematic of social change: Buck-Morss, Buck-Morss, Susan, *The Dialectics of Seeing: Walter Benjamin and the Arcades Project*, Cambridge, Mass. & London , England: MIT Press, 1989. References in this article are to the paperback edition, 1991, pp. 101. There is a discussion of his ambivalence in Jane Gaines & Charlotte Herzog (eds), *Fabrications: Costume and the Female Body*, New York and London: Routledge, 1990, pp. 1–27.

43. McDowell, Colin, *Galliano,* London: Weidenfeld & Nicolson, 1997, pp. 117. 'John, we are told, loves women, but it is not easy to avoid the thought that, within that love lurks a fear which must be laid to rest by pastiche or, even more compelling, the suspicion that it is a love so intense it also encompasses a degree of hatred.'

the preceding social system, have used the term to designate the enormous social and cultural changes which took place from the mid-sixteenth century in Europe.[44] For the sociologist Max Weber, the origins of capitalism lay in the Protestant ethic; its leitmotifs were modernization and rationalization but also, and crucially, ambiguity.[45] It is both this sense of ambiguity, and the concept of historical rupture, which inform my exploration of the links between women, fashion, modernity, the city and capitalism. It is beyond the scope of this chapter (and beyond me) to plot a precise and structural connection between Western fashion and modernity by tracking back through European culture. Furthermore, such an enterprise might construct a linear history which, in a sense, runs counter to my project.[46] As outlined earlier, I have instead drawn on Walter Benjamin's concept of dialectical images, juxtaposing the more spectacular manifestations of the consumer explosion of the nineteenth century against those of the late twentieth-century fashion show to illuminate the historical relay between past and present.

Throughout I have drawn extensively on Elizabeth Wilson's writing on fashion and modernity. Although Susan Buck-Morss discusses fashion in *The Dialectics of Seeing*, an imaginative reconstruction of Walter Benjamin's Arcades Project, published in 1991, only Elizabeth Wilson has focused exclusively on the nexus between women, modernity, fashion and the city.[47] Wilson argues that fashion and modernity share a double-sided quality, because they are both formed in the same crucible, that of 'the early capitalist city'.[48] It is this double-sided quality that informs my use of the term 'modernity'; it combines, on the one hand, fragmentation, dissonance and alienation with, on the other, euphoria, excitement and the pleasures of self-

44. Turner, Brian S., (ed.), *Theories of Modernity and Postmodernity*, Newbury Park, New Delhi: Sage Publications, London, 1990, discusses the major debates and cites key texts.

45. Bryan S. Turner, 'Periodization and Politics in the Postmodern', in Turner (ed.), ibid., pp. 1–13.

46. Benjamin, too, wrote: 'in order for a piece of the past to be touched by present actuality, there must exist no continuity between them' for the historical object is constituted as dialectical image by being 'blasted out of the continuum of history'. Cited in Buck-Morss, Susan, *The Dialectics of Seeing: Walter Benjamin and the Arcades Project*, Cambridge, Mass. & London, England: MIT Press, 1989. References in this article are to the paperback edition, 1991, pp. 219.

47. Wilson, Elizabeth, *Adorned in Dreams: Fashion and Modernity*, London: Virago, 1985. See too Wilson, Elizabeth, *The Sphinx in the City: Urban Life, the Control of Disorder, and Women*, London, Virago, 1991, which, like this paper, uses Walter Benjamin to connect the nineteenth-century city to the urban consciousness of the present.

48. Wilson, Elizabeth, *Adorned in Dreams: Fashion and Modernity*, London: Virago, 1985, p. 9.

fashioning and of novelty and artifice. This double-sided quality also, and specifically, characterizes the spectacle of women in the modernist period.

In *The Painter of Modern Life* Charles Baudelaire defined the experience of modernity in nineteenth-century Paris as 'the ephemeral, the fugitive, the contingent'.[49] These ideas were later developed in Georg Simmel's discussion of 'neurasthenia' and Walter Benjamin's concept of 'shock'. Simmel related fashion to the fragmentation of modern life and discussed its neurasthenia, that is, the overstimulation and nervous excitement which came with the growth of the metropolis. He associated fashion with the middle classes and with the city, as well as with the stylization of everyday objects (for him the *Jugendstil* movement in Germany) and he pointed to a close relation between art, fashion and consumer culture, a connection which became topical again in the 1990s. Benjamin's concept of shock also related to Baudelaire's *modernité* in his descriptions of life in Baudelaire's Paris – for Benjamin the ur-city of modernity – as being characterized by 'shocks, jolts and vivid presentness captured by the break with traditional forms of sociation'.[50] Again, one could point to present-day similarities in the changing social patterns of work, leisure and the family in the late twentieth century. The so-called weakening of the family structure was a feature of nineteenth-century Paris too, when populations drifted to the cities in huge numbers.

Both Simmel and Benjamin imply the idea of rupture with the past, a sense which could also be said to have characterized the last twenty years of the twentieth century. Hal Foster suggests that today Baudelaire's 'shock' has become electronic; he writes that we are *wired* to spectacular events and 'psycho-techno thrills'.[51] The question raised in Hal Foster's observation is whether our electronic shock is radically different from Benjamin's, or whether traces of the past still echo in the present.[52] Whereas Baudelaire, Simmel and Benjamin wrote about the effects of industrialization on urban populations, the late twentieth century has been characterized, rather, by an information revolution which started thirty years ago with the first satellites

49. Baudelaire, Charles, 'The Painter of Modern Life', *The Painter of Modern Life and Other Essays*, London : trans. Jonathan Mayne, Phaidon Press, 1964, p. 12.

50. Featherstone, Mike, *Consumer Culture and Postmodernism*, Thousand Oaks, New Delhi: Sage Publications, London, 1991, p. 65.

51. Foster, Hal, *The Return of the Real: the Avant-Garde at the End of the Century*, Cambridge Mass & London England: MIT Press, 1996, pp. 221–2.

52. Featherstone, Mike, *Consumer Culture and Postmodernism*, Thousand Oaks, New Delhi: Sage Publications, London, 1991, argues that postmodernism is a continuation of modernity, and that is why the writing of Simmel and Benjamin still resonate in the present: see his chapter 5, 'the Aestheticization of Everyday Life', pp. 65–82.

in space but has escalated in the last five to ten years with the spread of electronic and digital forms of communication.

This technological revolution, although very different in its effects, has produced a sense of upheaval and change which can be compared to the effects of industrialization in nineteenth-century Paris. Above all, the rise of the information society has produced a comparable sense of rupture in contemporary sensibilities and social practices.[53] The 'intoxicating dream worlds' of the nineteenth century, with its 'constantly changing flow of commodities, images and bodies'[54] was replaced in the late twentieth century by the rapid flow of signs and images. Although the contemporary experience was lead by communications and new technology, rather than by industry, both were periods of accelerated transition which perhaps explains the prominent role of fashion in each. Fashion itself is about rapid change, and can articulate modern sensibilities in a time of transition. Indeed, Gilles Lipovetsky has argued that the instability of fashion trains us to be flexible and adaptable, so that modern fashion is socially reproductive and not, as some would argue, irrational and wasteful. He writes that 'fashion socialises human beings to change and prepares them for perpetual recycling',[55] and argues that the kinetic, open personality of fashion is the personality which a society in the process of rapid transformation most needs.

Most theorists of postmodernism have posited it as a moment of absolute rupture with the past. Yet there are also enough similarities, as I have sketched, to suggest, as Lyotard does in *The Postmodern Condition*, that postmodernism is simply another stage, or development, of modernism and that there is no radical break with the past.[56] Galliano's retro-images, ushering back the historical styles of modernity, remind us of the way the past can continue to resonate in the present. His nostalgic designs conjure up an earlier period of idleness and luxury, yet the historical period he draws on was also, like the present, a time of mutability, instability and rapid change, when all fixed points seemed to be in motion, and in which the image of woman was correspondingly highly charged. For the image of woman as commodity and consumer is as ambivalently coded today, in the work of Galliano, as a hundred years ago in the Parisian woman of fashion.

53. For a discussion of the effect of new technologies on sensibilities and social practice see Antony Giddens, Antony, *Reith Lectures*, London: BBC Publications, 1999.

54. Featherstone, Mike, *Consumer Culture and Postmodernism*, Thousand Oaks, New Delhi: Sage Publications, London, 1991, p. 70.

55. Lipovetsky, Gilles, *The Empire of Fashion: Dressing Modern Democracy*, Princeton, New Jersey: trans. Catherine Porter, Princeton University Press, 1994, p. 149.

56. Lyotard, Jean-François, *The Postmodern Condition: A Report on Knowledge*, University of Minnesota Press, Minneapolis: trans. Geoffrey Bennington & Brian Massumi, 1984.

Yet, for all the similarities, there are also some fundamental differences related precisely to changes in technology around the image which have transformed modern fashion, including the marketing of Dior and Galliano, despite their nostalgic evocations of the past. It is the paramount and altered role of the image in contemporary culture, and particularly in fashion, which differentiates Galliano's practice from his nineteenth-century referents, however insistently he harks back to them in his design motifs. Whereas historically the imagery of fashion was an adjunct to fashionable dress, increasingly the relationship of the two shifted, so that fashion began to function equally as image and object, nowhere more so than in the spectacular fashion shows staged in London and then Paris in the 1990s. Only a very small number of people experienced the old-fashioned intimacy of a Galliano show, seated close enough to the models to see the fine detailing of the clothes, like the original Dior customers in the 1940s and 1950s. Yet many more people became familiar with the 1990s collections than in the 1950s, as these designs were increasingly conveyed to a mass audience through the new visual media: magazines, books and videos, on the television and on the Internet. An haute couture collection which would not appear in the shops, such as John Galliano's collections for Dior, or Alexander McQueen's for Givenchy, would almost certainly only be experienced through images. Susan Sontag has argued that in the modern period our perception of reality is shaped by the type and frequency of images we receive. Sontag writes that from the mid-nineteenth century 'the credence that could no longer be given to realities understood *in the form of* images was now being given to realities understood *to be* images, illusions', and goes on to cite Feuerebach's observation of 1843, also cited by Debord at the beginning of *The Society of the Spectacle*: 'our era prefers the image to the thing, the copy to the original, the representation to the reality, appearance to being'.[57]

But if the new technologies have altered our access to image and meaning, nevertheless many of the techniques of the image, in retailing and marketing, remind us of their origins in nineteenth-century Paris. In this there is an ambiguity. The new emphasis on the image contains within it the trace of the past. A feathered and sequined evening flapper dress by Galliano for Dior does not merely gesture stylistically towards the past but conceals deeper,

57. Sontag, Susan, *On Photography*, Harmondsworth: Penguin Books, 1972, p. 153. For more empirically-based studies of the impact of new visual technologies on sensibilities, see: Crary, Jonathan, *Techniques of the Observer: On Vision and Modernity in the Nineteenth-Century*, Cambridge Mass & London England: MIT Press, 1990; McQuire Scott, *Visions of Modernity: Representaion, Memory, Time and Space in the Age of the Camera*, Thousand Oaks, New Delhi: Sage Publications, London, 1998.

structural similarities beneath its surface. If there is a similarity, it is in the spectacular patterns of consumption of the nineteenth-century modernist city, specifically Paris, a city in which women frequently stage themselves as spectacle, be it the bourgeoisie consumers of the department stores, or the more ambiguously coded showgirl. Woman, like the image itself, is an unstable sign.

And if there is a difference, it is that the spectacle in the 1990s has mutated into pure image. Never before have so many seen so much of what goes on behind its closed doors; but only as a representation. Spectacle is not *represented* in these haute couture fashion shows, as the visits to the moon or the Far East were supposedly represented in the cinéoramas or dioramas of the nineteenth century; now the spectacle *is* a representation. Print and digital media have taken the space occupied by world fares, and we consume this kind of spectacle primarily through visual media: magazines, newspapers, television, the Internet and video.[58] If the technology improves to give pictures of high enough quality, even fashion photography could become digitalized in the future, banishing film. The photographer would licence the magazine to use the images he transmitted to them electronically, via the computer, making analogue techniques of reproduction outmoded, perhaps appropriately for a kind of fashion which can be consumed exclusively as image not as object. Couture clothing will never appear in the shops. Its appearance to us as image is phantasmagoric. And, appropriately, the role of the fashion show has changed with its increasing public visibility. No longer necessary to sell the clothes to buyers and clients, for the collection will have been sold a few weeks before the show, it remains a ghostly spectacle, a view into a designer's mind, captured fleetingly in images. As such, it evokes Susan Sontag's claim that 'a society becomes "modern" when one of its chief activities is producing and consuming images'.[59]

Yet these images are not free-floating signifiers but part of a network of signs which constitute an expanded 'society of the spectacle'. In the 1990s, Galliano was described by the British fashion journalist Sally Brampton as 'the greatest 3-D image-maker alive'. Brampton argued that he was partly responsible for the greatly increased attendance at the Paris shows, which she described as 'a media feeding frenzy as newspapers and television stations around the world give increasing prominence to fashion'.[60] These images do not exist in some rarefied realm of art for art's sake, but as a commercial

58. Throughout the majority of the twentieth-century the couture houses prohibited the use of cameras at the collections and press photographs of fashion shows only became common in the 1980s and 1990s.

59. Sontag, Susan, *On Photography*, Harmondsworth: Penguin Books, 1972, p. 153.

and marketing stratagem. Stéphane Wagner, professor and lecturer in communications at the Institut Français de la Mode said in 1997, 'If we accept that much of haute couture is about squeezing out maximum media coverage – good or bad – then the more spectacular the presentation and collection, the better. And from that point of view the English are the best by far'.[61]

Although traditionally Paris has been a centre of luxury, London has always had the edge in terms of imaginative presentation. This is due in part to the system of education in certain British art and design schools, in part to the comparative lack of infrastructure in Britain, so that young designers leaving college have nothing to loose and everything to gain by putting on spectacular and extravagant shows which will catch the attention of press and buyers. For them, as for their Victorian predecessors in the production of consumer goods, the spectacle is 'the theatre through which capitalism acts'.[62] Most practically, it is how they will get a backer. In rare cases, it may lead to them being recruited by a major Parisian couture house. Spectacle, therefore, does not function outside of the realms of consumption and discourse but, rather, from within those structures, as their 'voice'. What is new, however, is the way that new technology and communications have expanded the network of spectacle into the new visual media.

60. *Guardian*, 14 October 1998.

61. Quoted in: Stephen Todd, 'The Importance of Being English', *Blueprint*, March 1997, p. 42.

62. Thomas Richards provides a useful model of the application of Debord's ideas to nineteenth-century Britain in *The Commodity Culture of Victorian England: Advertising and Spectacle, 1851–1914*, London & New York: Verso, 1991, p. 251.

10

Luxury and Restraint: Minimalism in 1990s Fashion*

Rebecca Arnold

Simple, elegant and restrained, American designer Marc Jacobs' work epitomizes the 1990s minimalist aesthetic. His spring 1998 collection comprised a series of easy separates, little soft grey cardigans, flirty pleated skirts, contrasting fuschia macs and sporty clamdiggers. There was a slight hint at 1950s style in the cut, but not so much that the modern feel of the collection became swamped with nostalgia; there were enough references to trend-based shapes and colours that the potential consumer could feel comfortably fashion-conscious, but there was nothing too extreme, too difficult to wear. As such it seemed perfect for contemporary women's lives: streamlined, stripped of clutter, functional yet beautiful.

Importantly it also drew upon the undoubted allure of luxury fabrics. The cut of the clothes may have been restrained but the luxury of the materials, soft cashmeres, and fine wools meant that the wearer was able to indulge in the tactile pleasure of expensive fabrics next to the skin. Since the late 1990s we have liked to believe in the simplicity of the minimalist lifestyle, with its pleasing connotations of controlled rationality, which creates a tranquil space in the chaos of urban living, but we also crave the comforting embrace of luxury. While the idea of capsule wardrobes, made up of infinitely interchangeable key separates, may be enticing, there is also a desire to retain a sense of distinction, particularly from the mass-market copy. The look may appear democratically accessible, but the cost of such minimal styles is prohibitive. While high street fashion may have become increasingly quick at replicating the latest catwalk looks, quality has, however, remained harder to emulate. And as was pointed out in the *Observer Magazine* in July 1998,

---

* This chapter is based upon a section of the book *Fashion, Desire & Anxiety,* published by I.B. Tauris in spring 2001.

'[Fashion] has decreed a massive swing away from easy, throwaway fashion to divisive, elitist, luxury.'[1]

In this chapter I want therefore to unpick both the precedents of 1990s minimalist fashion, as well as questioning its deceptively simple style. It may appear to be an innocently easy way to dress, but as ever in fashion there is a web of contradictory meanings attached to its streamlined exterior.

Tyler Brûlé, the editor of *Wallpaper* magazine, wrote in an article entitled 'It's smart to be simple' in the *Independent on Sunday* in 1996 of the growing trend towards 'downsizing', 'voluntary simplicity', 'beyond basics'.[2] He felt the roots of this shift were on the West Coast of America, where it had become increasingly fashionable to discard unnecessary elements of your life, casting off excess in both possessions and lifestyle, and, influenced by both the economic impact of the recession, and the moral imperative to avoid extravagant display, lead a simpler existence. The term 'minimalism' was understandably appealing. He cited both the *Chic Simple* collection of books, and a Seattle newsletter *Simple Living*, as examples of this apparent emphasis on scaling down of both wardrobe and home. So powerful has this move been that even designers like Dolce e Gabbana, who are not usually known for their love of restraint, used advertising in their Autumn/Winter 1998/99 menswear campaign that evoked a simple, rustic lifestyle. A male model clad in a pale polo neck sweater and contrasting dark trousers and jacket stared out at the viewer from a blank, white interior; on the other side of the double page spread was a still life adding detail to this scene. On a rough wooden table a collection of simple bowls and eating utensils, a loaf of bread, fresh fish and olives were displayed. They spoke of a rural Italian lifestyle, a simple, honest and healthy existence, unhampered by the pressures of the city, the constant drive of commercialism. Minimalism had become a lifestyle that could be sold on this very contradiction: it seemed to offer an escape from constant consuming, from the confusion and violence of contemporary society and yet, ironically, as Tyler Brûlé pointed out, this frequently involved buying more.

Another element in the shift by many fashion designers towards this restrained style, is the rejection of overt display that had been seen as characterizing the 1980s. The glittering excess of designers like Gianni Versace was felt by some to be too vulgar, too brash for the intelligent consumer. His eveningwear was cut to slip around the body, revealing the figure to the eager eye of the tabloid press. Its extravagance attracted celebrities, keen to be turned into curvaceous femme fatales. However those who sought the

---

1. Rumbold, J. 'Cashmere', *Observer,* Life Section, 1998, p. 62.
2. Brûlé, T., 'It's Smart to be Simple', *Independent on Sunday,* Real Life Section, 1996, p. 7.

apparent cool rationality of simple clothes rejected designs that flaunted this image of women as spectacles of sexually charged flesh and glamour. Simpler dress seemed to offer women freedom from culturally defined notions of the body that focused attention constantly on the ability to fulfil current physical ideals.

It was not just the obviousness of sexual provocation that led to minimalism becoming an alternative to the Versace aesthetic. Designers wanted to move away from ostentation and the perceived bad taste of the gilt logo, which was seen as too blatant a symbol of wealth and excess. This represented a turning away from the ethos of conspicuous consumption as the motivating force when buying fashion. For the designers I will be concentrating on, a much subtler, but no less powerful form of status assertion was brought to play. This could perhaps be called inconspicuous consumption: wearing clothes whose very simplicity betrays their expense and cultural value, when quiet, restrained luxury is still revered as the ultimate symbol of both wealth and intelligence. This contradictory consuming is apparently untainted by slurs of vanity, and brashness, since its style seems so clearly to be about restraint and abstinence.

Douglas Coupland's satirical definition of the significance of Armani's appeal mocks the contained sophistication of the designer's unstructured, modern tailoring, but it betrayed the potential, covert meanings of this style, 'Armanism: After Giorgio Armani: an obsession with mimicking the seamless and (more importantly) *controlled* ethos of Italian couture. Like *Japanese Minimalism*, Armanism reflects a profound inner need for control.'[3]

While Armani appeared to snub the decadent extravagance that is such a feature of high fashion, its focus on detail, on Armani's desire to demonstrate an intellectual distancing from trend-led fashion's frivolous ephemerality, his work constructed an alternative set of expensive obsessions. This was noted in the *Sunday Times Magazine* in 1990: 'Armani can measure his success as a series of subtractions'.[4]

An advertisement from his campaign of 1994 epitomized the unstructured tailoring that is Armani's signature. Both male and female models were clad in muted fluid linen, their posture conveying a feeling of relaxed confidence; even the collars of the women's suits were smoothed away, reducing the jackets to their most essential form. Nothing was allowed to distract from this reduced silhouette – the models' hair was swept back tidily from the

3. Coupland, D., *Generation X, Tales for an Accelerated Generation*. London: Abacus, 1997, p. 92.

4. Howell, G., 'Giorgio Armani: The Man who Fell to Earth', *Sultans of Style, Thirty Years of Fashion and Passion*. London: Ebury Press, 1990, p. 122.

faces, their sunglasses added to the air of rational anonymity of their figures. Their natural surroundings reinforced ideals of simple, authentic design, echoed in the organic unforced lines of their clothes. This aloofness offered a protective sense of security to the wearer, who was well dressed but never calling out for attention, never a spectacle of display. Armani's clothes were at once anonymous in their simplicity yet recognizably expensive when inspected up close, their fabric and cut betraying their elite status.

Armani's need to strip designs to their most basic form expressed not only an admirably modernist aesthetic, but also his desire to police definitions of 'good' taste. Indulgence in clothing is allowed only within the realms of those knowledgeable enough to appreciate the subtlety of a well-cut jacket, the sensuality of luxurious, yet deceptively plain, fabrics. Financial and personal indulgence is as much a part of consuming the sleek trouser suits made by Armani, as it is in the purchase of a sparkling Versace outfit, but the former wear the mask of puritan abstinence, of rational, functional design and the longevity of the 'classic'. Such clothes are, Rosalind Coward commented, 'designed to make a statement about what they feel like. They are designed to connote a sophisticated sensuality, that enjoys touching itself all the time.'[5]

Designers like Jil Sander whose signature style is pared down, minimalist design is seen as producing clothing for women with careers, women too busy, and too powerful to wish to dress in the decorative or the spectacular. Abstinence from such traditionally feminine pursuits is perceived as a sign of this power, perhaps because it has for so long been seen as a masculine trait. This essentially is what designers like Armani, Jean Muir and Nicole Farhi have sought to do: to give women a sense of ease and confidence in their clothing, a rational anonymity that belies the quality and expense of their garments. This modesty and understatement provides a 'neverending dialectic of status claims and demurrals,'[6] at once ascetically simple, yet decadently expensive.

Minimalist fashion is concerned with more than its surface simplicity, which is really an inscrutable mask presented to the world as a feint, belying the undercurrents of sensuality hidden in the soft fabrics which shift against the skin. This mask also disguises the wearer's aspirational desires, their search not just for tactile experiences, but also their wish for legitimate status, valid unquestionable identity, which is traditionally associated with 'old money', stability increasingly hard to find in the fluid job market of the late twentieth century. As Bob Colacello noted in an article on Sander in *Vanity Fair* in 1996, 'As with [Ralph] Lauren behind all the restrained good taste is a

5. Coward, R., *Female Desire: Women's Sexuality Today*. London: Paladin, 1984, p. 31.
6. Davis, F., *Fashion, Culture and Identity*. Chicago: Chicago University Press, 1994, p. 64.

romantic yearning for something more, not less.'[7] In Jil Sander's view the worst thing is to be judged déclassé, to expose any trace of lowly status, any slip into bad taste.

This ideal has a series of noble precedents that illuminate the attitudes that have built up around this manner of dressing. The dandies of the early nineteenth century allowed for no indulgence in decorative detail or unnecessary elements in a design. Beau Brummell, who personified the minimal style of the first dandies in London, viewed dressing as a ritual of washing and preparing the body and then clothing it in the most exquisitely restrained examples of each garment: austerely cut dark cloth coat, perfect pale pantaloons, plain waistcoat and shirt and simple accessories, yellow leather gloves, hessian boots and a neat hat. The only area left for any sartorial expression was the white cravat, which was to be dexterously tied in the most modishly elaborate manner.

The dandy was obsessed with self-adornment, even though the end result was so simple in its appearance that it was viewed with deep suspicion by the popular press at the time. This can be seen in a French caricature of the 1820s, when dandyism crossed the channel to Paris. The caption 'Egotism personified' reinforces the cartoon's satirical view of the dandy as a self-absorbed narcissist. The dandyish young man seated at the centre of the image seems so concerned with collecting the chairs in the room together to support his elaborately graceful pose that he has rudely allowed the women to stand. He appears oblivious to the fact that his spurs have ripped one unfortunate woman's gown and that his walking cane is poking another in the eye. This lack of attention to anything other than his own appearance was an affront to the nineteenth-century ideal of active manhood, prompting the historian and writer Thomas Carlyle to ask 'And now for all this perennial Martyrdom, and Poesy, and even Prophecy, what is it that the Dandy asks in return? Solely, we may say, that you would recognize his existence; would admit him to be a living object; or failing this, a visual object, or thing that will reflect rays of light.'[8]

It is ironic therefore that such sobriety was to become a defining feature of much nineteenth-century menswear, coming to be seen as the mark of the respectable bourgeois male. Heaven forbid though that men should seem too preoccupied with achieving this sober ideal, masculine attire was to appear effortless, demonstrating the gentleman's ease with his status. Brummell's close attention to detail and fanatical allegiance to the puritanically austere was a lesson in control and restraint that Coco Chanel later transferred to

7. Colacello, B. October 1994. 'The Queen of Less is More', *Vanity Fair*, p. 165.
8. Carlyle, T., Sartor Resartus. Oxford: Oxford University Press, 1987, p. 207.

the female body. Fashion designers' desire for a simple style that would sweep away the multi-layered excess of the early years of the twentieth century was epitomized in Chanel's work. Her designs were at the cutting edge of couture fashion, mocking bourgeois sensibilities that still clung to the more obvious wealth of rich fabrics and complex designs. Utilitarian fabrics like jersey were given high fashion status by virtue of the image and ideals conveyed by their designer. Chanel worked within the rarefied atmosphere of couture, but she attracted avant-garde and daring customers at the start of her career. Potential wearers had to be willing to risk the misunderstanding of onlookers, unversed in the coding of inverse status symbols. There is a history of artists and intellectuals adopting simple, utilitarian clothing as a symbol of their contempt for fashion's constantly shifting whims and a sign of their loftier concerns. However, the bourgeois fashion consumer needed to be sure of the unassailable nature of her status to embrace such simplicity of style. Chanel provided women with clothing that was appropriate to their new, more active lifestyles, and which viewed femininity as confident and streamlined, rather than as a decorative confection. She encouraged women to dress as plainly as their maids, but this did not mean that they should necessarily be mistaken for such lowly creatures. Chanel's sleekly minimal designs fused the tenets of dandyism: close attention to detail, high quality, basic forms, with an irreverent attitude, simple black dresses and separates were piled with the previously déclassé glitter of fake jewelry.

Another earlier form of pared-down design is exemplified in the work of American designer Claire McCardell who rose to prominence in the 1940s. In her work we see minimal fashion as an expression of laid-back functionalism rather than any adherence to introspection. Her clothing is about allowing the body to move and work, to take part in an active and healthy life. The simple shapes and utilitarian fabrics she favoured came to epitomize American style, based as they were upon a belief in democratic ready-to-wear, not the elitist couture of the Old World. As one commentator remarked, 'She thought the couture mode too structured, too formal and wanted to create accessible, easy clothes for busy women in a fast world.'[9]

McCardell dressed the proto-career woman of the 1940s and 1950s, freeing her from the New Look and giving her instead an easy-to-care-for wardrobe of sports-inspired separates. In a Louise Dahl Wolfe photograph of a McCardell bathing costume of 1948, the soft grey tones enhance the feeling of harmony between body and fabric. The model wears a clingy knitted jersey costume which forms around her figure, its patterned weave echoed in the gentle ripples of the sand she lies on.

9. Yusuf, N., 'Form and Function', *British Elle*, June 1990.

A McCardell empire line dress of 1946 shows her commitment to clothing that allowed for a variety of body sizes, the definitions of its line provided only by drawstrings at the bust and neckline, rather than by cut. Its simple silhouette also exemplifies the timeless quality of this type of dressing: its 1940s heritage is given away more by the evening gloves and costume jewelry that it has been accessorized with, than by its style. McCardell sought to include certain key pieces in each of her collections, decrying the usual fashion imperative for seasonal trends. She wanted to make clothing easier, providing women with six-piece travel wardrobes, popover dresses that just slipped cleanly over the head, durable denim and gingham outfits that could be worn year after year. For her such basic forms expressed the vitality of the wearer, and the vitality of modernity. In the 1954 entry of *Current Biography*, McCardell's approach was described thus: 'The designer's idea is that clothes should fit the individual and the occasion, and should be comfortable as well as handsome. The color and line should flow with the body.'[10]

Even her more obviously glamorous eveningwear draws its allure from the use of a few striking elements. In an example from the Metropolitan Museum in New York's collection, rose-red pleated silk, and the wrapover form of a kimono, add sophistication and allure to a simple column dress, rather than any elaborate decorative devices that might distract from its essential silhouette.

Anne Hollander sums up this easy style and potential problems relating to simplicity of form by saying, 'American modernization allowed women's clothing to participate equally with men's in the new impersonal character of American modern design itself. When a designer's original idea can so easily be adapted to mass production and can become familiar to many people in many different contexts, it quickly loses the look of an individual invention.'[11]

The democratic nature of simple designs can make it hard for consumers to distinguish between brands, or indeed to discern the need to pay more for minimalist clothing. Townley, the firm McCardell worked for, lost money on one of her most dramatically pared down designs, the 'monastic' dress, a basic a-line style, cut on the bias to swing down from the shoulders and flatter the figure. Customers could see no difference between her version and the cheaper copies that soon filled the stores, and chose economy over the cachet of owning one of the originals. For later American designers this need to distinguish the brand became paramount.

10. Dent Candee, M., (ed.), *Current Biography, Who's News and Why, 1954*. New York: The H.W. Wilson Company, 1954, p. 423.

11. Hollander, A., *Sex and Suits, The Evolution of Modern Fashion*. New York: Kodansha, 1994, p. 144.

In the 1950s Robert L. Steiner and Joseph Weiss revised Thorstein Veblen's theory of conspicuous consumption to demonstrate the elite's need to constantly create new status symbols to maintain their position as taste-makers, in an increasingly prosperous America, where more and more could afford the obvious splendours of luxury. Steiner and Weiss wrote, 'As a result of the long practice of conspicuous consumption, ornate objects have become associated in the common mind with vast wealth. Therefore, if the old elite is to demonstrate a disinterest in money, it must deplore ornateness and adore simplicity.'[12] This so-called 'counter-snobbery' ensured that the old elite maintained the moral high ground, able to assert their superior style, through their apparent contempt for such base instincts as the accumulation and display of vast wealth. However, as the authors pointed out, 'underneath the shy, retiring, unassuming ways and masquerading as quiet, good taste, shines forth a distinctive exhibitionism quite as flagrant as the pomp and circumstance of former years'.[13]

This contradiction was encapsulated in the 1970s by Roy Halston's designs. Halston's work was the favourite of fashion insiders, who enjoyed the contrast of minimalist clothing worn in the context of the decadent extremes of New York's Studio 54 nightclub. He added sensuality to McCardell's utilitarian aesthetic by using fluid luxurious fabrics to enliven his trademark twinsets and wraparound skirts. In a double page spread from a 1975 edition of American *Vogue*, Halston's easy daywear is displayed in the clean lines of a mulberry car coat and olive suedette trouser suit. His eveningwear was more daring, for example in a purple dress which is slit to the waist, seemingly held together only by the broad yellow belt, the restrained feel of the silhouettes undercut by provocatively revealed flesh. His work stood out as coolly sophisticated, at a time when most designers were dabbling in hazy images of romantic nostalgia.

However by the end of the 1980s simple clothing, had come to be associated with a conservative need to ensure the validity of the status claim rather than as a preoccupation of the fashion cognoscenti. While McCardell, like Chanel, had been regarded as avant-garde, labels like Donna Karan and Calvin Klein were viewed as taking a 'safe' approach to design, providing the essential wardrobe for those who wished to be viewed as serious and career-minded. American designers' more casual diffusion lines were also signifiers of a functionalism and conformity that sidestepped the flamboyance of much of the era's fashions. Even in the 1990s the New York collections are famous for making the more outlandish trends from European catwalks

12. Steiner, R. L. & Weiss, J. vol.IX, no.3, March 1951. 'Veblen Revised in light of Counter-Snobbery', *Journal of Aesthetics and Art Criticism*, p. 263.
13. Ibid., p. 265.

palatable to the consumer, rather than for their innovative ideas. A Calvin Klein outfit of spring/summer 1997 demonstrates this commercial talent. The influence of Helmut Lang's layering is discernable but here it has been translated into shiny stretch fabrics rendering the ensemble sportier in feel than the Austrian designer's edgier style.

While Klein has sought notoriety for his label via controversial advertising campaigns, Donna Karan has emphasized her empathy with the female consumer. Also drawing on the McCardell look, she has, like her forerunner, been seen to personify the easy elegance of her style. Using a limited palette of mainly blacks, greys and soft putty colours and simple shapes she has created an empire of clothing and home ranges. In a 1993 coatdress, she paid homage to McCardell in the basic wrapover style and the 'important belt' McCardell advised adding to plain dresses to enliven them for social events.

Karan's eveningwear is equally laid back – a supple dress of 1993 comprised a column of greige fabric, illuminated by the subtle glow of a pale gold collar. However, there is a need to create an aura of exclusivity and glamour around such simple clothes, since they lack the instant status cachet of more elaborate designer fashions, enticing consumers with the visual images attached to the designer's name. Both by association with glamorous star names, (Demi Moore and Bruce Willis for Donna Karan, Jodie Foster and countless other Oscar candidates for Armani), and using lifestyle-enhancing marketing campaigns, the prestige of such labels was raised. The crucial links between editorial, social and advertising pages that this publicity created forged a link in the consumers' minds between image and reality, elevating the status of simplicity. Halston, himself a purveyor of reworked classics, remarked at the height of his fame that, 'You're only as good as the people you dress.'[14] This is a dictum that has helped many of the designers discussed to raise their turnover. Mass market brands like Gap's utilitarian basics fulfilled a need to 'downsize', to strip away unnecessary objects that cluttered up already complex and confusing lives, in a manner that was cheap and accessible. However designer goods provided the rational cachet of the stripped-down lifestyle, with the cocooning feeling of exclusivity.

In 1995 Lisa Armstrong wrote in *Vogue*, 'Eighties snobbery may have been simplistic, but. . . it was democratic, easily grasped by everyone. This new version, by contrast, has taken to its heart a completely different system of status symbols that, far from being recognized from the other end of Bond Street, couldn't be identified from next door.'[15]

14. Gaines, S., *Halston, The Untold Story*. New York: G. P. Putnam's Sons, 1991, p. 15.
15. Armstrong, L., 'The New Snobbery', British *Vogue*, 1995, p. 172.

For many designers and wearers of minimalist clothing though there is a series of subconscious meanings hidden beneath the surface. It is clear that simplicity of form can be a more deliberate search for new definitions in dress. In Rei Kawakubo's work for Comme des Garçons, the relationship between body and fabric, and the spatial planes they create in combination are intrinsic parts of her design approach. In an outfit from her Spring/Summer 1994 collection layers of black linen cloak the body. The silhouette was reduced to a simple column, but within this there was a play of dark and light, transparent and opaque as the folds of tunic and skirt met and crossed over. For Kawakubo designing is always about questioning and testing the boundaries of fashion; in this case the asceticism of the resulting garments is a means of forcing the viewer to concentrate on the forms and textures of the clothing. The Western couture tradition of extravagance and overt luxury as the key signifiers of wealth and status are challenged by this erasure of decoration and the contemplation instead of simple, clean shapes. As Harold Koda has demonstrated she draws upon Japanese philosophy of sabi 'poverty/ simplicity/aloneness', and wabi 'transience/decay and rusticity' to produce 'an aesthetic of external denial and internal refinement'.[16]

In Yohji Yamamoto's work a similar philosophy of design is in operation. As with Kawakubo, colour is often negated, leaving only shades of blackness, or garments are drenched in a wash of colour in a full-length dress of 1998 warm golden yellow, that adds richness to the felt fabric. In contrast to Sander and Armani who tend to favour expensive fabrics to add dimension to their designs, for these Japanese designers the poverty of the material speaks of the reflective nature of their work, and potentially of the wearer who looks inwards too, the austere shell of her garments a symbol of inner thought and tranquility. The simple forms provide the space for introspection and higher thought, once again, as with the European designers discussed, minimalism is held to be a sign of intelligence.

Hussein Chalayan's work is another example of this belief in asceticism, in the denial of flamboyance and distracting decorative elements, as a tenet of an alternative form of beauty. The forms of a grey, caped, sleeved jacket photographed for *Frank* magazine in September 1998 had an organic feel, heightened by the illuminated fronds of the leaves in the background of the image. The curving line of the sleeves drew the eye inwards towards the deep black of the skirt, revealed beneath the rounded hem of the jacket. In this example a minimalist aesthetic was used to give a sense of purity to the

16. Koda, H. vol. II, 1985.'Rei Kawakubo and the Aesthetics of Poverty', *Dress*, 1985, p. 8.

forms, of unity and wholeness, and an invitation to seek meaning, rather than a mask to conceal the codes hidden under the simple designs.

By the 1990s there was a growing anxiety, exacerbated by the economic recession, about fashions that flaunted their expense too flagrantly. Consumers' feelings of exhaustion with obvious labels compounded this after the huge rise in awareness surrounding designer fashion, which had become so closely tied into the entertainment business and gossip columns in the previous decade. People at all levels of society were more familiar with prestige fashion brands than ever before. Designers at the cutting edge of fashion's elite like Helmut Lang were able to assert minimalist style as the obverse of 'vulgar', obvious designs that by the 1990s seemed so unfashionable. His subtle style is shown in an outfit from 1993 where narrow-cut leather trousers and single-breasted jacket were teamed with a synthetic printed tee-shirt. While excessive designs continued to make headlines for Versace and Mugler, it was Lang's cool, urban silhouettes that married basic shapes with edgy colour combinations and advanced technological fabrics, which were both the crucial look for fashion insiders, and the key influence on other designers, eager to find a new vision of the modern.

Lang helped to reinvigorate the fashion for simplicity. By using cheap, industrial fabrics, and discreetly complex construction methods, he added an urban sophistication to his designs, a feeling that the consumer had to have greater fashion knowledge to appreciate the complexity of such seemingly basic items. His clothes suggested cultivated taste, and, as Bourdieu noted, in the case of consuming to demonstrate knowledge, rather than just wealth, 'What is at stake is indeed "personality", i.e. the quality of the person which is affirmed in the capacity to appropriate an object of quality. The objects endowed with the greatest distinctive power are those which most clearly attest the quality of the appropriation, and therefore the quality of the owner.'[17]

Prada was the other label which helped to bring minimalist style to the forefront of 1990s fashion consciousness. The designers' need to construct an identity which spoke of both cultural and fashion capital was acute at a time of anxiety and insecurity, both the etiolated, androgynous chic of Lang's work, and the ironic subtlety of Prada's inverted status symbols, enabled consumption that was gratifyingly fashionable, yet eluded the taint of obviousness. A red coat from Prada's Autumn/Winter 1998/99 collection showed her attention to detail in horizontal slits that broke up the smooth surface of the coat, adding a dissonance to its simple form.

17. Bourdieu, P., *Distinction, A Social Critique of the Judgement of Taste*. London: Routledge, 1996, p. 281.

However, as the decade wore on, the understatement of minimalist style became increasingly influenced by, on the one hand the revival of luxury and detailing that came via couture's newcomers, and on the other the desire to possess less easily pirated objects, that relied on the supreme luxury of expensive fabrics. Narcisco Rodriguez created midnight blue or oyster cashmere separates that glimmered with the iridescent shine of constellations of self-coloured sequins; and Gucci played with the minimalist aesthetic, fusing it with a sense of decadence shown in an advertisement of 1996. The two models pose languidly in a fashionably simple interior, the stark lines of which are softened by the natural light shining onto the stone walls. They are clad in Halston-style columns of white, betraying the 1970s nostalgia of the Gucci look. The woman's tubular dress is broken only by a neat circular gap in the fabric at her hip, revealing the white strap of her underwear and an oval gold buckle that sits against her tanned skin. The image conveys an underlying sexuality that belies the simplicity of the style.

This sensuality became more explicit in Gucci's 1998 collection that revelled in the contrast between the simple lines of the minimalist and a love of excess. The tailored structure of one catwalk model's midnight blue coat and pencil skirt were defused not just by the flesh revealed beneath her semi-transparent top, and visible bikini pant strap, but also by the blinding glitter of the rhinestones that lined the coat. As the model walked down the runway the ensuing light show teased the seriousness of minimalist design, injecting a glittering brashness into its normally sober contours.

This love of luxury has meant that late-1990s minimalism has been less and less about the denial of tactile pleasures in dress. Even the starkly utilitarian ethos of workwear was reinvented. The appeal of Ralph Lauren's white cashmere cargo pants of autumn/winter 1998/99 was based at least in part upon their very impracticality, the delicious irony of this military basic being transformed into a decadent status symbol.

Sportswear was given the same treatment, its status as the ultimate functional form of dress once again hijacked by high fashion, and translated into slouchy sensuality in Marc Jacobs's cornflower blue hooded tops of 1998/99. Once again cashmere was used to add the distinguishing mark of luxury, of expense. The ambiguity of such simple garments and their omnipresence at all levels of the fashion industry was a motivating force in this shift towards quality fabrics rather than the cheaper more durable materials of earlier designers discussed, like Chanel and McCardell. As has been noted, minimalist fashion is never as simple as it seems and it constantly shifts between the seemingly opposing values of luxury and restraint, reflecting in its balance between these elements of decadence and abstinence the fears and desires of contemporary culture.

Figure 10.1. Marc Jacobs, Spring/Summer 1998. Copyright Niall McInerney.

So how might the meaning of the style be assessed? The various attitudes that are reflected in minimalist designs discussed – the controlled, confident elitism of Armani and Sander, the avant garde modernity of Chanel and McCardell, the intellectual introspection of the Japanese designers, the edgy urban cool of Prada and Lang, and finally the decadence sparked within the recent trend in pared–down–dressing presents an interesting complex of meanings. What do all these strands imply about the contemporary minimalist? Minimalism may strip down garments to their basic form, provide an escape from clutter and confusion, but is the resulting ambiguity of pervasive simplicity fulfilling in itself?

In Calvin Klein's advertisement campaign of autumn/winter 1998/99, the mood was not languid and confident as in the earlier Gucci campaign. The models appeared tense, the outside world of grass and trees seemed distant and cut off from them, as they sat in a claustrophobically Spartan interior.

Amy Spindler of the New York Times described these Steven Meisel images in terms of alienation, saying, 'they are images depicting the height of isolation, figures in close proximity but their eyes never meeting'. For her minimalist designs had become a distancing device, the blankness of the clothes' surface hiding the wearer's identity from prying eyes. The pervasiveness of these basic garments turned them into conformist anonymity rather than allowing the space for introspection. Indeed for her there was anxiety rather than tranquillity in the scene. She went on, 'What if nothing was happening, and we finally had time to sit and think, but our minds were as minimalistic as the room, as blank as our faces, and as empty as our eyes?'[18]

So is the escape into minimalism of the last years of the twentieth century a mask for our anxiety? Perhaps, but this style also provides a space that can generate new ideas, new definitions, that are harder to create in more defining fashions. Marc Jacobs's designs for Louis Vuitton of autumn/winter 1998/99 demonstrated the easy-to-wear forms that minimalism generates, and the gentle lines they create around the body, flowing softly around the figure, rather than restricting or idealizing it. These clothes also marked a shift in attitude towards prestige brands, and at the end of the decade a number of more progressive designers were recruited by luxury brands to revive their profiles, most notably, Martin Margiela at Hérmès. His first collection for them in 1998, consisted of deceptively simple reversible short-sleeved sweaters, worn with soft suede gauntlet gloves, and gentle long skirts. Rather than the challenging designs that he is known for, the look created was simple and luxurious. But, as Sarah Mower wrote, 'What more mordant

18. Spindler, A. M. 24.3.1998. 'Tracing the Look of Alienation', *New York Times*.

a put-down of current Paris runway sensationalism than a statement of wearable classics for older women?'[19]

And this is the key to a more positive reading of such designs. Their simple forms and subtle colours do not try to dictate a particular ideal of beauty, either in terms of body shape or age. As Donna Karan's advertisement campaign for autumn/winter 1998/99 showed in its images of a statuesque fifty-something woman clad in a thickly knitted sweater and slim black skirt, these clothes allow a space, a break from seasonal fashion. Inherent in the cut of the clothes is a reverence for longevity, for the notion of timeless classics, which are wearable by any woman, not just the modelesque. And in an era obsessed by the perfection of the body, the chasing of idealized youth, this may still be considered liberatingly avant-garde.

19. Mower, S. June 1998. 'Margiela does Hérmès', *Harper's Bazaar*, p. 147.

11

Italy: Fashion, Style and National Identity 1945–65

Nicola White

The Italian fashion industry is currently one of the leading players on the international fashion stage, and ranks parallel with Paris and New York.[1] Yet before 1945, there was no industrial production of fashionable womens-wear in Italy, and little innovative made-to-measure haute couture. The well-known Italian fashion style currently seen in the world's glossy fashion magazines rose seemingly from nowhere in the post-war years, and was not widely recognized until the early 1980s. It is perhaps not surprising therefore, that the early post-war period has been seen simply as a preparation for the recent "miracle" of Italian fashion. This chapter considers whether a distinct Italian fashion look existed in the mind of the international fashion industry well before this date, in fact, by the mid-1960s. It attempts a definition of Italian fashion style in the two decades after the Second World War, through the top three levels of production: haute couture, boutique and quality ready-to-wear. It is confined to the upper levels of Italian fashion manufacture for women, because these led the move towards international recognition, and can be more accurately documented.

The "style" of objects has been the subject of a lot of recent research, not least, as Stuart Ewen has explained, because it is 'a basic form of information' and 'has a major impact on the way we understand society'.[2] Although the

1. This chapter uses Christopher Breward's definition of fashion as 'clothing designed primarily for its expressive and decorative qualities, related closely to the current short-term dictates of the market, rather than for work or ceremonial functions'. Breward, Christopher, *The Culture of Fashion*, Manchester: Manchester University Press, 1995, p. 5.
2. Ewen, Stuart, 'Marketing Dreams: the Political Elements of Style', in Tomlinson, Alan (ed.) *Consumption, Identity and Style: Marketing, Meanings and the Packaging of Pleasure*, London: Routledge, 1990, pp. 41–56. See also Ewen, Stuart, *All Consuming Images: the Politics of Style in Contemporary Culture*, New York: Basic Books, 1988.

relevance of style to national identity has been addressed by a number of authors, the evolution of a specifically Italian national style in fashion has never been defined.[3] The three principle sources which offer evidence for an international commercial understanding of a distinct "Italian look" in these post-war years are: analysis of surviving garments in museum and private collections, the opinions of witnesses and contemporary press coverage.

Traditionally, well-off Italian women looked to Paris for their fashion. The alternative to French couture was the extensive network of Italian dressmakers, many of whom had very good reputations, and achieved very high technical standards, especially with embroidery.[4] Despite their quality, it was normal practice for the top professional dressmakers to import designs from Paris, and copy or "translate" them. By the interwar years there were three principle agencies, known as "Model Houses" (Modellisti) which facilitated this process. Maria Pezzi, now in her 90s, worked for an agency from 1936, and has a unique private archive of her designs. She described both the process and her role within it in interview.[5] Translations were made in two principal ways: firstly, concentration on the decorative element as testimony to the Italian tradition of great craftsmanship, and secondly, simplification of the original idea in line with the so-called 'poorer market'. Although these two themes can be traced through the post-war years, it is the latter, simpler look which triumphed in the late twentieth century. According to Pezzi, these "translations" were shown collectively to the smarter Italian dressmakers, who purchased them in the form of toiles or patterns, and then copied them for the Italian market.

Reduction of the dependence of Italian dressmakers on Paris style was integral to the Fascist pursuit of self-sufficiency in this period and, as Grazietta Butazzi has established, there was a determined government effort to establish an Italian style, based on regional peasant models.[6] From 1933, designers received both financial and promotional government support (including official exhibitions of both Italian textiles and fashion), which was given on the condition that the designers created original styles. In 1941 *Bellezza* was established as the "official magazine" of Italian fashion, and published many articles in support of an independent Italian style.

---

3. The relationship between America and Italian fashion style is addressed in White, Nicola, *Reconstructing Italian Fashion: America and the Development of the Italian Fashion Industry*, Oxford: Berg, 2000.

4. This is corroborated by the contents of the Pitti Palace Costume collection, Florence.

5. Maria Pezzi in interview, Milan, 13.10.95.

6. Butazzi, Grazietta, *1922–1943 Vent' Anni di Moda Italiana*, Florence: Centro Di, 1980. The Fascist period in Italy was 1923–43.

In September 1942, *Bellezza* ran a piece entitled 'Collections Prepared for Strangers' which used Italian topography as a metaphor to describe the progress of Italian fashion.[7] The text encapsulates the ambitions of the regime:

> When you climb a mountain, you can look back and see how far you've come. Many people saw the path as un-climbable. They thought that real elegance could only reach the Italian woman from across the Alps (*France*) or across the ocean (*the United States*). Italy used to use foreign models, to copy or adapt to Italian taste. To continue on this path would not have been useful to Italy's economy.

It was claimed that Italy was, instead, producing 'refined and practical models which are perfectly in tune with the new rhythm of life. Italian fashion has achieved a prominent position in Europe, and will know in future how to use this position.'

This claim to eminence was clearly misguided and overstated for propaganda purposes and it is now clear that the whole operation was fundamentally ineffective. By the outbreak of war, there was no Italian fashion industry, nor an independently innovative "Italian style" recognisable to the international market, peasant-inspired or otherwise. Nonetheless, the references to refinement, practicality and modern life are important indicators of the future development of Italian style.

After the Second World War, France recaptured its reputation as the global centre of elegance. Although the Paris couture industry experienced difficulties when it reappeared immediately after the armistice, in 1947 the world's eyes were firmly refocused on Paris when Christian Dior launched his famous "New Look".[8] Dior's opulent and formal style with its long full or pencil skirts, narrow waists and rounded shoulders formed a stark contrast to the box-jackets and short, straight skirts of the War and was eagerly accepted by women in both Europe and America.

Most Italian dressmakers reverted happily to imitation of Paris style and the "trickledown" nature of the dissemination of fashion in this period meant that French fashion still led the whole of the Italian market. Analysis of the middle-market Italian magazine *Linea Italiana* clearly illustrates this typical Paris orientation in the late 1940s. There are articles on the latest Paris styles in each issue, including coverage of the Paris collections. It is not unusual to see Italian fashion integrated with the latest French couture styles, perhaps in the hope that some of the prestige would rub off.[9] Moreover, some Italian-

---

7. *Bellezza*, September 1942, pages unnumbered.

8. See for example, Cawthorne, Nigel, *The New Look: the Dior Revolution*, London: Hamlyn, 1996.

9. See for example *Linea Italiana*, Autumn 1948 and *Linea Italiana*, Winter 1948.

made garments are presented as Italian, but the name of the Italian "designer" is printed alongside the source of direct Parisian inspiration. For example, in summer 1948 one model was sold by couturier Galitzine, and worn by the Italian socialite Countess Crespi, but was described as a 'modello Christian Dior'.[10] This means that either Galitzine was buying in Paris and simply reselling in Italy, or, more likely, had bought a toile or a pattern and was reproducing copies or adaptations. Evidently, either way, this represented excellent publicity value for Galitzine.

Yet by Autumn of that year, *Linea Italiana* claimed that Italian dressmakers were fed up with paying the prices charged by French couturiers for the right to copy; some, they said, had paid 'incredible figures'.[11] In the same period there was also a marked increase of interest in the international position of Italian fashion. Even before Italy's collective international shows of the 1950s, commentators began to notice both a conscious effort to move away from Paris dominance, and the emergence of a discernible Italian style. For example, following the liberation of Italy, but before the end of hostilities, the young and elegant editor of US *Vogue*, Bettina Ballard, visited Rome and wrote in her memoirs that she was astonished by the 'lovely, warm-skinned Roman women in their gay pretty print dresses . . . and Roman sandals' and felt instantly unfashionable.[12] Ballard recounts how she quickly found a local dressmaker 'to bring my civilian clothes up to Roman standards of fashion', and 'sent all the information I could to Vogue about the way the Romans lived and dressed and entertained'.[13]

As early as January 1947, US *Vogue* covered the major fashion houses of Italy, and offers an invaluable insight into the American perception of Italian style just after the War.[14] This is crucial, because the US represented the

10. Brin, Irene, 'Fashion in the eternal city', *Linea Italiana*, Summer 1948: 14, 'La Contessa Consuelo Crespi indossa "flamme en rose" (modello Christian Dior)'. See also Perkins, Alice, *Women's Wear Daily*, 31.3.50, p. 7, 'Stein and Blaine custom originals and interpretations of Paris models. Examples include a bouffant taffeta dress adapted from Balmain (and a) Balenciaga printed taffeta with a slim skirt'.

11. 'Moda d'Autunno a Roma', Brin, Irene, *Linea Italiana*, Autumn 1948, 'una certa amarezza ha accompagnato i sarti italiani nel loro viaggio di ritorno da Parigi; alcuni avevano speso cifre incredibili' (a certain bitterness has accompanied Italian dressmakers on their return trip to Paris; some have spent incredible figures). This piece also features the key Italian dressmakers of 1948: Tizzoni, Fiorani, Rina Pedrini, Noberasko, Biki, Veneziani, Fercioni, Battilochi, Fontana, Carosa, Simonetta, Gattinoni, and Fabiani.

12. Ballard, Bettina, *In My Fashion*, London: Secker and Warburg, 1960, p. 184.

13. Ibid.

14. Mannes, Marya, 'The Fine Italian Hand', US *Vogue*, January 1947, p. 119. The same article was published in British *Vogue* in September 1946, 44–9, p. 81.

major international market for fashion in these years. The definition of Italian style begins: 'Italian clothes are inclined to be as extrovert as the people who wear them – gay, charming, sometimes dramatic, but seldom imaginative or arresting – it was difficult to discover any strong native current, except in the beach clothes.' The competitiveness of Italian prices was also stressed and this remains a recurrent theme in the reporting of Italian fashion over the following decade. The article concluded that 'Italy has everything necessary to a vital and original fashion industry – talent, fabric and plenty of beautiful women.' Since US *Vogue* was available in Italy at this point, it is highly likely that many of those working in Italian fashion would have been well aware of this type of constructive criticism, and indeed of this particular piece.

In fact by this stage, Italian fashion journalists were also devoting attention to stylistic emancipation from France. *Bellezza*, for example, continued to cover the French collections in detail, but simultaneously stressed the innovation of Italian collections, and pointed out that there was little justification for what it called 'pilgrimage to Paris' or copying foreign models.[15] Over the next few years, French haute couture found that a combination of overt protectionism and high prices was beginning to have a negative effect on exports. According to one French newspaper, by 1955, Paris couture prices had risen 3,000 per cent compared to their pre-war level, and the international market was getting a little tired of it.[16] With their relatively low prices, there was thus a small gap which, if they could manage to prize it open, the Italians might be able to fill.

The first collective presentation of Italian fashion to the international market took place in Florence, in 1951. It was organized by an Italian buyer of Italian goods for the American market, named Giovan Battista Giorgini. Whilst this was clearly not the first attempt to promote an Italian fashion industry, it marks both an awakening of international consciousness, and a very deliberate effort to sever stylistic links with Paris. Italian haute couturier Micol Fontana recalls that in return for his financial and organizational input, Giorgini demanded that there would be 'no more going to Paris', and no more imitation of French designs.[17] Fontana says that this represented a request to literally 'sever their lifeline', because of course, all wealthy Italian ladies traditionally wanted French style. It also meant operating in direct

15. *Bellezza* 16, 1947, p. 15, 'we want to recall the period in which, encircled by war, the Italian collections were all without duplicates, and the dressmaker cut and detailed in her own way'.

16. *Les Femmes D'Aujourd'hui*, 3 April 1955, page unknown.

17. Micol Fontana in interview, Rome, 23.10.95.

competition with France. There followed a period of intense deliberation amongst the three Fontana sisters (Sorelle Fontana), before the final decision to take part was reached. According to Fontana, this was the precise moment when Italian style emerged on the international stage.

Nonetheless, it should not be assumed that all Italian couturiers suddenly forgot Paris and designed entirely independently thereafter. There was no abrupt break from Paris style at couture level, and adherence to the general seasonal stylistic prescriptions of Paris continued throughout the 1950s and early 1960s. The move away from Paris gathered momentum from 1951, but it was not consistent at all levels of production and with all designers and was seen less in terms of silhouette than in use of colour, fabric and surface decoration. However, it is significant that the links between Italian designers and Paris fashion (which were stressed in the Italian fashion press before 1951) are difficult to find after this date.

Deviations from French dictates can be detected not only through innovations mentioned in media coverage, but also through analysis of individual surviving garments and amalgamated testimonies of witnesses to the early collections. Carla Strini, for example, was Head of Emilio Pucci's foreign operations and attended the very first collective show. She remembers the embroideries, fabrics and colours especially vividly, and says, for example, that 'the colours were very striking, especially the soft pastels of green and aqua which was very unusual'.[18] Micol Fontana recalls particularly that 'Italian couture was simpler in line than the French. Draping good quality soft materials was an important part of this, but the real secret was in hidden construction; the garments were very carefully cut, and this was not shown.'[19]

These key points can be illustrated through examination of extant garments. Italian evening wear was the most important export sector of Italian couture in this period, and typically followed the French lines of Dior's sharp New Look. However, there are few surviving Italian creations as extreme as most Paris designs, and the following examples represent the typically moderated Italian interpretation. The first example is a startling scarlet gown designed by Fontana in 1953, in draped soft crepe chiffon, with a simple, curvaceous silhouette, exactly in line with Fontana's recollections (figure 11.1).[20] According to Micol Fontana, it was vital that the gown fitted the individual body perfectly without discomfort. The structure is very intricate, with a firmly boned silk underbodice.

18. Carla Strini in interview, near Florence, 18.10.95.
19. Micol Fontana in interview, Rome, 23.10.95.
20. Held at the Fontana archive, Rome, number n.17/F 1953. Label reads 'Sorelle Fontana Roma'.

Figure 11.1. Scarlet chiffon gown by Sorelle Fontana, 1953. Source: Fontana archive, Rome, n. 17/F 1953. Courtesy of Sorelle Fontana, Alta Moda SRL.

Reflecting Italy's reputation for exquisite craftsmanship, intricate hand-worked beading was already long known as an Italian specialization and this continued strongly in the post-war years. The M.H. De Young Museum in San Francisco has several fine examples. The earliest is a 1949 cream satin evening gown by Ferrario.[21] It is decorated with all-over scrolled embroidery

21. M.H. De Young Museum, San Francisco, number 1991.83.2a–b. Label reads 'Ferrario Milano'. Spaghetti straps are knotted and dropped inside the dress which indicates that the dress was worn strapless at least sometimes. An American-made underwired strapless bra was added to the bodice by the original owner.

using toning silk thread, cream sequins and amber glass. The front has a false-wrap which suggests it was meant to swing open as the wearer walked, perhaps offering a glimpse of the lower leg. It was worn by Naz Mardikian, an Armenian emigré who was involved with the Italian resistance during the War, and was very keen to help resurrect the Italian industry after the War. Mrs Mardikian was given a ball gown every year by Ferrario in recognition of her efforts. She received this particular example for the 1949 opening of the San Francisco opera, a major social and sartorial event in the San Francisco calendar.

Another significant extant example of evening wear was designed by Galitzine in approximately 1962 (and is particularly interesting because two variations of this outfit are held in museum collections, one in the Pitti Palace and one at the Victoria and Albert Museum in London). The first is a suit comprising a short, sleeveless, waisted cocktail dress with a matching jacket.[22] The second variation is a three-piece and includes the same jacket, but matched with both green "capri pant" trousers, and a maxi wrap-around overskirt.[23] It shows an aptitude for combining elegance with practicality; trousers were rarely seen in French couture collections until the later 1960s. The fabric is very striking, an exotically coloured and patterned satin, with stylized flowers, leaves and butterflies, which incorporates both pastels and brights. The jacket is very heavily beaded in accordance with the fabric pattern and is lined with fine green crepe de chine. There is great attention to detail; even the internal poppers are covered with different colour crepe to match the fabric pattern beneath. These are important examples of Italian use of colour, fabric, surface decoration, and the simple lines which were beginning to distance Italian fashion from French. This reading is substantiated by the contemporary press. In *Women's Wear Daily*, for example, in 1952, it was noted that 'richly embroidered evening gowns . . . and fabrics play a big role in fashion interest in these showings'.[24]

An interesting example of a further important facet of Italian couture eveningwear was published on the cover of American magazine *Life* in January 1955.[25] The feature, entitled 'Gina Lollobrigida: a Star's Wardrobe',

22. Pitti Palace, Florence, number TA 3898/9. Label reads 'Irene Galitzine Roma'.

23. Victoria and Albert Museum, London, number T220-74 and T220A. Label reads 'Irene Galitzine Roma'.

24. *Women's Wear Daily*, 18.1.52, p. 3.

25. Gina Lollobrigida: a Star's Wardrobe', *Life*, 10.1.5, p. 38. After the Second World War a significant proportion of Hollywood films were made in Italy, especially in and around Rome, as Hollywood faced declining audiences and sought to cut costs. American stars poured in, and together with the new Italian Hollywood stars, offered an important and particular market for Italian couture, both for their film and private wardrobes.

shows the famous Italian film star in a relatively simple gown of figured satin, with no surface decoration, but a carefully constructed swathed cut which fully emphasizes the star's celebrated physique. The accompanying article reported on 250 gowns in her wardrobe, saying that 'Lollobrigida's clothes, which she had all made in Italy, most of them by Rome's Emilio Schuberth, and are made with an eye on Gina's figure, rather than on the season's new silhouettes'. They are made of luxurious stuffs, such as velvet and satin, and many of the designs involve considerable surface decoration. Lollobrigida's clothes can be seen to epitomize a valuable sector of Italian high fashion which was created for Hollywood stars from the late 1940s and which can be described as figure-hugging, glamourous and above all, sexy.

Although Italian couture became increasingly well known for its evening wear, formal day dress was always produced and sold successfully in the US. Broadly, like the eveningwear, daywear followed the Paris "New Look" line, which can be seen in a tailored black and grey stripe suit by Paris couturier Jean Dessès, featured in a *Linea Italiana* editorial in Spring 1951.[26] However, another Spring 1951 tailored suit, this time in maroon rayon by the Italian Baruffaldi, is a softer, more wearable garment than the more extreme French style of the same date, and this is typical of the stylistic development of Italian daywear.[27]

Few examples of Italian couture daywear survive in museum collections, partly because donors and curators did not feel them worthy of collection and partly because they tended to be more frequently worn. Probably the most memorable day outfit in a museum collection is a dress-suit by Fabiani, circa 1965, held at the Victoria and Albert Museum.[28] The suit is in a very heavy woven wool, with navy and red horizontal stripes. It consists of a double-breasted unfitted jacket, with a rounded collar, and a shift-dress with a high waist. The suit is visually striking because of the juxtaposition of strong colours with simple shape. It is these very factors which seem to link the surviving examples of Italian couture daywear and which distinguishes much of Italian style of this date from the sharper French look.

The daywear featured in contemporary press coverage further emphasizes these factors. For example, in 1961 US *Vogue* typically chose to emphasize Italian use of colour, at the spring collections.[29] The article prosaically explained that 'there were apricots in every shade of ripeness, pinks in every

26. *Linea Italiana*, Spring 1951, p. 58.
27. *Linea Italiana*, Spring 1951, p. 61.
28. Victoria and Albert Museum, London, number T322.78. Label reads 'Fabiani Roma'.
29. 'The Good Word on Italy and Italian Fashion', US *Vogue*, 1.4.61, p. 135.

blush of pinkness, strawberry and camelia reds, pale blue and periwinkle blue, pistache and jade greens, oranges, yellows, bronzes'. The use of vibrant colour predates that of London and Paris, and became an important part of Italian fashion style early in its development.[30] Nor did Italian designers restrict themselves to bright hues. Another daywear example illustrated in this article is a coat by Fabiani, described as 'a loose coat that's camel-coloured on one side, charcoal-grey on the other'.

Just below the level of made-to-measure couture was high fashion ready-to-wear, known as "boutique". Boutique fashions were produced in Italy (by both couturiers and specialized boutique designers) and sold abroad in the late 1940s, but it was not until the Florentine shows from 1951 that collections of boutique began to be presented to an international audience of buyers and press.[31] They are well remembered by witnesses. Gianni Ghini, who helped set up the shows, defines boutique fashion as 'different, novel and fantastic, though not extreme. It was also comfortable, simple and more wearable than the couture. Fabric and colours were important.'[32] Ghini also makes the important point that 'it was much easier for the press to state that the boutique was innovative, because the French did not have it'.

Boutique style represented a niche which Italy could carve out in the international market, without standing in direct competition to Paris, or copying it. Luigi Settembrini, who was a fashion PR in this period, echoes these ideas, writing that even in the 1950s 'Italians stood out for their greater simplicity, their sophisticated use of colour and their attention to decorative details . . . features like wearability, practicality, and simple cut were even more pronounced in the boutique collections which accompanied the high fashion showings. They were also more in tune with the "modern woman", especially the American woman who was understood to be active and working.'[33] He continues, 'It is these collections that represent a truly new

---

30. Although there are examples of bright hues in French couture (for example, 'Le Rouge en Marche', French *Vogue*, November 1957, p. 55, an article which presented scarlet coats and suits by couture houses such as Patou, Heim and Chanel), sombre and pastel tones predominate until the early 1960s.

31. Although some French couturiers were already designing what may be termed "boutique" clothing before 1951 (for example, 'Peignoirs de Plage', French *Vogue*, July 1949, pp. 62–3, including Dior trousers and beachsuits by Lanvin and Ricci), a systematic survey of French *Vogue*, between 1947 and 1963 reveals few examples compared to the stress laid on this area of production in press coverage of Italian fashion.

32. Gianni Ghini in interview, Florence, 17.10.95.

33. Settembrini, Luigi, in Celant, Germano (ed.), *Italian Metamorphosis 1943–68*, New York: Guggenheim, 1994, p. 485.

understanding of how women dress. They were also forums for freer experimentation, in material, production and cut.'[34]

The most frequently cited example of such experimentation in the contemporary press is Emilio Pucci's casual jersey printwear. It is generally accepted that Pucci was the first and most successful Italian designer to work in the boutique sphere in the two decades after the Second World War. With great fervour, ex-employee Carla Strini, claims that 'Pucci didn't just create Italian sportswear, he created sportswear, period. Before this, sportswear had meant a combination of slacks or skirts with tops and blouses. Pucci linked it with sport and made it fun.'[35] Strini cites Pucci's ski-pants, his first garment, in support of this. She described previous ski-pants as 'unflattering and baggy garments', which made 'women look like a bag rolling downhill', and explained that Pucci created 'tight flattering ones, which women could look good in'. This new approach to shape was combined with unusual colours and patterns, and unusual fabrics such as light silk jersey, which were easy to wear and care for.

Pucci's signature garments were narrow capri pants, loose long square-cut shirts (figure 11.2) and pared-down shirt-dresses, all in unusual brightly coloured prints.[36] They were seen as 'spare, sexy, liberating' and 'relaxed and sleek, comfy and neat, well-fitting and flattering'.[37] The relaxed sexuality of Pucci's designs was perhaps the most important factor in their success. Certainly, the clothes and the lifestyle for which they were designed, were very different from the restrictive and formal designs of contemporary Paris fashion. Whilst it must be remembered that these garments were very expensive (and were beyond the reach of all but the wealthy), for the international jet set, Pucci's easy-to-pack designs became symbols of their lifestyle and exclusivity. The fashion editor of US magazine *Life* summed it up in 1951, when she wrote that 'Pucci has made it chic to be casual'.[38] This concept is crucial in the development of Italian stylistic identity.

It is difficult to make an assessment of boutique style in this period through analysis of surviving garments, because so few survive in museum collections. However, there are three important examples. The first is an example of boutique fashion by a couturier (figure 11.3).[39] It is a semi-fitted day coat

34. Ibid, p. 487.

35. Carla Strini in interview, near Florence, 18.10.95.

36. Bath Costume Museum, number BATMCI.42.98. Label reads 'Made in Italy, Emilio, Capri SRL, Florence'.

37. Kennedy, Shirley, *Pucci: a Renaissance in Fashion*, New York: Abbeville Press, p. 8.

38. Kirkland, Sally, 'Italy Gets Dressed Up', *Life*, 20.8.51, p. 104.

39. Fontana archive, Rome, number n.31/F. Label reads 'Fontana Alta Moda Pronta'.

Figure 11.2. Printed silk shirt by Emilio Pucci, mid-1950s. Source: Courtesy of the
Museum of Costume, Bath, BATMCI.42.98.

worn by Giovanna, one of the three Fontana sisters, and made in 1964, under
the "Fontana Alta Moda Pronta" label. Made of thick wool in plain grey
and a geometric monochrome design, the coat makes striking use of fabric
pattern, through its simple construction, and an uncluttered line. The
fastenings are simple black buttons with a gold rim. This approach, combining
simple form with unusual details and/or use of fabric, can also be seen in a
photograph of two Fontana boutique day dresses taken in the Piazza di
Spagna, Rome, a few yards from the Fontana atelier in 1964.[40] The dresses

40. Fontana archive, Rome, photographic records, entitled 'collezione boutique Primavera-
Estate 1964'.

Figure 11.3. Wool day coat by Sorelle Fontana, 1964. Source: Fontana archive, Rome, n31./F. Courtesy of Sorelle Fontana, Alta Moda SRL.

are both simple shifts, in two different colours, which use drawn detail to indicate buttons and seams, in the Surrealist manner.[41] These examples all contribute to the definition of Italian boutique style; the designs are restrained, yet offer detail which catches the eye, at sub-couture prices. Another example of boutique design by a couturier has been recently donated to the Costume Museum at Bath. It is described as a ski-suit, but was probably worn for

41. This method was pioneered by Italian-born couturier Elsa Schiaparelli, who worked in Paris in the inter-war period.

informal winter-wear. It dates from the mid-1950s and comprises an unfitted jacket, rollneck sweater and matching ski-pants. Clearly, it contrasts very strongly with French couture.

The only identified examples of boutique garments by a boutique designer are by Pucci. However, more Pucci garments have been unearthed than by any other Italian designer, at either couture or boutique level. This is probably because so very many were sold, and also because they were seen to be so very directional. In 1998, for example, the Fashion Institute of Technology in New York, for example, had twenty-seven Pucci garments dating from the 1950s, and a massive eighty-seven from the 1960s. Such numbers testify to the increasing popularity of Pucci in America in these years.

Because there are so few examples in existence, contemporary media coverage of boutique style is especially important. *Bellezza* covered this level of production from the late 1940s. A typical example was published in July 1953, and was called 'The Wind on the Beach'.[42] This piece included beach shots of a young model with loose hair and no shoes, wearing a jersey two-piece (trousers and a loose stripe top) by Simonetta and a halter top by Antonelli, worn with shorts. This is a very different fashion ideal to that proffered by haute couture.

Boutique coverage by *Linea Italiana* began in Winter 1949, with a feature for ski-resort wear, entitled 'Sport below Zero'. The magazine featured swimwear and beachwear for the first time that summer, with items by both well-known couture houses and boutique firms.[43] There is a variety of outdoor and holiday settings: on deck, on the quayside, and on the beach. Young girls are dressed in afternoon dresses, playsuits, smocks, capri pants, wraps, bikinis, and hooded tops (figure 11.4). In another feature, two years later, one jacket by Bronzini is described as a 'rustic jacket' in 'green-red-azure-yellow towelling, garnished with fringes'.[44] The use of such practical fabrics for fashionable wear was also unusual and was a new post-war phenomenon in Europe. The trend towards "easy elegance" continued through the 1950s.

A subset of this boutique sector, which fits into this trend very neatly, is Italy's fashion knitwear. In Summer 1954, the knitwear magazine *Linea Maglia* published an editorial entitled 'Holiday knitwear synthesised for the modern taste'. The feature included a range of beachwear by boutique

42. 'Il Vento sulla Spiaggia', *Bellezza*, July 1953, pp. 22–3.

43. *Linea Italiana*, Summer 1949, p. 9. Beachwear by Marucelli, Gallia Peter, Ferrario, Brunelli, Alma, Rina, Veneziani, Alda, Moro, Lilian and Rina, Tico Tico, Montorsi, De Gaspari and Zezza.

44. *Linea Italiana*, Spring 1951, pp. 37–8.

Figure 11.4. Boutique beachwear by Veneziani, Moro, Lilian and Rina. Source: Linea Italiana, Summer 1949: 9.

designers such as Pucci.[45] For example, Emilio Pucci's printed 'fishtail' cotton capri pants and thong sandals, are worn with a fisherman's-style jumper and set against an evocative backdrop of boats and fishermen. The article concludes that 'knitwear is an ideal complement to today's wardrobe' and is not only 'the basis of the sporting wardrobe in every season' but also 'the ultimate news in elegance, which, for its line and colour fits in well with high fashion'. Clearly, colour and practicality combined with elegance was the selling point.

This ethos was taken further in a 1955 *Linea Italiana* editorial which proposed 'refined knitwear, which enables you to dress from morning to night.'[46] This suggests a completely new way of dressing for the smart woman of the 1950s. Instead of a formal fitted suit for day, and perhaps a full-length, strapless gown for evening, a one-step alternative is suggested in knitwear. This was multi-functionalism and refinement combined. Another example

45. *Linea Maglia*, Summer 1954, pp. 42–7.
46. *Linea Italiana*, Spring 1955, pp. 27–72.

of this was proposed a year later by *Linea Maglia*. A Spagnoli cross top, in azure blues, was decorated with a 'worked edge' and worn with plain capri pants. It is described as 'knitwear for elegant occasions'.[47] In the same issue there is an article featuring city dresses and suits in jersey wool for the first time.[48] The Veneziani Sport model is especially elegant, yet relatively unrestrictive. A simple mustard dress with a stand-up collar, belted waist and three-quarter sleeves, it was designed by a couturier for ready-to-wear production. Also featured are high-quality ready-to-wear city suits by Avolio, Modella and Wanda. All are loosely fitted and simple in effect, yet with interesting detailing, such as contrast collar and cuffs, a Chinese-style collar and check fabric jacket edging to match the skirt. Although the feature is shot in monochrome, the colours 'strawberry pink', 'green and maroon stripes' are stressed and are clearly a selling point. These examples indicate that the properties of knitwear, previously used predominantly outside fashion for practicality and warmth, now offered the key stylistic elements noted in Italian fashion success. Moreover, it could also bridge the gap between formal and informal wear.

Women's Wear Daily drew attention to boutique as early as 1951, the year of the first collective Italian presentations and it is generally mentioned with greater enthusiasm than the couture. At the beginning of the 1960s, Emilio Pucci was interviewed by *Women's Wear Daily* about the future of Italian fashion, and offered his perception of Italian style, under the revealing headline, 'Pucci Sees Couture Doom, [and] Ties High Fashion to Ready-to-Wear'.[49] The journalist stated that 'Mr Pucci has a very definite idea of what the immediate future cycle will be: an increasing trend towards the casual look.' Pucci defined this, saying, 'casual to me means a woman who perfectly co-ordinates her clothes but still gives the air of great nonchalance'. The implication is that the essence of Italian boutique style rested not only on fresh simplicity, but also on the appearance of indifference created with the utmost care. By this time, the disparity between Italian style and that associated with Paris was increasingly evident. The distinctions were captured by *Women's Wear Daily* two years later in 1962: 'The French base design on formal, elaborate indoor parties, the Italians stress the carefree outdoor life, against a backdrop of nature. For the gala evenings, the "important" dress must come from Paris, for the unconventional parties one should wear Italian clothes'.[50]

47. *Linea Maglia*, Autumn 1956, pp. 52–5.

48. Ibid, pp. 36–9.

49. 'Pucci Sees Couture Doom, Ties High Fashion to Ready-to-Wear', *Women's Wear Daily*, 25.10.60, p. 26.

50. Massai, Elisa. *Women's Wear Daily*, 20.7.62, page unknown.

Although US *Vogue* offers a more select perspective of Italian fashion, stress was placed on informality from the start. In 1951, for example, the magazine equated Italian style very firmly to outdoor casuals, with the headline 'Resort Fashions – the Italian Look'.[51] Under the sub-heading 'Italian Ideas for any South', the article recommended Italian boutique design, such as that by Pucci, for its 'fabrics of great variety and beauty, colours unconventional and full of character, and original taste'.

By 1960, even French *Vogue* devoted six pages to 'Shopping in Italy', its first acknowledgement of Italian fashion.[52] Not surprisingly, Italian couture was ignored in favour of 'Italian purchases which speak of happy holidays', featuring Italian boutique designs, such as silk trouser suits with slim, cropped legs. Presumably, the French felt that such clothes posed little threat to the bastion of high fashion that was still Paris. Such media coverage demonstrates that from the immediate post-war years the boutique collections were seen to be the most stylistically interesting category of Italian fashion production, and with hindsight it is evident that they were the most directional.

The stylistic evolution of Italian ready-to-wear is much more difficult to pinpoint than that of couture or boutique. This is because there is no published assessment and press coverage is limited, even in Italian magazines, until the mid-1960s. Therefore the evidence for this section is in the form of a case study of one of the leaders of the development of Italian ready-to-wear, MaxMara, founded in 1951. The information for the case study comes predominantly from interviews with the founder Achille Maramotti, as well as the contents of the MaxMara archive.

MaxMara products were confined to coats and suits until the mid-1960s and were aimed predominantly at the upper middle class. There was little contact between the embryonic clothing industries of Europe when MaxMara was established, so it was probably inevitable that its founder Achille Maramotti looked to America for his initial stylistic inspiration. Maramotti perused a copy of US magazine *Harper's Bazaar* (which was available in Italy in the bigger towns and by mail order), and was very interested by advertisements for American ready-to-wear companies. Indeed, the first MaxMara coat was a copy of one advertised in *Harper's* by a smart American ready-to-wear company called "Lilli-Anne of San Francisco". It was a bell-shape cut all in one with kimono sleeves. Figure 11.5 shows an example of MaxMara's style in the mid-1950s.[53] It is a relatively simple tailored suit, photographed with a copy of *Vogue* for high-fashion kudos.

---

51. 'Resort Fashions: the Italian Look. Italian Ideas for any South', US *Vogue*, November 1951, pp. 124–7.

52. 'Shopping en Italie', French *Vogue*, May 1960, pp. 103–9.

53. MaxMara archive, Reggio Emilia.

Figure 11.5. MaxMara suit, 1956. Source: MaxMara archive Reggio Emilia, photographic records. Courtesy of MaxMara SRL.

Between about 1956 and 1963 the company took its stylistic lead directly from French fashion. Designs purchased from Paris couture houses were "translated" for ready-to-wear production. Balenciaga's creations were preferred for their easily translatable clean lines and strict proportions and his approach was seen as being closest to the MaxMara attitude.[54] The exaggerated styles of the House of Dior had to be more carefully 'reduced for industry'. Examples of this "translation" process can be seen in figure

54. For further details see Miller, Josephine, *Cristobal Balenciaga*, London: B.T. Batsford, 1993.

Figure 11.6. Four versions of 'Base 11', drawn by Gianni Iotti for MaxMara in
1962. Source: MaxMara archive, Reggio Emilia, photographic
records. Courtesy of MaxMara SRL.

11.6, four versions of "Base 11", drawn by Gianni Iotti for MaxMara in
1962.[55] Although this process was already the norm in the UK and the US,
it was new in Italian ready-to-wear. In the early days at least, MaxMara's
competitors were operating at a lower price level, and it would not have
been financially viable for them to go to Paris. Analysis of contemporary
media indicates that the rest took inspiration from the international and
domestic fashion press as they reported the Paris collections. There is therefore
no evidence that Italian ready-to-wear companies were following the Italian
catwalks in the 1950s and early 1960s.

This chapter has stressed that there was an internationally recognized
Italian stylistic identity at couture, boutique and ready-to-wear levels by 1965.
Initially, foreign buyers were attracted to Italian fashion for the combination
of French-led style and low prices at couture level. They were pleased with
the high quality of Italian couture, particularly its fabrics, and the hand-
sewn decoration, which was highly sophisticated. Increasingly, simple lines
and effective use of colour were also noted. Although the buyers came at

55. MaxMara archive, Reggio Emilia.

56. Breward, Christopher, *The Culture of Fashion*, Manchester: Manchester University Press,
1995, pp. 226–7.

Figure 11.7. Gold metallic shift dress, Gucci, Spring/Summer 2000. Source: Niall McInerney.

first to see the couture, even in the 1940s, the casual yet elegant nature of Italian boutique style was highly praised. Boutique was seen to fit the mood of the times, and offered something very different to French couture, whilst developing the Italian reputation for quality, fabric and colour. It is this sector which most obviously pointed the way forward towards the mass-produced, fashionable, high-quality casuals, for which Italy is so famous today. By the mid-1960s, the casually elegant look was also emerging at ready-to-wear level.

The allure of internationally sold Italian fashion in this period remains an important facet of Italy's national stylistic identity in fashion. Today, as Christopher Breward points out in *The Culture of Fashion*, 'The power of clothing itself to communicate difference in terms of nationality' is becoming 'muddied', as the Western world becomes increasingly conscious of fashion, the migration of designers between countries continues and collections are often manufactured and presented outside the designer's home nation.[56] Nonetheless, it is still possible to discern the fundamental elements of Italian style which have been identified here. Both the colourful sexuality of Versace and the restrained sophistication of his rival Armani are internationally recognized and celebrated; good quality, soft tailoring in innovative cutting-edge fabrics remains the backbone of Italian fashion style. What is not widely recognized is that the roots of these styles can be traced directly to the flowering of Italian style in the immediate post-war decades. Even the ever-metamorphosing "must-have" styles of Prada and Gucci (figure 11.7), with their emphasis on luxurious, high-status modernity through the clever use of fabric, pattern, hue, texture and decoration, are clearly connected to the easy, sexy designs of the pioneers of Italian "boutique". Despite the muddied waters, the style of fashion presented in Italy can still be seen to contrast with that presented in France, for example, which tends to focus on experimentation rather than wearability. The significance of America to Italian fashion style continues to develop, as American designers and executives are increasingly employed in Italian fashion, and as American stars become an increasingly important form of publicity.

There can be no doubt that the foundations for Italy's contemporary success in the sphere of "sport's chic" were laid during the 1950s and early 1960s, and that there was an internationally recognizable and recognized "Italian style" by the end of this period. Pucci's 1960 predictions reported by *Women's Wear Daily*, under the title 'Pucci Sees Couture Doom, Ties High Fashion to Ready-to-Wear' were accurate; at the start of the twenty-first century, mainstream Italian fashion is known precisely for its wearable elegance in high-quality ready-to-wear and it is through this national stylistic identity that the secret of Italy's fashion success lies.

Index